DISASTER RECOVERY TESTING
Exercising Your Contingency Plan
(2007 Edition)

Philip Jan Rothstein, FBCI, Editor

ROTHSTEIN ASSOCIATES INC., Publisher
Brookfield, Connecticut USA
www.rothstein.com
info@rothstein.com
203-740-7444

ISBN 1-931332-42-8
(978-1-931332-42-2)

Library of Congress Catalog Card Number 94-066555
Rothstein, Philip Jan, FBCI, Editor

Disaster Recovery Testing:
Exercising Your Contingency Plan
(2007 Edition)

ISBN 1-931332-42-8

(978-1-931332-42-2)

The chapters "The Test Plan" and "The Test Report" by David Sobolow have been adapted with permission from the book Recovering Your Business, Copyright © 1993, TAMP Computer Systems Inc.

The chapters "Closing The Loop" and "The Emergency Management Exercise Process: A Step-By-Step Blueprint" by Patrick LaValla, Robert Stoffel and Charles Erwin have been adapted with permission from the publication Exercise Planning and Evaluation, Copyright © 1990, Emergency Response Institute, Inc.

The chapter "Psychological Issues in a Crisis Simulation Exercise" has been adapted with permission from an article in Industrial and Environmental Crisis Quarterly, 7 (1993): Doepel, D. G.: Psychological Preparedness and Crisis Management: Theory and Practice.

The chapter "Testing Methods" has been adapted with permission from the book Disaster Proof Your Business: A Planning Manual for Protecting a Company's Computer, Communications & Records Systems & Facilities, Copyright © 1991, Probus Publishing Company, Chicago, Illinois.

The chapter "Testing Public and Internal Communication" is Copyright © 1994 by James E. Lukaszewski and is used with permission.

The chapter "Disaster Plan Simulates Plane Crash into High-Rise Building" is reprinted with permission from N.F.P.A. Journal® (Vol. 87, #6), Copyright © 1993, National Fire Protection Association, Quincy, MA 02269. N.F.P.A. Journal® is a registered trademark of the National Fire Protection Association, Inc.

The chapter "Rehearsing Your Crisis Management Plan" is Copyright © 1994, DIA*log Management, Inc. Used with permission.

The chapter "Vital Records Testing" is adapted from the publication Disaster Planning Guide for Business and Industry, Federal Emergency Management Agency (F.E.M.A.) Publication 141.

INTRODUCTION TO THE 2007 EDITION

This edition of Disaster Recovery Testing: Exercising Your Contingency Plan is a reprinting of the version originally published in 1994. In the fourteen years since I first began development of this book out of a sense of frustration with the lack of published resources on the subject, Business Continuity as a discipline, as an industry, and as a professional practice has evolved dramatically. In addition, the role of exercises in the continuity management program has grown in importance.

And yet — more aspects of business continuity have stayed pretty much the same over the years. Of course, there have been some changes — in 1994, the Internet was incidental to most organizations; today, it is indispensable. Email use was limited. Cell phones were prohibitively expensive and impractical. Amazon.com was a struggling startup. And don't get me started on iPods! On the other hand, there are still plenty of organizations who have yet to implement meaningful continuity structures, let alone to conduct effective exercise programs.

Nevertheless, two factors prompted me to agree to reprint this book:

- Upon rereading this book, I was pleased to see that most of the concepts, processes, issues and recommendations remain current and effective with, of course, some allowance for current technologies; and,

- After fourteen years, nobody else has stepped up to the plate and written a book to replace it.

The second factor concerns me greatly. Having authored, edited or published around ninety books over the past fifteen years, it amazes me that there are no other books in print on this subject. To address this gap in part, I welcome your submission of articles, white papers or other relevant resources which we can share through our Business Survival™ Newsletter as well as at www.rothstein.com. We are working on development of a completely new book on this subject over the next few months.

So, what has changed since I first set fingers to keyboard? Technology, certainly — both as a recovery issue and in offering recovery and exercising opportunities that did not exist in the mid-1990s; for example, there are now numerous web-based recovery planning and exercise management solutions. The Internet, of course, has become a major consideration to most any business, regardless of size; VoIP telephony, satellite phones and cellular phones have changed the way we think about and use telephones, and have provided new recovery support options as well as contingency issues. Remote workplaces as well as outsourcing have affected recovery options and exercise strategies. Ubiquitous dependence upon email and wireless networking have not only complicated recovery strategies but also the management of vital business records. As Walt Kelly said in the comic strip Pogo years ago, "we are confronted with insurmountable opportunities!"

I have said for as long as I can remember, "An unexercised contingency plan can be worse than no plan at all." I believe this more than ever. It is far too easy to document a plan which looks good on paper (or on an LCD screen), tuck in lots of impressive content, and assert an enterprise is protected from disruption. In reality, without exercise, there is no evidence that your plan and its supporting procedures will be functional when called upon; even more critical, there is no assurance that the underlying assumptions and strategies would be appropriate and effective.

The exercise process assures your team members fully understand your plans and procedures, along with their roles and relationships; that your resources and infrastructure will be in place and sufficient; that your plan and its underlying assumptions are up to date and adequate. There is no substitute for exercising your contingency plan!

As a profession, we have learned a great deal about exercising every type of contingency plan — from community emergency management to IT disaster recovery to departmental and business unit continuity to trading floor recovery to telecommunications network recovery, crisis management/communication, and more. I hope that this book will provide you with the benefit of the collective experience and wisdom of the thirty contributors. As I have been fond of saying over the past 25 years as a management consultant, "A consultant's job is to have made all of the mistakes already — at somebody else' expense."

ACKNOWLEDGEMENTS

'What do you have on recovery testing?" The dozens of people who have called, faxed or written to The Rothstein Catalog On Disaster Recovery started me on a frustrating search of our library, archives, inventory and industry contacts. Curiously, as critical as I firmly believe testing is to recoverability, remarkably little has been published on the subject.

Therefore, I offer my sincere appreciation to those seasoned professionals and beginning contingency planners alike who have confirmed the need for this book.

More specifically my heartfelt appreciation to Paul F. Kirvan (The Kingswell Partnership, Turnersville, New Jersey); Judith Hinds (Depository Trust Company, New York City, New York); and, Marvin Wainschel (McWains Chelsea, Inc., Morristown, New Jersey) for their diligent and ruthless editing and feedback.

To save the very best for last, I extend my profound appreciation to my partner in business, marriage and life, Carla, whose support, encouragement and inspiration made this book possible.

Philip Jan Rothstein, FBCI
Brookfield, Connecticut
October, 2007

TABLE OF CONTENTS

Introduction To The 2007 Edition iii
Acknowledgements iv
Preface vii
    by Alan Freedman
Introduction ix
    by Philip Jan Rothstein

I.   MANAGING RECOVERY TESTING

1   Justifying Recovery Testing 1
    by Dan Muecke
2   Managing The Testing Process 9
    by Marvin Wainschel
3   Budgeting for Recovery Testing 21
    by Robbie Atabaigi
4   The First Test 25
    by John Nevola
5   The Test Plan 31
    by David Sobolow
6   Hot Site Recovery Testing Checklist 37
    by Judith Hinds
7   Choosing and Developing the Test Scenario 47
    by Melvyn Musson
8   The Politics of Recovery Testing 57
    by Philip Jan Rothstein
9   Closing The Loop 61
    by Patrick Lavalla, Robert Stoffel and Charles Erwin

II.   TEST PARTICIPANTS AND RESOURCES

10   The Test Team 69
    by Michael G. Courton
11   Management's Role 75
    by Dan Muecke
12   The Psychology of Recovery Testing 83
    by David Doepel
13   The Consultant's Role In Disaster Recovery Testing 93
    by Marvin Wainschel
14   The Recovery Vendor's Perspective 105
    by John Sensenich
15   Client Participation In Testing 113
    by Michael G. Courton
16   Recovery Planning Software's Role In Testing 119
    by Kenneth J. Bauman
17   The Recovery Plan Document In Testing 127
    by William J. Krouslis

18   The Restoration Vendor's Perspective 131
       by Ronald N. Chamberlain
19   The Risk Management Perspective 135
       by Melvyn Musson

III. TESTING METHODS AND PROCESSES
20   Testing Methods 141
       by Geoffrey H. Wold and Robert F. Shriver
21   Testing Levels and Resources 155
       by William J. Krouslis
22   The Test Report..159
       by David Sobolow
23   Surprise and Unannounced Testing 163
       by James Certoma
24   Disaster Recovery Testing Cycles 175
       by Judith Hinds

IV. WHAT IS BEING TESTED
25   Data Center Recovery Testing 183
       by Joan Blum
26   Data Communications Recovery Testing 189
       by Paul F. Kirvan
27   Voice Communications Recovery Testing 203
       by Paul F. Kirvan
28   Local Area Network Recovery Testing...219
       by Paul F. Kirvan and Philip Jan Rothstein
29   Trading Floor Recovery Testing..233
       by James N. Loizides
30   Testing Public and Internal Communications 239
       by James E. Lukaszewski
31   The Emergency Management Exercise Process 255
       by Patrick LaValla, Robert Stoffel and Charles Erwin
32   Disaster Plan Simulates Plane Crash into High-Rise Building 263
       *by William H. Johnson, Warren R. Matthews
       and Casey Cavanaugh Grant*
33   Rehearsing Your Crisis Management Plan 281
       by Alvin Arnell
34   Testing Emergency Plans and Capabilities: Two Case Studies 295
       by Roger W. Mickelson
35   Vital Records Testing 303
       by The Federal Emergency Management Agency
36   The Bottom Line 307
       by Philip Jan Rothstein

V. CONTRIBUTORS' BIOGRAPHIES
      311

PREFACE

In December 1992, a Northeaster ripped its way through the east coast of the United States causing severe flooding and business disruption. Some companies were put out of business or significantly hampered to the extent their business could not function.

On February 26, 1993, a bomb exploded in the World Trade Center in New York City. The result of this disaster included six people dead; over one thousand injured; 50,000 people displaced from their work locale; and 950 businesses put on the street. In addition to spending eight weeks around-the-clock and significant dollars to make the World Trade Center habitable, an additional $70 million was spent to erect an interim air conditioning plant to provide temporary cooling to the World Trade Center during the summer. Business loss was estimated at $600 million and many believe that figure to be conservative.

Perhaps the World Trade Center disaster had an even greater impact than described above. It took away whatever innocence we had that a terrorist attack would ever befall us at home. It also reinforced in a most tragic way the need for preparedness in the event of catastrophic circumstances.

Most disasters are not the work of terrorists but of mother nature or human error. The impacts of disasters take many forms with human and business devastation all too often the result. In business, we refer to these phenomena and the ability to recover from them as disaster recovery or contingency planning or business continuity. Regardless of label, this translates to the ability to conduct business at an alternate location when the primary business facility is no longer functional.

Business continuity is a necessity. Testing is crucial to business continuity. This book will help you work through a variety of testing scenarios and methods to better understand the requirement for a workable contingency plan. In examining these alternative test scenarios, you will in turn be able to better plan for your own business.

Viable business continuity plans need not be a three-inch book. They should only contain what is absolutely necessary for business resumption. First and foremost they must always address life-safety of the individual. Interviews with those who lived through Hurricane Andrew and other catastrophes have articulated two common themes: the well-being of the employee and immediate family is paramount; and, the recovery plan book is not used when it represents a symbol of an audit or regulatory requirement. It is used when its contents define what is required to recover.

No two businesses are identical. One business' needs may be very different from those of another. This book will walk you through various test scenarios and approaches. It is designed to be a guide, to help you gain optimal results in business preparedness, to identify and quantify base needs, to facilitate response to the difficult questions of who, where, what, when, and how.

A business continuity plan that is not tested is of little to no value. Testing and learning from the experience is the only way to perfect the plan; to ensure the business needs are addressed. Ideally, a perfect test addresses all business requirements and thoroughly involves the real users. Anything less than optimum presents levels of business risk.

This book has been written to allow the reader to focus on a particular or multiple concerns (at the discretion of the reader); to examine and study one or a series of test scenarios. As this preface is being written, the Midwest United States is trying to recover from the worst flood in its experience. The human devastation is incalculable, while business losses have been estimated as high as eight billion dollars. The ability to recover in an appropriate time after a catastrophe is imperative. One difficulty has been creating a document and test mechanism that will do just that. You will discern what it takes to be prepared, to experience a catastrophe and survive without sacrifice of life-safety or going out of business.

Alan Freedman
August, 1993

INTRODUCTION

There are those of us who would argue that testing the business continuity or disaster recovery plan is at least as critical as actually developing the plan in the first place. Without testing, the continuity plan is little more than an exercise in speculation – or even futility. After all, how else could any organization assess the effectiveness of a continuity plan, short of the "ultimate" test – living through an actual disaster?

Regrettably, many organizations find it difficult enough to develop a plan, let alone to find the resources and time to conduct meaningful testing. Recovery testing has, for these organizations, held many similarities to the classic data processing dilemma of application software documentation: always budgeted at the end of the project, yet seldom enough time or money left to do a decent job. Why is it that some organizations never get around to recovery testing, and others test aggressively?

Where recovery testing is planned, budgeted and conducted, the predicament is as often as not a dearth of practical experience or knowledge. If one turns to the typical disaster recovery book, one will find a chapter near the back entitled "Testing and Maintenance," or something like that. In a handful of pages, the author communicates the desirability of testing, the basic types of tests, and little more. This is not meant to be a criticism of these valuable books, so much as an observation that they are usually focused on plan *development and implementation* rather than testing. To the contrary, this book does not attempt to convey the process of recovery plan development – it is assumed that the reader at least understands the mechanics of disaster recovery / business continuity / contingency planning.

Among the clients of Rothstein Associates Inc.'s management consultancy, recovery testing has been a hot topic for some time. As publisher of **The Rothstein Catalog On Disaster Recovery**, recovery testing has been the single most requested subject, yet our extensive research has shown that precious little has been published on the subject.

From this book, the contingency planner can understand more than just how to test: *why* to test, *when* to test (and *not* test) and the necessary participants and resources. Further, this book addresses some often-ignored, real-world considerations: the justification, politics and budgeting affecting recovery testing. By having multiple authors share their respective areas of expertise, it is hoped that this book will provide the reader with a comprehensive resource addressing the significant aspects of recovery testing.

Philip Jan Rothstein

I.

MANAGING RECOVERY TESTING

1

JUSTIFYING RECOVERY TESTING

by Dan W. Muecke

The justification for disaster recovery testing has the same basis as almost every other decision in the business world — economic benefit. Determining the cost of a particular disaster recovery testing procedure is usually a straightforward process of identifying the resources that will be used during a test, determining the usage cost associated with each of the resources used, and totaling the individual costs to obtain an overall total cost. The problem with performing a standard cost / benefit analysis is in determining the true benefit of the test. The balance of this chapter offers some guidance on determining these benefits and discusses the issue of when not to test.

THE COST OF NOT KNOWING

In most business problems, costs are associated with acquiring knowledge or acquiring objects that will allow the company to better perform its mission. If the cost to acquire and use this knowledge or object is less than the additional value the company obtains through increased production or some other quantifiable measure of performance, then a rational person or company would make the acquisition. With disaster recovery testing, this normal view is basically turned inside out. To see this problem in perspective, consider the situation as it typically exists before the first disaster recovery test is performed:

- a disaster recovery plan has been prepared. Assuming that the preparer has tried to prepare a comprehensive and usable plan, all concerned expect that this plan will meet the company's needs should a disaster occur.

- all necessary contingency arrangements have been completed.

- the design of computer systems, networks and applications conform to the requirements set forth in the disaster recovery plan and the company's application design standards.

- procedures are in place and followed in normal processing that will facilitate recovery should a disaster occur, e.g., backups are regularly made, backup tapes are stored off-site, provisions are in place to recover tapes as required, etc.

Any consultant reviewing the situation at a company in the above situation would be pleased to report that this company has done a good job at disaster recovery *planning*. But, is this company really ready for a disaster? The answer is an emphatic, NO! Until the disaster recovery plan and its procedures are thoroughly tested, this company is only marginally more prepared than the company that has done nothing.

The reason — this company does not know what is missing from its disaster recovery plan. If a company conducts its disaster recovery plan implementation without testing, it is very likely to encounter major problems. When a problem is encountered, there will be no prepared response to resolve this problem. In the vernacular, the company will be forced to "wing it." Clearly, no company wants to "wing" its disaster response.

The whole purpose of disaster recovery testing is to expand the company's knowledge base. By conducting tests, the company will find gaps in its knowledge base for response to a given situation. It will also find areas where it needs to acquire knowledge in order to properly respond to an unpredictable situation. It is obviously much better to find these gaps under controlled conditions which do not threaten the company's viability rather than trying to do so under the pressure of real disaster.

Impact of having a plan that does not function when it is needed

The purpose of disaster recovery testing is to reduce the level of information that a company does not know it does not know. Therefore, one way to establish the economic benefit (value) of performing disaster recovery testing is to estimate the cost of having the disaster recovery plan fail, either in part or totally. In the extreme, this may mean that the company will cease to exist. In many cases, it will mean that the company will suffer significant loss of business as customers move their purchases to competitors who can meet the customer's needs or in whom the customers have confidence that product can continue to be delivered in the face of disaster.

To obtain this data, the disaster recovery management team will need to work with the principal business units of the company to establish a time-based estimate of actual losses (or potential lost revenue) if there is a failure to recover data processing capability or business functionality following a disaster. Typically, this data will follow a curve similar to that shown in *Figure 1.*

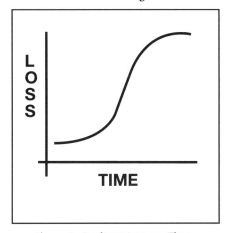

Figure 1 *Business Loss vs. Time*

Initially, there will be little impact to the business. As the length of the time the company lacks data processing capability or business functionality increases, there is likely to be a sharp increase in revenue impact. That revenue impact then levels out because virtually all revenue in a given area is lost.

Each business unit will also need to assess whether the business impact will be long-term or short-term. For example, if a company is in the business of providing information, there may be little long term impact to the business if the information being provided is unique and can only be obtained from this single source. However, if the information being provided is more generic or available from multiple sources, then the long term business impact is likely to be very significant since customers will move to alternative sources. Trying to regain these customers will likely prove to be difficult.

It is critical that the business units are involved in this process. This will provide the required degree of credibility to the cost-benefit analysis.

Can the plan be improved?

In a similar vein, subjecting a completed disaster recovery plan to an actual test will allow the test participants to determine not only whether the plan works, but whether it can be improved. In performing disaster recovery tests, the participants often determine that the plan will work; however, with modifications to the plan, the process can be improved, thereby raising the overall probability of a successful recovery or reducing the time to complete recovery.

While it is certain that the disaster recovery process will be improved through a regular testing program (practice makes perfect), it is doubtful that such improvements can, of themselves, be used to justify a testing program. However, the projected improvements can be used as a source of soft benefits that contribute to the justification of an overall disaster recovery testing program.

TESTING CRITERIA

As previously discussed, it is necessary to establish the cost of not performing a disaster recovery test (and the potential for associated failure) with the cooperation of the company's business units. As part of this process, it will become evident that certain applications and business functions are more important to the company that others. While such knowledge is largely intuitive, the process of establishing the cost of failure will provide an objective basis for categorizing business functions and concentrating efforts where they are likely to be most productive and cost-effective.

Categorize application / business functions

As part of the effort of establishing a disaster recovery plan, it is likely that the team putting together the plan considered some type of priority ranking methodology for the applications or business functions being supported. If this occurred, then the involvement of the business units in determining the impact of the loss of availability of an application or business function will allow refinement of the categorization process. If the original plan was developed without the use of any type of application or business function prioritization, this will be the time to address this prioritization. Using the analysis relating business impact to time developed as part of the test justification process, this information can now be applied to determine logical groupings of applications and business functions. For example, one grouping of applications that resulted from this process was as follows:

CRITICAL	Full recovery required within 24 hours of disaster
URGENT	Full recovery required within 72 hours of disaster
IMPORTANT	Full recovery required within 30 days of disaster
OTHER	Recovery not required or may exceed 30 days from disaster occurrence

Table 1   Example of Application Criticality Ranking

In addition to the business impact of each application, the importance of the application to the ongoing functioning of the business must be considered. For example, the inability to process the payroll application may have little impact on revenue or loss; however, it will be very important to the morale of the company, especially following a disaster. the other hand, depending on the payroll cycle (and the date when the disaster occurs), it may be possible to defer recovery of the payroll function for several days.

An aside that needs to be highlighted at this point is that the criticality ranking of applications is not static. Indeed, the actual categories themselves are likely to change. As an illustration, the company that used the above ranking system recently changed to the following categorization following an intensive reassessment of their business functions:

ESSENTIAL	Full recovery required within 5 minutes of disaster
CRITICAL	Full recovery required within 3 hours of disaster
URGENT	Full recovery required with 24 hours of disaster
IMPORTANT	Full recovery required within 72 hours of disaster
NORMAL	Full recovery required within 7 days of disaster
OTHER	Full recovery required within 30 days of disaster

Table 2   Revised Example of Application Criticality Ranking

A review of these disaster recovery categories would show that this business has become much more of an on-line transaction driven business than was previously the case. Furthermore, many applications that had been previously categorized as "Other" had been eliminated. If an application is not required within 30 days of a disaster, one has to question what business function is being served by this application.

Concentrate on high priority applications and business functions

With the assistance of the company's business units, applications and functions have now been categorized as to their importance to ongoing functioning of the company. Further, this categorization is credible because the business units themselves have done the categorization. Remembering that the purpose of this exercise is to justify a disaster recovery testing program, it is now possible to develop a multi-faceted testing program that concentrates on the highest priority business applications or functions. The cost-benefit analysis should be developed for each of the application prioritization categories chosen. This set of cost-benefit analyses will show clearly which applications should be included in the disaster recovery testing program and which should be eliminated from the program. This analysis may also point to alternatives for developing a disaster recovery testing program that is comprehensive yet less expensive than a total test.

For example, in the example noted above for classifying the priority of applications, any application that required recovery in 24 hours or less was required to have identified back-up resources available. These resources had to be in place and continually functional. These resources could have alternative uses (for example, the development processor could serve as the back-up processor for a production application provided the two processors were not in the same location). If the recovery period was 72+ hours, then this company assumed that some of the resources required for the application could be purchased and installed within that period. Under this plan, it is unlikely that these applications would be tested in a full disaster recovery plan because this would force the company to actually make the purchase of the back-up equipment — something it was obviously trying to avoid.

However, an alternative to the full disaster recovery testing of these applications would be a series of controlled tests for each of these applications. In this instance, it is possible that a single set of back-up equipment could be purchased and used to test each of the 72+ hour application's back-up plan individually. While this would not be a full test of the company's ability to recover all applications simultaneously, it would demonstrate the soundness of each application's disaster recovery plan. This process would materially increase the probability of making a full recovery within the allotted time for this class of applications.

THE NEED TO MAKE ROUTINE TESTING A LINE ITEM IN THE BUDGET

Assuming the success of the cost-benefit analysis process in convincing senior management to establish a disaster recovery testing program, it is necessary that this program become an ongoing part of the normal functioning of the business. It is vital that the cost of performing disaster recovery tests be included as a line item in the budget. In this process, the cost of disaster recovery testing becomes a normal cost of doing business.

Until disaster recovery testing is considered a normal cost of doing business, the disaster recovery team cannot consider itself successful. Many companies schedule a comprehensive disaster recovery test for each data center or critical business function on an annual basis. Some companies schedule two tests for each data center – one that is scheduled and one that is unscheduled.[1] This author's position is that any disaster recovery testing program that does not include scheduled tests on at least an annual basis for the highest priority applications is simply not viable.

WHEN *NOT* TO TEST

To this point in the chapter, the discussion has been on the process of actually justifying a disaster recovery testing program. For the testing program to be credible, it is essential that the program include criteria that show what tests should *not* be performed. It is a very rare company that would have a set of applications or business functions of sufficient priority that all of them need to be included in a disaster recovery testing program.

The preceding cost-benefit analysis should have provided the basis for excluding applications or areas from the disaster recovery testing program. Obviously, any application where the cost to test exceeds the benefit of performing the test should not be included.

One aspect of the testing program which may not be self-evident from the cost-benefit analysis is the need to exclude applications or processes from the disaster recovery testing program which are covered in the normal course of doing business. For example, the company that developed the need to recover applications within 5 minutes of a disaster, routinely shifted the processing for these applications between the primary and secondary data processing sites. This switching between sites was done for the operating convenience of the data centers involved. However, each time the switch was accomplished, it had the effect of testing the disaster recovery plan. Since this switch was accomplished many times a year on a routine basis, this set of applications did not require an explicit disaster recovery testing program.

In a disaster, the switch-over would occur in exactly the same way that had become routine practice. Thus, as application systems, and the resources supporting them, become more robust and self-healing, the need for a formal disaster recovery testing program may actually diminish.

This process has proven successful in numerous companies in establishing a credible and comprehensive disaster recovery testing program that meets the needs of the company. It is not a magic process, but it does require perseverance and determination. Even in companies which could be characterized as information providers (those whose business really is providing information to others), it is not unusual to find resistance to the expense of a disaster recovery testing program. However, making the case for such a program on the basis of a sound business analysis often turns skeptical business unit management into staunch supporters of the program.

---

[1] It should be noted that only companies truly serious about disaster recovery planning and execution perform unscheduled tests. These companies are most likely to be willing to risk potential disruption to a normal day's processing to ensure successful recovery of applications and business processes should a real disaster occur.

2
MANAGING THE TESTING PROCESS
by Marvin S. Wainschel

Managing any process means setting objectives, identifying resources required to achieve those objectives, assigning responsibilities to participants, allocating resources, coordinating participants, and reporting results. Of course, management status reports are expected all along the way, and senior management approvals and/or intercession may be necessary at any point. Testing a recovery plan on an ongoing basis is a process that follows precisely this management format.

SETTING OBJECTIVES

Testing a recovery plan is one of many elements in building and maintaining a plan designed to protect a particular organization. The recovery plan is a deliverable to some "customer" who represents this organization. As in all healthy customer-supplier relationships, the supplier seeks to meet customer requirements. Testing the plan has the dual purpose of satisfying the customer that requirements are being met and working out the kinks in the plan. Setting testing objectives presumes a thorough understanding of customer specifications and the resultant deliverable — the effective recovery plan.

Meeting Customer Requirements for Recovery

While testing a recovery plan is an ongoing process, the plan itself is a system — an orderly way of getting things done. Testing a system is an elemental part of its development. No self-respecting system would allow itself to be turned over to a production environment without being tested. This requirement is especially true in cases where errors in actual use could severely affect corporate objectives. In the case of a recovery plan, a corporation may not have a second chance to make the system (plan) work once disaster strikes.

Making a plan work does not imply a perfect plan or even that all possibilities have been taken into account. No system (or plan) is flawless. Military strategists will attest that combat plans never work perfectly in battle. Basic strategy, however, is crucial and proper tactical training along with leadership understanding of base objectives is what makes the strategy work. Testing a plan strengthens the plan by contributing to the training of participants in the use of procedures and by building awareness of the basic strategy.

The goal of a business continuity plan is the continuity of mission-critical business processes. The adequacy of the plan needs to be measured against whether its basic strategy and procedures support the continuity of these processes sufficiently, as defined by customer specifications.

Testing Against Spec

System success indicators are derived from customer specifications. To test for the adequacy of a recovery plan, it is necessary to properly determine what the customer wants. The first step in this endeavor is to identify the customer. Who is the customer in Business Continuity Planning?

Business continuity plans protect the corporation from operational failure. Who stands to benefit from this protection? In general, corporations benefit their Customers (big "C"), i.e., the people to whom they provide products and services. They also benefit shareholders and employees. All of these people are represented within the organization by Senior Executives. These "representatives," responsible to their constituency for operational continuity (among other business issues), are the customers of the "service" called Business Continuity Planning, resulting in a "system" called a Business Continuity Plan.

According to the "systems development" formula, wherein customers provide specifications, specs for business continuity planning must be obtained from senior executives. Executives seek information with which to make decisions in these matters via a business impact analysis. Customer specifications are created through that analysis by identifying the following planning elements: mission-critical processes, acceptable downtime for these processes, resource loss-tolerances, recovery resource requirements, and procedures needed for recovery. In effect, the customer specifications provide depth to Business Continuity Planning objectives:

"We will recover such-&-such processes because they are the ones we feel are mission-critical. Each of these processes has a time limit within which it must be recovered, and the time limit is _____. We cannot afford to lose more than "x" amount of data or other resources. To accomplish these objectives, we need such-&-such resources and procedures."

The skeletal statement above represents the detailed plan objectives against which test results are to be measured. Therefore, success indicators for testing are summarized in the following question:

"Are sufficient resources being applied, according to appropriate procedures and criteria, to recover mission-critical processes within acceptable time-frames?"

The recovery plan must be designed to answer this question in the affirmative, and a successful test shows either that it does or that it needs improvement to do so. Of course, a business continuity plan cannot be founded upon a single test. A testing program is needed.

TESTING PROGRAM

The first test of a recovery plan verifies the basic strategy. After planners are satisfied that the strategy is sound, a program of trials, training, and exercises is in order. Tests need to be scheduled that include strategic combinations of these elements, which have the following objectives:

TRIALS	Assure that component resources come together to produce expected results and that written procedures are in place to bring those resources into play efficiently
TRAINING	Assure that personnel assigned specific recovery responsibilities are prepared to carry out the tasks needed to fulfill these responsibilities
EXERCISES	Bring the resources, procedures, and personnel together to make the recovery plan work on an ongoing basis

Testing is a never-ending obligation of recovery planners. Especially when business continuity plans support a dynamic, growing business environment, plans need to keep pace with changes to the environment. Not only are trials needed to assure that resources are sufficient to support a changed environment, but training is required to keep recovery personnel in tune with their responsibilities and to orient new personnel. Exercises are needed to assure that the modified plan still works.

An organization can schedule periodic tests, hoping that one or more of the above objectives will be met in the process. Where the testing program is based upon more than just hope, however, tests need not be periodic. Instead, they should be scheduled to meet specific objectives.

TEST TEAM

Recovering even a single business process usually involves a variety of skills and disciplines to achieve the following objectives:

- acquire and allocate resources, such as space, furniture, cash, personnel, and equipment
- re-establish data, voice, and other systems of communication
- install equipment
- restore data from backups and recover computer operating systems
- execute procedures to assemble and use required resources.

Likewise, testing the recovery process requires a similar diversity of skills and disciplines. But as important as having the people to do the job, is to develop those people into a team—a team that can buy in to the needs and expectations of senior management, who can believe in the viability of the plan, and who are willing to improve the plan through the testing process.

Team-building is largely a matter of choosing the right people for the right tasks, contacting them individually to discuss objectives, availability, and commitment, bringing them together as needed for planning purposes, and getting them to pull together toward a mutual objective. Membership of the team may change over time as objectives change—and they will. The initial construction of the team should be based upon a preliminary set of objectives. Among these objectives would be mapping out the test program, probably for the first year or two.

Setting objectives never ends. There are objectives for the testing program, there are objectives for each test, and there are objectives for each meeting leading to and following a test. For each event, it is appropriate to remain flexible in setting objectives, but once objectives are set, the team needs to stand behind them. Therefore, it is particularly important to reach consensus among team members for objectives of the testing program. As indicated previously, the testing program needs to verify *procedures* to recover *resources* for *mission-critical processes* within *acceptable time-frames*. This statement could be the basis for initial discussion.

Even before planning the first test, it would be wise to have a full-team meeting to determine objectives of the program and ground rules for how the team will operate. Thereafter, when the team meets to discuss specific tests, the members will have a perspective of the whole program and why they are being asked to handle certain responsibilities.

A testing program is basically a *schedule* for testing the plan and its components. Plans change over time depending upon the needs of the business, many of which are predictable over a two-year period. Therefore, it is possible to build a testing program on a two-year plan, extending the program annually or as further plan objectives materialize. Various types of tests can be scheduled, for example:

TEST TYPE	DESCRIPTION
NOTIFICATION	Determines adequacy of internal recovery notification procedures, accuracy of call lists, and the responsiveness of personnel notified
OPERATIONS	Determines adequacy of operational procedures, facilities to restore mission-critical services
VAULT INVENTORY	Spot checks that key resources, such as data backup tapes, are stored off-site according to the latest inventory and pick lists
PICK LIST DATA	Verifies the accuracy of data used periodically to construct lists of data backup tapes to be stored off-site
PROCEDURES	Performs a run-through of recovery procedures by recovery-team managers based upon a simulated disaster
VENDOR RESPONSE	Determines vendor's ability to provide anticipated turnaround on critical recovery items
MOCK DISASTER	Usually a surprise to most participants, verifies the ability to pull it all together

Pre-Test Meetings

Each test requires at least one meeting of the entire team prior to the test. Pre-test meetings assure that participants are reading from the same sheet of music, that team leaders understand the base recovery strategies, and that all team members know what is expected of them. At the meeting, the scope of the test will be confirmed. The next order of business is to set objectives for the test and their feasibility. In setting objectives for the test, it is important to assure that:

- normal operations are not jeopardized. It is unacceptable to cause a disaster while running a test to recover from one

- objectives are well within the capacity of the people who must fulfill them. It is advisable to set some challenging "optional" objectives

- participants understand that "failure" to meet an objective is acceptable — that one purpose of testing is to uncover inadequacies in the plan so that configurations and procedures can be corrected.

Team members will often have other pressing matters which could interfere with their ability to prepare for the test. It is important as manager, team leader, or facilitator of the team to be sensitive to membership constraints. Going so far as to reschedule a test in order to accommodate a single team member could go a long way in fostering cooperation. Rarely does a single person want to be the sole obstacle in accomplishing a major objective.

Running team meetings to prepare for a test is like running any other successful meeting. Formality and structure will save people time and foster productivity. The team leader will want to:

- announce all meetings well in advance

- establish the purpose, agenda, and time-limit of the meeting at the start of each meeting

- assure that everyone is heard who wishes to be heard

- have a clear set of meeting objectives and make sure they are met

- review all decisions and end the meeting on a positive note.

At the conclusion of the first meeting for any given test, participants should go away feeling certain of their responsibilities, understanding the test objectives and how people will interact, knowing the problems that need to be resolved or at least addressed before the next meeting, and knowing the date, time and place of the next meeting. Timely and thorough minutes of the meeting will serve as a reminder of what is expected of each member and will reinforce the importance of fulfilling individual responsibilities in order to meet team objectives.

The importance of publishing minutes which contain a clear description of individual responsibilities and credit for specific ideas and achievements is worth emphasizing here. It is too easy to believe that everyone heard what was said, feels elevated by their performance, and will do what they promised to do. Typically, team members do not report to the team leader day-to-day. Their primary motivation for supporting a successful test is to be good team members. Team building is the only way to success. Part of team building is the acknowledgment of what the team is doing. Therefore, copies of the minutes should be sent to managers to whom team members report. Also, these managers are a step closer to the "customer," and it is wise to keep the customer informed.

It is important to follow the progress of preparatory measures right to the point of testing. Dependent upon the complexity of the test, several smaller meetings may be required. Where objectives must be changed, the new objectives should be published for all team members, prospective test participants, and pertinent managers. By test time, a complete hour-by-hour time-line of activities should be published and agreed to by participants. A final memo to participants should include this time-line, a map to testing locations and information about personal identification required at the testing sites.

SHOW TIME

Running the Test

If preparations have been properly carried out, the test should almost run itself. Based upon pre-test meetings and briefings, participants will understand their roles. Team leaders will understand basic strategy and other team members will know what to do. The test coordinator/manager needs to allow flexibility for team members and leaders to use this opportunity to try out their roles. One of the prime benefits of testing is the training of participants. In actual recovery efforts, the best team members are usually those who have participated in testing.

The principle responsibility of the test coordinator is to assure that everything is done that could be done to meet testing objectives. To carry out this responsibility, the test coordinator must observe activities, make sure participants have the resources they need to do their jobs, identify all test participants and make sure they are logged in and out, see that all major events start on time and are logged, assure that food is available at planned break periods, and see that all problems are fully documented.

Often, operational tests (like real disruptions) run for days, and many conscientious technical people, responding to the need for their critical talents, have a tendency to burn themselves out at the early stages. The test coordinator must assure that key people observe rest periods so that they will be available when needed. Furthermore, after long periods of tedious activity, participants will try to take short cuts in order to go home and rest. The test coordinator needs to be sensitive to this need but strong in determination to meet all realistic objectives. When presented with the dilemma of starting a test process that is likely to take more time than is planned for the test, the coordinator should have the attitude that getting things started is a good experience even if the process cannot be completed.

Users often get involved in testing by developing procedures to exercise recovered systems, by executing those procedures, and by verifying results. For each of these tasks, users may need assistance. Especially during a test, observers should be on hand to support users in diagnosing certain problems.

During the test, management should be kept informed to the extent that they need or want to be informed. Even if a manager has indicated prior to test time that all that is needed is a post-test report, most managers will appreciate a mid-test update, whether or not things are going as well as expected.

At the conclusion of the test, the test coordinator has a number of responsibilities which may or may not be delegated. The most important consideration is that resources required for normal operations be returned to their appropriate place. Secondarily, since a disaster can occur at any time, resources need to be placed in readiness for such an event. For example, data backups, if any, need to be returned to the appropriate vault and, if a commercial recovery center was used, all lockers should be replenished and inventoried. Network elements should be restored to some optimal configuration. Where confidential data was used, it should be removed, erased or secured. Finally, all test results, whether printed or on a machine-readable medium, need to be picked up.

Auditing the Test

Can testing be valuable without publishing the results? Certainly! Testing is an opportunity to practice procedures and build awareness among participants. However, not publishing results is like burning a painting on the premise that the artist's experience is sufficient benefit. Reporting test results serves two purposes:

- team building

- informing senior management.

To report results, it is necessary to track problems and accomplishments. While each participant can assist in documenting problems and other events, one person should be responsible for producing the final audit report. "Auditing" is sometimes a dirty word. It implies that an observer has free reign to be critical of trivial problems and ignore the achievements. Some audits are like that—because some auditors are like that. Happily, most auditors are not.

To qualify for the position of test auditor, the candidate must be able to fully understand the objectives of the test, express ideas in writing, and be concerned with details. Further, in order to document the management of problems at test time, particularly technical problems, the test auditor needs to be able to probe and analyze without being disruptive. During a test, situations are simulated, and procedures may not be executed exactly as they would be following an actual disaster. A test auditor must recognize the difference. EDP auditors are not necessarily the best candidates for this position, unless they have worked closely enough with the test coordinator to be thoroughly familiar with the details of recovery procedures and objectives.

As soon as possible after the test, the auditor should produce a chronology of events. This record of events is not for the eyes of senior management. It may contain some analysis, but it should avoid personal judgments. A meeting of participants within a few days after the test will use this report to discuss problem resolution and how management is to be advised. Resulting from this discussion will be a report to Senior Executives, the customers of the Business Continuity Planning process.

Communicating to the Customer

Meeting customer requirements is the basis for planning and for testing. The manager of the testing process must maintain focus on customer requirements. The customers of Business Continuity Planning, (i.e., Senior Executives), need to know that the funds they have allocated to this project are resulting in satisfaction of their recovery needs (i.e., that sufficient resources can be recovered after a disaster to maintain continuity of mission-critical business processes). That message needs to be sent with every test.

Follow-up

Once the test coordinator is satisfied with the post-test analysis, an executive memo should be issued. The first page of the memo should bring the test into the perspective of the Business Continuity Planning program and list the specific objectives of the test and whether each was achieved. This test summary may be the only page a busy executive gets to read, although the complete memo is likely to be several pages long.

The remainder of the memo should include a detailed list of achievements and problems with resolutions, preferably organized by department. The resolutions should be listed with expected resolution dates and cross-referenced to the problem list. In this way, department heads who need to address the problems will have a comprehensive list of their areas of responsibility and expected deliverables. A response form should be attached for department heads to verify feasibility of expected resolution dates and to list the parties to whom specific tasks have been delegated. The memo should provide basic testing statistics and the purpose and date of the next test.

Once the memo is issued, the test coordinator or manager of the testing program/process needs to track the corrective action. A commitment for problem resolution should be expected from department heads and a report on such resolution should be submitted to higher levels of management. Changes to recovery plan documentation that results from the test or the corrective action must be implemented. If additional tests are required, they should be added to the two-year plan for testing.

Tracking Test Results

A complete set of post-test executive memos represents the detailed history of the testing program and its achievements. However, it may be desirable to maintain a database that lends itself to several views of test results. For example, it may be interesting to see a complete list of problems by Department, which problems are still outstanding, and how soon problems have been resolved. Likewise, management may wish to see a list of all mission-critical computer applications, the last time each has been tested, and elements of success for each application, e.g., database restored, on-line transactions executed, complete cycle of production completed, remote user access achieved, reports generated. Reports from this database could be made available to EDP auditors on demand. This might eliminate any ambiguity in reports to management regarding the readiness to support mission-critical business continuity in the event of a disaster.

PROOF IN THE PUDDING

As the last step in the development of a recovery plan, testing is the measure of a plan's fitness to perform in the event of a disaster. However, testing is much more than "the last step," because development of the recovery plan never really ends and the resources required to run a successful test usually drive enhancements to the plan. While recovery requirements should be considered for each new or revised system, often they are overlooked. A well-managed plan testing process assures that recovery requirements are not overlooked, which leads to an effective recovery plan.

3

BUDGETING FOR RECOVERY TESTING
by Robbie Atabaigi

Although budgeting is never painless, the guidelines below should make the process a little less dreadful, at least for disaster recovery testing. Like most businesses, you probably plan your budget during the middle of the fiscal year for the following year. So when you are looking into your crystal ball, use the guidelines below to help you hit your target, because if you miss, you may have to wait until next year to get what you want. Ouch!!!

One item I would like to emphasize up front. My mentor, Jim Kolinsky, taught me many years ago that although disaster recovery is a serious subject, add a little 'fun' for your test participants (but be serious with management). Although the main goal of a test is typically to meet the stated objectives with minimal problems, it should also be a bonding experience for you and for the test participants. Chances are you will be testing together many times in the future. So, emphasize team effort.

Back to business. Price ranges are not listed in these guidelines due to the fact that there are too many variables (contract agreements, geographic locations, etc.). Here are some of the items to consider when developing your budget for recovery testing:

- ***Test Site Fee*** - if you are conducting a hot site test, you may be lucky and already have a hot site contract in place with a professional recovery vendor which would make this item part of your negotiated contract (hence: free, that is up to a certain number of hours per year). If you have already used up your annual test time, you will be charged for blocks of time, usually in 4- to 8- hour blocks. Check with your vendor for the price per block. Beware — some professional recovery vendors 'charge' you an hour of your test time for setup and cleanup.

  If you do not have a hot site, you may have a reciprocal agreement with a sister office, or with a business with a similar computer system as yours. In this case, you will have already determined the 'test site fee' in your agreement. As you are aware, this type of agreement is not usually a good idea. Chances are the business you have a reciprocal agreement with, has enough resources on their computer system to handle their needs and not yours as well.

  If you are thinking about conducting a cold site test, think again. This may be the most expensive of all the testing alternatives. You would have to secure a cold site location (which you may already have if you are contracted with a professional recovery vendor), or have the extra real estate available. You would have to contact the hardware vendor and arrange the computer equipment to be shipped and tested prior to turning the system over to you.

  If you are conducting a walkthrough test, you can either use a conference room in your building, or better yet, use a conference room at a nearby hotel. You need to get all test participants away from interruptions (e.g., temptation to go to their desk during breaks, secretaries pulling people out of the room, etc.).

- ***Meals*** - ensure you have plenty of the good stuff (fruits, vegetables, etc.) and some of the bad stuff (pastries, fast food, chips, etc.). Again, don't be stingy in this area. You want to give your test participants as many nice touches as you can. Common Sense — no alcohol until the exercise is complete, and only if your company condones this practice.

- ***Auditor Expense*** - test time is an excellent opportunity to develop a strong relationship with your auditor (internal and / or external). Get them involved in the planning process of the test. In many cases, they can state whether your objectives are too vague or on target. Their feedback can be invaluable. Unless your auditor is located in the same city, budget for airfare, and a per diem charge for meals and hotel. Remember - your auditor can be your 'best friend.'

- *Tape and / or Documentation Shipping Fees* - items from offsite storage are to be used for both walk through and live tests. Whenever you conduct a test, you are also testing your off-site storage vendor's response time in delivery of your off-site storage items (i.e., system backups, critical documentation, etc.). Typically this is going to be a 'high ticket' item. Do not try to 'save money' and make arrangements to deliver these items yourself. You are to make only one call to your off-site vendor. They will take care of the rest. Of course, you will have investigated beforehand to know what the vendor will do in this situation (i.e., pull the tapes, pack, ship with a vendor who is reputable for handling critical media, delivery of off-site items to the test site, etc.).

- *Appreciation Gifts* - Your test participants have worked hard, right from the planning phase through the end of the test. Now it is over, and they should be recognized. You take them to an appreciation luncheon, but something tangible is always preferred (e.g., T-shirts or caps with an inscription of the event, some disaster recovery related item such as mini first aid kits, Swiss Army knife, pocket flashlight, etc.).

- Other budget considerations for an out-of-town test:
    - *Airfare* - ensure team members travel on two separate flights. No one wants to be morbid, but you don't want to put all of your eggs in one basket.
    - *Ground Transportation* - van rental, car rental and mileage is a consideration if one or more of your test participants will be driving to the test site.
    - *Lodging* - although it may be tempting to double up people in a room - don't. Everyone prefers their privacy.
    - *Telephone* - this expense could become significant. Rules vary from company to company, but generally a call home when you arrive at your destination, a call every day you are on location, and a call prior to leaving is appropriate.
    - *Microfiche Fee* - it is a good idea to test the microfiche vendor while conducting an exercise at an alternate site.

- *Telecommunication Fees* - this relates to the testing of the telecommunication network. There may be an activation fee for the test or at the very least a fee based on a 30 minute rate. Consult your telecommunications analyst and vendor.

- *Hand-Held Recorder* - if you do not have a hand-held recorder, budget for one. Not only is it very helpful during the actual test, but especially afterwards when you have to refer back to a problem. What do you record during the test? Not everything. Whenever you hit a milestone, use your recorder to state the time the milestone was reached, as well as any problems encountered.

- *Photo Processing Fees* - record the event using a camera or video camera. If the video camera is implemented, the tape from the test can be useful for future training, and as a tool to critique future tests.

There are many other considerations, but these are the ones you will likely encounter. Hope you hit the bulls-eye with your budget!

4

THE FIRST TEST
by John E. Nevola

There is hardly an adult alive who cannot recall, with excruciating clarity, the trauma and trepidation they experienced on the occasion of their first date. The desire to make a good first impression, the need to get off on the right foot and the advantage of establishing a strong foundation are universal objectives for that fateful first date. And, fear of failure is the compelling motivator. Sound familiar?

The unknown and unfamiliar often cause great stress and anxiety. These emotions can decrease effectiveness unless properly managed and channeled. Did that first date begin with a perspiring handshake followed by a stammering explanation for being late or was it well choreographed with compliments and flowers? Were the evening's plans made with your date's preferences in mind? Did you know what those preferences were? Did you care? And if the choice was left up to you, was it pizza and a movie or dinner and the theater? And finally, were expectations met and was the date a success?

The first disaster recovery test, like a first date, can be very successful if approached with an equal measure of anticipation and preparation. The anticipation can heighten awareness and sharpen the senses while reflective preparation can remove many of the pitfalls of the unexpected. On the other hand, stumbling into a first test without a plan, unprepared and without reasonable goals and expectations can provoke a fiasco. In addition, a failure in the first test can have serious consequences in subsequent tests and can even debilitate the entire testing strategy.

There are some characteristics that are uniquely associated with the successful first test. A sound first test plan will contain modest but meaningful objectives, emphasize elements dealing with location and people familiarization and minimize risk in order to assure success. It is imperative, for reasons which will become evident, that the first test has a successful outcome.

Mainframe disaster recovery testing can be segmented into three distinct entities, each building upon the previous ones. The first phase involves restoring the base system and completing a successful IPL (Initial Program Load). In addition to restoring the system, this stage also verifies the integrity of the hardware configuration; the addresses of all of the peripheral devices; and, the operability of all of the systems software including all program products and utilities. Once this has been accomplished, the second phase can begin.

The second phase is the part of the general testing strategy that entails the testing of applications. The data required to process all of the applications that have been identified as critical in the business recovery plan is restored along with the application programs. This phase is intended to prove that all of the programs and data required to run the critical batch applications have been backed up in the production site and restored at the test site. This phase also validates that the processor defined in the recovery plan has sufficient power to restore and run these applications within the prescribed timetable. The results of this processing, of course, are compared to production results or expected test case results. Once these test objectives have been achieved and the test results verified or proven, the next phase of testing can be attempted.

Having built a base operating environment and tested selected critical applications, the last phase requires the establishment of the backup network and the testing of the on-line applications. This includes the participation of both local and remote end users who normally rely on the network to access the production applications in a normal production environment.

Backup networks vary widely in design. Some backup networks use "hot nodes" at the recovery site that simply re-route the network traffic to that site. Others use dial backup lines to the recovery site as a substitute for dedicated lines to the production site. The latter network recovery plan is likely to be complex and to require significant end-user involvement to implement. Therefore, it must be tested exhaustively and thoroughly. The entire test plan can be viewed as constructing a pyramid, with each phase being built upon the previous one. The foundation is phase one, the base operating system part of the plan. This can be tested alone. Once successful, the application layer can be added and the first two phases can be tested together.

After all of the programs and data are successfully tested, the network test plan can be added and all three can be jointly tested. Upon achieving all of the objectives of testing all three phases together, the test plan goes into maintenance mode. Future tests can now be scheduled after major changes or at fixed intervals to train new test personnel. The pyramid is now complete. The entire testing process is often arduous and replete with problems whose solutions may call for major changes to the test plan. After all, this is why plans are tested. Therefore, a first test should not be too ambitious nor adopt objectives that are unlikely to be attained. The first test should focus exclusively on successfully completing phase one (restoring the base operating system, verifying the systems software and program products and validating the configuration): the foundation of the pyramid.

At first blush, these objectives may not appear worthwhile nor aggressive enough. When combined with all of the other "learning experiences" of a first test, attaining these objectives would definitely make the effort worthwhile. The key, however, is preparation and avoiding some of the more common errors that have plagued first-time testers in the past. Whether the test site is a commercial hot site or another computer center within the enterprise, prudent preparation can assure the first test gets off to a good start.

The selection of the test support team well before the scheduled test is the first important task to be accomplished. Rather than select "second team" players, the best systems programmers are more appropriately assigned to the first test. The reason more than one programmer is proposed is to provide backup should one of them become unavailable on the day of the test. Test teams for the first test usually consist of a team leader (the recovery test coordinator), operators and the all important systems programmers. Representatives from the software and / or hardware vendor often attend the test and their presence sometimes makes the difference between success and failure.

Internal or external auditors as well as company executives sometimes accompany test teams but their participation is more meaningful in later tests than the first one. Executives and auditors are usually more interested in more tangible results than the foundation being built in the first test. Once the test team has been formed, it is imperative that a dialog is established with the support staff of the test site. This can be accomplished by meetings, video conference or teleconference calls.

If the test team is required to run "native" at the test site, the addresses and configuration must be made known to the test team. An IOCP (Input Output Control Program) must then be created by the test team ahead of their visit to the test site. If the test site runs the recovery system as a VM (Virtual Machine) guest, the test team must provide the test site with their production site configuration and addresses. The test site support personnel can then create a directory entry for the test system prior to the team's arrival.

Whichever method is employed, it is essential that constant and continual communication exist between personnel of both locations during the period immediately preceding the test. This should include an exchange of both work and home phone numbers of all key personnel and management at both sites. Many a test has been doomed because one individual not present possessed a vital piece of missing information.

Once teams have been identified, logistics becomes the next most important consideration. Getting all of the people, data and documentation to the test center on time is fundamental. If the test team had not previously visited the test center, it is smart to make a trial run. If the trip requires air travel, flight arrangements should be arranged to allow arrival a day early, especially during winter months. In spite of these precautions the unforeseen may still occur. However, equipping the test team with several cellular phones will ensure that instant communications can always be attained. These precautions will ensure that precious test time is not wasted while the test team is wandering around, lost and searching for the test center.

The most critical part of the first test is the timely arrival of a complete set of backup tapes. The data vaulting vendor should be instructed to deliver the backup tapes the day before the scheduled test. Drivers have been known to get delayed or lost delivering tapes to a testing site. Beyond this precaution, another complete set of backup tapes should be made at the production site immediately prior to the test. They can either be carried to the test center (by the test team) or delivered through a different messenger. Whether or not an audit of the tapes was made at the vital records location (another recommended precaution), bringing duplicate tapes to the test center is essential to assure a successful test. This is the single most important caution in preparing for a first test.

The same preemptive measures should be taken with the test plan documentation. More than a few tests have gone belly-up because of missing documentation or a single unreadable tape. There is usually insufficient time to cut a replacement tape, even if the production site is within driving distance. Assuming that all of the data and all of the people have arrived intact and on time at the testing center, the test can get off to a good start. While the operating system is being restored, test team members should compare the two sets of backup tapes. Any discrepancies should be noted and corrected.

A successful recovery from a real disaster may rely solely on the integrity of the backup files from the off site vault. Therefore, the vital records must be a complete set of the latest version of the operating system. The first test is a good opportunity to verify this. Some companies keep a duplicate set of the operating system backups at the test site. This measure is also highly recommended.

There are several common problems in a first test that can be avoided with some forethought. The first problem is the licensed software program products which check the serial number of the CPU (Central Processing Unit) to be sure they are running on the same machine for which they were licensed. In recovery testing, the serial number of the test machine will obviously fail this test and the program product may abort. Software vendors will usually provide a work-around or bypass if they are consulted in advance of the intended purpose. The test team leader should, however, receive written permission from the software vendor to avoid any legal questions associated with running the products on a machine other than the one for which they were licensed. This problem, while not normally a show stopper, can delay testing if not anticipated. This and many other start-up problems can be addressed smoothly as long as the entire test team is present at the test site. This means that remote testing must be avoided in the early stages of testing.

Remote testing has become a popular method of conducting recovery tests in recent years. With this method, key team members direct the test from a remote center with consoles, printers and tape drives connected by channel extenders to the main site. The main site houses the mainframe and its attached disk storage. Current network technology and capacity are usually insufficient to support restoring large amounts of data from remote locations. Therefore, most of the data is sent to the test site where it can be restored locally at maximum channel speed. This splitting of the test team staff and the difficulty of coordinating activities in two separate sites makes this method better suited for later tests.

Remote testing is strongly discouraged until the entire test plan has been successfully executed. The first test should be conducted by the entire team assembled at the test site. On test day, the team should arrive early at the test center to inventory and sort the back up tapes. The team leader should arrange for food to be delivered so that the team can focus all of their energy and time on the elements of the test. While a test of this nature usually can be scheduled to be completed within eight to twenty-four hours, more time may be needed if problems are encountered. The test coordinator should determine whether additional time could be made available to the team if necessary. On the other hand, if the primary test objectives are achieved early, the team could test elements of future plans. With this in mind, the team should bring a limited amount of application data or be prepared to establish a minimal network environment. It would be better to accomplish more than less.

It is also important to develop some level of team spirit and camaraderie within the group. Some companies accomplish this with a memento or an inscribed T-shirt to commemorate the success of the event. After the conclusion of the test, a thorough and deliberate post-test review can reveal shortcomings, solutions and suggestions to avoid mistakes, improve timings and facilitate the success of the next test. It is helpful to establish a rapport with test center support personnel, who possess a wealth of knowledge gleaned from past test experiences. It won't be easy; it seldom is. But, with careful preparation, reflective planning and a healthy dose of fervor, that frightening first test can become a resounding success: an accomplishment of which the entire team can be proud. The accomplishment will create significant momentum and build confidence for future tests.

Getting off to a good start and knowing it is the best way to lay the groundwork for what is to follow. The first test, like the first date, need not be a "blind date." And an unqualified success can be just as rewarding as getting that symbolic but elusive "first date" goodnight kiss!

5
THE TEST PLAN[1]
by David Sobolow

Before you conduct any test, you should have a test plan. A disaster recovery test plan document provides the following information about the test:

Identification information, e.g.:
- test number
- from / to dates and times
- test locations

Logistical test objectives, e.g.:
- become familiar with the recovery facility, surrounding facilities and how to get there
- identify the resources (vital records, personnel, supplies, etc.) needed for the test
- determine if the organization's personnel could find their way to the recovery facility(s) within the planned time frames

Operational test objectives, e.g.:
- recover and reestablish [___] mission critical operations at [___]
- bring up [____] technical systems on the recovery facility's hardware

- institute [_____] application processing on the recovery facility's hardware
- run selected batch and on-line jobs for [_____] application processing
- establish dial-up communications to the recovery facility from [_____] location(s)

Secondary test objectives:

In addition to the primary test objectives, you may decide to identify secondary test objectives. You would try to complete these objectives only if time and resources permit. For example, most test planners would not attempt to test data communications during their first test. However, they may identify establishing dial-up data communications as their first test's secondary test objective.

Preparatory activities, e.g.:

- resolve contract issues
- coordinate test planning
- verify recovery facility's system compatibility
- develop test scripts
- conduct conference calls with your test participants and recovery facility personnel
- obtain a copy of the recovery facility's handbook, which would complement your recovery plan for logistical information on directions, nearby hotels, supply and service companies, etc.
- copy and distribute the recovery facility's handbook. (*Be sure the recovery facility contract provides authorization for copying the handbook*)
- identify a "Freeze Date" which would be the processing date used for the test, as well as the date of the backup files to be used for the test
- identify travel routes and make travel arrangements
- identify communications resources required for the test
- obtain and install required communications resources
- obtain and fill out "Test Worksheets" from the recovery facility vendor

- identify serial-number-dependent software products and their vendors

- identify serial number of the mainframe being used for the test

- obtain software patches for serial-number-dependent software products from their vendors

- apply software patches for serial number dependent software products

- notify serial-number-dependent software vendors of the planned test, and the possibility of needed hot-line support

- identify and apply any other software fixes for the test

- verify off-site stored backup resources (magnetic media, documentation, etc.) for completeness

- identify tape and document transport containers, including keys, to be used to carry test resources

- develop a duplicate set of the magnetic media to be used. The first set would go to your off-site storage location, as normal. The second (duplicate) set would be sent to the recovery facility several days before the test, and would act as a backup to your off-site stored magnetic media.

- identify and obtain other resources such as scratch tapes / disks, special forms, etc.

- verify arrival of backup resources at the recovery facility

- identify all the technical tasks that can be completed before the day of the test, and make arrangements to have them accomplished. Any extraordinary technical measures taken should trigger a review of the appropriate section of the recovery plan

Details concerning the vital records/supplies needed for the test, e.g.:

- identification of stored magnetic media files, and their locations (off-site and on-site)

- initialized magnetic scratch tapes and diskettes

- tape and document containers / carriers, including keys

- forms and stationery

Identification of the personnel to be involved and their planned involvement, e.g.:

- operate recovery facility hardware
- oversee test operations
- verify vital record arrival
- provide technical systems support
- provide information security support
- verify recovery facility's system compatibility
- establish outside communications connectivity
- process [_____] applications
- monitor and document success levels
- consider inviting EDP Audit to attend and to provide post-test comments

A description of the planned activities including test tasks, e.g.:

- orientation and tour of recovery facility
- unpack and set up tape library
- load and submit restore jobs
- restore operating system
- apply patches / fixes for serial number dependent software
- restore application processing
- verify system functionality
- correct system inconsistencies
- verify ability to establish remote communications connectivity
- test remote communications
- begin test scripts
- complete test scripts
- verify processing results
- create a test file that can be read at your home facility
- scratch and clean recovery facility disks used during the test
- schedule post-test meeting

An agenda of the recovery test schedule including a description of the pre-test activities by date and responsible individuals, e.g.:

- create a duplicate set of the freeze date's off-site stored tapes. These tapes would be sent to the recovery facility as a backup to the off-site stored tapes. Keep in mind that in the event of an actual disaster, these tapes would not be available. If their use becomes necessary during your test, consider what your options would have been without them. Adjust your off-site storage requirements as necessary

- conduct pre-test conference calls with recovery facility representatives to finalize test agenda, required resources, and outstanding items for the test

- confirm test attendees, including recovery facility representatives, hotel reservations and other resources required for the test. Planning for meals in advance may be of some help in the control of this expense

- make final arrangements to deliver the backup tapes, documentation and other resources for the test

- make arrangements to have the tapes and resources used during this test returned from the recovery facility after the test

- confirm travel arrangements for personnel, tapes, manuals, etc. Each test attendee may make his / her own travel arrangements; however, the associated expense may be greater

- arrive at the recovery facility

- become oriented with recovery facility

- begin test

- document test activities

- end test

- schedule post-test meeting

A description of the planned post-test activities including post-test tasks, e.g.:

- verify that test files created at the recovery facility can be read at your home facility

- write and distribute the Test Report
- conduct post-test meeting
- update disaster recovery plan with lessons learned from the test

---

[1] This chapter has been adapted with permission from the book <u>Recovering Your Business</u>, Copyright © 1993 TAMP Computer Systems Inc., which contains comprehensive 'how to plan' information and tools for business recovery planning.

6

HOT SITE RECOVERY TESTING CHECKLIST

by Judith A. Hinds

This checklist is a tool for the test coordinator of a large data center disaster recovery test. It can easily be customized. Its purpose is to highlight the range of activities frequently involved in disaster recovery testing, particularly when using a hot site. Policies, strategies and scenarios all shape the process. Many of the tasks can be delegated, though the overall coordination is more than a clerical responsibility. The items may not all be applicable to a given situation. There are many variables to consider. Moreover, some types of tests, such as an unannounced test, for example, may require specifically not communicating some of the steps.

SIX MONTHS PRIOR TO THE TEST

Goals and Objectives

____ Review what systems and applications are new or significantly changed since last test.

____ Develop test goals.

____ Consult with auditors about any special areas of concern.

Data Processing and Media Issues

___ Ensure that tape librarian is informed about test dates and schedule, and about the media requirements for the test. Estimate number of scratch tapes required both in production and at the test. Order and initialize any extra tapes required.

___ Determine if any licensed software has CPU ID dependencies. Obtain addenda to licenses and/or code modifications to run at the hot site. Obtain CPU ID's from hot site, if necessary.

Hot Site Issues

___ Determine if hot site contract provides adequate configuration for readiness. If not, recommend contract adjustment and / or upgrades.

___ Verify configuration at hot site, including device addresses and capacities.

___ Obtain from hot site and circulate a list of available manuals. Place orders for any additional manuals that will be needed and arrange shipping.

Logistics

___ Select preferred test dates. When possible, avoid dates with known peak workloads and critical production upgrades. Keep federal and religious holiday dates in mind. Circulate test dates.

___ Estimate probable length of test and schedule test shifts at hot site.

___ Estimate probable size of test team and book a block of hotel rooms, if necessary. Obtain corporate rates where advantageous. Arrange for direct billing to the company.

FOUR TO THREE MONTHS PRIOR TO THE TEST

Goals and Objectives

___ Establish specific objectives for the test.

___ Conduct walkthrough and/or other simulation of the test in order to identify and assign the specific preparations required.

Data Processing and Media Issues

___ Determine if any datasets, schedules or other resources need to be set up for documentation or other purposes. If so, establish and publicize them.

___ Establish a "target" or "simulation" date for the test.

___ Determine whether normal media shipments and / or retention cycles will be affected by test plans.

___ Determine if any special backups and / or data capture will be required.

___ Remind test teams to develop their own technical Recovery Procedures Checklists.

Hot Site Issues

___ Check recent configuration changes at the hot site that may impact the test.

___ Ensure that equipment addressing changes are circulated and incorporated in the I/O gens.

___ Make arrangements for a permanent storage cabinet at the hot site for special manuals, markers, masking tape and paper for signs, pads, Post-It™ notes and other supplies and small equipment. Put together a box of such supplies and arrange shipment.

Test Participation

___ If external entities will participate in the test, determine if a customer support area will need to be involved in recruitment and / or training. Ensure that dates and schedules are communicated well in advance.

___ If internal end-users will be needed, confer with managers and supervisors about requirements. Make sure test dates are sent to them.

___ Establish Master Lists of external and internal users, allowing space/fields for names, dates of contact, special requirements, work phones, beepers and other details.

___ Establish Master List of test team members, including space / fields for beeper and home numbers, location assignments, test coverage times, any special assignments and / or needs.

Logistics

___ Schedule planning meetings, reserve meeting space and circulate this information to all concerned.

____ Determine whether staff will be deployed in more than one location.

____ Prepare preliminary test schedule and / or time line, showing test dates and times, simulation dates, related deadlines and major phases and objectives of the test.

____ Develop tracking mechanism for problems that come up during tests.

TWO MONTHS PRIOR TO THE TEST

Goals and Objectives

____ Continue to refine test objectives and draft a Test Script. Fill in details as they emerge in meetings and discussions.

Data Processing and Media Issues

____ Review input requirements by dataset and jobnames, making detailed plans for tapes and/or cartridges, if necessary.

____ Set deadline for additions / changes to be incorporated in backups for the target date.

____ Set shipment dates for media.

____ Establish deadline for changes/revisions in telecommunications resources.

Hot Site Issues

____ Make adjustments in timing of test shifts, if necessary.

____ Contact the appropriate hot site staff to outline test plans, alerting them to any special assistance that will be needed.

____ Determine whether any special equipment will need to be shipped and ensure that the shipping arrangements are in place.

Test Participation

____ Compose and distribute (mail, express, courier) initial background information and schedule to external users.

____ Plan some recognition of test participation. Order 'incentive' items.

ONE MONTH PRIOR TO THE TEST

Goals and Objectives

____ Keep reviewing the Test Script, highlighting any changes that have come up.

____ Discuss test evaluation plans and prepare questionnaire or other form.

Data Processing and Media Issues

____ Specify deadline and assembly point for all media and documentation to be shipped.

____ Ensure that media cases are suitable for shipping, and that any test-related labels for cases and media are available.

____ Prepare a memo fixing the dates of the media shipments to and from the hot site. Assure that copies of these instructions are sent to all relevant parties, including tape librarian, data center manager, off site storage vendor, dispatcher, hot site personnel.

____ Decide whether broadcast messages and / or header messages will be sent to external users. Work out details with network technical support staff.

____ Decide how data on storage devices at the hot site will be purged at the end of the test. Assure concurrence from auditors. Develop any necessary procedures. Allow sufficient time in test schedule to do this work.

Test Participation

____ Request names of test team members and add them to Master List, noting hotel and travel arrangements.

Logistics

____ If team members will be in multiple sites, find out what arrangements must be made for security access and building services (heat / air, lighting, rest rooms) for each location.

____ Decide what catering will be needed, request quotes, and find out deadlines for placing final order. Discuss billing arrangements.

____ Begin assembling test packet materials: envelopes or folders; travel information such as maps, directions, train schedules; expense reimbursement form; evaluation form.

TWO WEEKS PRIOR TO THE TEST

Goals and Objectives

____ Keep refining Test Script including time estimates for major phases.

____ Write up major test milestones on newsprint sheets for final review meeting.

Data Processing and Media Issues

____ Verify with off site media vendor that shipping instructions and dates are clearly understood.

____ Decide how media will be staged at start of test.

____ Contact tape librarian about extra hardcopy media listings, if needed.

Hot Site Issues

____ Mail in any hot site pre-test documentation, including telecommunications patching instructions.

____ Find out from hot site whether there are any specific requirements for the media shipment, such as loading dock location and hours and required signatures.

____ Schedule a conference call with hot site to review status of test plans.

____ Discuss whether pagers and two-way radios would be helpful; contact hot site about providing them.

____ Determine if any test team members want / need time prior to the "official" start of test shift for staging activities. Discuss any special site access requirements with hot site.

____ If test scenario will involve having different times, arrange for two clocks with "WALL TIME" and "MACHINE TIME" signs.

Test Participation

____ Prepare final instructions for external customers participating in the test. Where possible, obtain names of individuals specifically assigned to cover test at customer sites.

____ Inquire whether there will be any observers from senior management and / or external auditors. Make any necessary special arrangements.

___ Complete roster of test team members and send / fax it to hot site and hotel.

Logistics

___ Agree upon date for post-test Debriefing Meeting and reserve space.

___ Distribute to test team members a card or slip with contact information - hot site and hotel. Remind them to leave this information at home, in case they need to be reached while they're away at the test.

___ Follow up on all arrangements for security access and building services.

___ Assemble items / reminders for final memo to test team. Highlight any arrangements that are new since previous test. Include date of Debriefing Meeting.

___ Begin duplication of materials for packets.

___ Place catering order and check arrangements for payment.

___ If petty cash will be needed, fill out appropriate forms and get signature.

ONE WEEK PRIOR TO THE TEST

Goals and Objectives

___ Hold final review meeting: agree upon Final Test Script, including test milestones

Logistics

___ Before phoning in last minute changes to hotel, find out if any test team members have special needs such as early or late check-in / check-out requirements. Give these updates directly to hotel registration staff where possible.

___ Phone in last minute changes and arrival times to hot site.

___ Complete and duplicate final memo, Final Test Script, team rosters, other hand-outs, and assemble test packets

___ Hold final logistics meeting to hand out packets, arrange carpooling, etc.

___ Arrange to distribute packets to team members who cannot attend.

___ Confirm catering order - final count and delivery times.

___ Pick up petty cash.

ONE HOUR BEFORE THE TEST

___ Put up signs directing specific teams to designated work areas.

___ Post names of hot site staff who will be covering the test for each shift.

___ Tape up the newsprint with milestones.

___ Review Final Test Script with hot site staff.

___ Unlock storage cabinet and distribute supplies and materials as needed.

THE TEST ITSELF:
TEAMS EXECUTE THEIR TEST PROCEDURES

BEFORE LEAVING THE HOT SITE

___ Make tape / cartridge backups of test data, logs, etc., e.g., Syslogs and SMF data. Keep separate from media returning to scratch pool.

___ Write up details of any hardware or software problems encountered at hot site.

___ Return all beepers and two-way radios.

___ Collect non-hot site manuals and other materials, return them to storage cabinet or arrange to have them shipped back with media.

___ Lock storage cabinet.

___ Fill out any preliminary test evaluation forms requested by hot site.

FIRST WEEK AFTER THE TEST

Test Evaluation

___ Compose executive summary of test for senior management.

___ Load Syslog, SMF and other data from the test and communicate how to access it for analysis.

___ Collect evaluation forms, annotated team checklists and other reports.

___ Hold Debriefing Meeting for review of test problems, results and for other feedback.

___ Mail in post-test evaluation forms to hot site. Document all software and hardware difficulties that are responsibility of hot site.

Logistics

___ Verify that all media has been returned in proper order, including any media that must be returned to off site storage to complete retention cycle.

___ Arrange for return shipment of any extra equipment.

___ Set deadlines for making permanent corrections to problems encountered during the test.

___ Submit expense reports related to catering and petty cash.

SECOND WEEK AFTER THE TEST

___ Review all test results and evaluations, identifying possible future test goals.

___ Follow up on any open items.

___ Update test procedures.

___ Recognize participation of test team members.

___ *Take a vacation!*

7

CHOOSING AND DEVELOPING THE TEST SCENARIO

by Melvyn Musson

Specific scenarios should be used in all tests. They provide realism and help to foster "buy-in" among the participants. Merely saying that you are going to test the "X" and "Y" business functions or the "ABC" applications is not likely to bring enthusiasm to the process. Instead, if a scenario is developed for a test to which the participants can relate, it will likely create a more realistic test as well as more enthusiasm. In addition, the scenario may be used to test the more likely situations which could occur by basing them on specific situations and information developed from the risk and business impact analysis process.

Testing is principally a means to identify that:

- the contingency plan is complete, viable and accurate to meet the organization's overall business continuity goals

- the plan is being maintained and updated to meet changing situations in the organization's operations.

As a result, the test scenarios used must be

- *practical* - not "pie-in-the-sky," but related to actual circumstances which could occur, or threats which have been identified. Using situation which have been identified from the risk and business impact analysis process can form the basis for the scenarios and provide realistic situations. Consultants may provide the additional perspective based on experiences of other similar or related organizations.

- ***specific*** to the organization's needs at the time of the test. This will vary from test to test. For example,

  - the initial series of tests may concentrate on individual critical business units, departments or business functions

  - subsequent tests must cover all critical business units, departments or business functions to ensure that they coordinate their operations in the recovery mode.

  - major changes to company operations must be reflected in the tests.

Scenarios must also reflect and support the overall goals and benefits of the testing program.

Normally, the amount of detail in the scenarios will be dependent upon the type of test that is being held. Table-top, walkthroughs and support function testing will likely utilize limited scenarios. There should be just enough detail to make the exercise seem realistic and to enable the participants to base their thoughts, comments and decisions on realistic assumptions. A narrative description and some "what-if" requirements may be more than sufficient. However, with simulation and resource testing, much more detail and specific requirements will be necessary.

The main concerns in choosing a scenario for any testing are to provide:

- sufficient scenario information to enable the participants to grasp the situation

- challenges to test their reactions, flexibility and their willingness to adapt to deal with situations not specifically addressed by the contingency plan.

Scenarios should take into account:
- Purpose and objectives of the test
- Type of test
- Plan sections or components being tested
- Participants

- Duration of the test (actual and time compression)
- Constraints and assumptions
- Main events of the test

Scenarios should identify and describe:

- The type of disaster which has occurred
- Extent of damage or disruption to the facility and area
- What recovery capabilities are available
- What personnel and equipment are available
- Status of backup or recovery resources
- Time of the event and the duration of the test

Scenarios must enable the following to be tested:

- notification procedures
- recovery management
- temporary operating procedures
- backup and recovery operations

and, specifically such plan elements as:

- personnel
- MIS
- data / voice communications
- procedures
- supplies and forms
- documentation
- transportation
- utilities
- alternate site processing

There are also likely to be limitations on what can be done in the test mode and these must be accommodated by the scenarios. Such limitations may include:

- travel restrictions

- inability to move or affect equipment

- maintenance of voice and data communications for normal operations

- need to maintain sufficient staffing to continue normal department operations (unless the test is held when the organization is ordinarily closed)

- financial or budgetary constraints.

Although personnel who were involved in the development of the contingency plan may assist with the development of the tests or scenarios, care should be taken to involve others so that the tests and scenarios are not limited to strengths or weaknesses already identified by the plan developers.

There is no single criteria for choosing and developing scenarios to support the test program. Each company must develop its own criteria based upon the factors described previously.

SIMULATIONS

Simulations are the ultimate form of testing (short of an actual disaster). Simulations provide the capability for actions which other forms of testing do not permit, such as role playing or decision-making. These enable the simulation to test not only the recovery management procedures but also the anticipated perception of the company's actions by the outside world, including customers, vendors, financial community, media, etc.

However, simulations are not simple to produce. They require a carefully researched, richly detailed and highly realistic scenario with a specific supporting script. These must allow flexibility and changes to the plan during the test in order to accommodate differing circumstances and recovery management decisions. It is therefore important that sufficient time be allowed for the preparation of the scenario and supporting script.

TEST PLANNING CHECKLIST

- ✔ date & time of test established
- ✔ test planners appointed & notified
- ✔ test planning meeting held
- ✔ agreement on plan elements to be tested
- ✔ agreement on scope of test
- ✔ agreement on type of test
- ✔ objectives of the test established
- ✔ initial cost estimates prepared & approved
- ✔ agreement of the participants obtained (where necessary)
- ✔ statement of purpose & objectives prepared
- ✔ scenario narrative developed
- ✔ Master Sequence of Events List developed (see below)
- ✔ review meeting held
- ✔ scope, objectives & expected actions reviewed & refined
- ✔ facility / equipment / logistics requirements defined
- ✔ facility / equipment / logistics requirements, suppliers & contractors notified & commitments obtained

✔ test messages, problems developed & prepared
✔ test simulation materials prepared
✔ test evaluation materials prepared
✔ MIS & telecommunications needs identified
✔ hot site & other vendors notified; commitments obtained
✔ final costs, budget established & approved
✔ final review meeting held
✔ pre-test briefing held

TEST SCENARIO CONSIDERATIONS

General:

What is the intended purpose of the test? What objectives is the test intended to achieve? Can these objectives be measured? If they cannot, the objectives should be reconsidered.

Which business units / departments or parts of the plan are to be tested? This will identify the

•plan sections

•business units / departments

•individuals

•procedures, checklists, action plans, etc.

•recovery resources

that are to be tested. The scenario must therefore support this requirement.

- *What situation narrative is to be used?* This will detail the situation leading up to the disaster, the damage, the impact and assumptions made.

- *What is the scenario script?* This is the script that will be followed during the test. It must provide step-by-step information on how the test will be held.

- *How will results be measured?* The measurement criteria that will be used during and after the test must be identified and coordinated with the scenario to ensure compatibility.

- *What test results report format will be used?* Details of the objectives, scenario and results must be incorporated in a report to management. Recommendations for plan changes must also be included in the report. They may form the basis for subsequent test scenarios.

Specific:

- What disruption will be caused to the company's operations?
- What resources will be needed internally and externally?
- Will these resources be available?
- What is the cost of using such resources?
- Has the cost been approved?
- What is the intended length of time of the test?
- What business functions will be tested?
- What support is needed for these functions, e.g.,
  - MIS?
  - telecommunications?
  - support functions (mail, transportation, human resources, etc.)?
- How will these be covered in the scenario?
- What assumptions are to be made?
- How extensive is the test to be?
  - business unit, department or business functions?
  - entire building operation?
  - new operations?
  - support operations?
  - specific teams or individuals?

SCENARIO DEVELOPMENT WORKSHEET

Prepared by: _____ **Date** _____ **Test Reference #:** _____

Purpose and Objectives:
Provides details of the specific testing goals (e.g., measurable deliverables, areas / functions to be tested, support activities / resources to be tested, etc.)

Type of Test:
The type of test to be performed (table-top, walkthrough, simulation, etc.)

Section of Plan Referenced:
Details which part of the plan is to be tested (section, page number, etc.)

Business Units / Departments to be Tested:

Business functions to be Tested:

Equipment / Procedures to be Tested:

Test Date / Time:

Duration *(ACTUAL AND THE TIME COMPRESSED IN THE TEST): Specifies (1) the actual duration of the test (1 hour, ½ day) and (2) the time compression covered by the test, e.g., 1 day, 5 days.*

Probable Participants:
Details the management and senior department personnel who will be involved.

Constraints:
The scope of the test is defined and those plan and test elements which are to be included or excluded are detailed.

Assumptions:
The assumptions that are to be made relative to the operating conditions that will apply during the testing process.

Timing of Disaster:
Scenario Narrative (add separate description if appropriate): A description of the situation leading up to the activation of the plan.

Major Events *(add MSEL - Major Sequence of Events List - if appropriate:*

EVENT:	ACTION:	RESPONSIBILITY:
_____	_____	_____
_____	_____	_____
_____	_____	_____

Details the major events that will occur during the test and indicates the expected actions and the person(s) responsible for such actions. The events and actions can be sequential or parallel.

DEVELOPING THE SCENARIO NARRATIVE

The following should be considered in developing the scenario narrative that is to be used as the basis of the test:

1. What is the hypothetical moment of the disaster (time of day, day of month, part of the year)?

2. What event has triggered the disaster? Describe the type of event (fire, explosion, tornado, power failure, etc.) and how it developed or occurred.

3. How was notification given. Was there advanced warning?

4. If there was advanced warning, what procedures or actions were implemented prior to the disaster?

5. Describe the sequence of events which have occurred leading up to the disaster declaration and activation of the contingency plan.

   Alternately, if there is to be a continuing series of events which will form the basis of the test, describe not only the sequence of events leading up to the activation of the plan but also the sequence of events and their duration that must be anticipated during the test. This will apply particularly if a regional or national disaster such as an earthquake or hurricane is the trigger event, or if a transportation accident prevents building access.

6. Will the disaster have any geographical or regional implications? If so, describe (how fast, strong, dangerous).

7. What response has been taken or is being taken at the time of the activation of the plan?

8. What damage has occurred both internally and externally? Can future damage be anticipated?

9. What is the status of all personnel?

10. What comments should be made about the status and availability of:

    • alternate or backup locations

    • vendors and suppliers

    • backup storage arrangements

- emergency operations center
- utilities.

11. What other predictions for the future affecting the recovery process should be included in the scenario narrative?

MASTER SEQUENCE OF EVENTS LIST

Test Reference #: _____   **Date:** _____

Actual Time:	Simulated Time:	Event (Including any cue actions or events)	Expected Action:	Responsibility:

SAMPLE TEST MESSAGE FORM

Message #: ME- _____   Time Issued: _____

To: _____   From: _____

How is the message to be communicated? (verbally, written, telephone, etc.): _____

_____

_____

Simulated time of the message: (within the test time compression) _____

_____

_____

Text: _____

_____

Action Taken: _____

_____

_____

Special Instructions: _____

_____

_____

SAMPLE TEST PROBLEM FORM

Problem #: PR-_____   Actual Time Issued: _____

Time of occurrence: (within the test time compression) _____

Situation at the time of the problem: _____

_____

Description of the problem or event that has occurred: _____

_____

How will information on the problem / event be transmitted or simulated to the test participants? _____

_____

Are there specific actions which it is anticipated the test participants will take? _____
If so, describe. _____

_____

Do the anticipated actions lead to another problem? _____

_____

If so, what is the problem number? PR _____

_____

Comments from the test controller / simulator / witnesses: _____

_____

_____

8

THE POLITICS OF RECOVERY TESTING
by Philip Jan Rothstein

It should be no surprise to anyone in the business world that disaster recovery testing is susceptible to the inter-personal and inter-departmental give-and-take which characterize most any significant organizational endeavor. In that the degree of maneuvering, posturing and negotiating seem to correlate to the importance of (and effort required for) most any corporate undertaking, it should not be surprising that disaster recovery testing engenders more than its share of controversy. Moreover, the all-too-common perception that disaster recovery testing (let alone planning) is a discretionary investment adds to the difficulty in traversing the minefield of corporate politics.

At this point in this book, a fair assumption is that the reader has in place some semblance of a disaster recovery plan, whether tested or not. It should be noted that many of the issues addressed in this chapter are not unlike those faced in developing and implementing the recovery plan in the first place.

COMMITMENT AND MOTIVATION

It is absolutely essential to the process that the commitment to recovery testing be authentic and clearly communicated prior to beginning the testing process. All too often, the commitment is either shallow or implied, thereby dooming the testing program, and likely the entire disaster recovery capability, to failure. The direct result is most certainly to be failure of the disaster recovery program when it is needed most, that is, as a critical tool during an actual disruption.

A critical distinction between effective or ineffective recovery testing programs can be observed by answering the question:

Is the disaster recovery testing program designed and implemented as a tool to be used during an actual recovery, or as evidence?

The incompetent recovery testing program is, as often as not, a direct result of a powerful, organizational incentive to produce tangible documentation rather than to produce less visible (but far more critical) changes to the organization. In other words, given the task of putting together a testing program, a manager or staff member is most likely to be motivated to deliver an impressive paper document. Of course, the same incentives apply to recovery plan development.

That paper document may or may not be important to the organization during an actual disruption. Far more likely to be vital to recovery is the team experience and process shakedown from exercising the actual testing program. Therefore, one should be conscious of this common, underlying pressure to produce evidence to satisfy management, auditors, regulators or others — evidence which appears to meet the stated demands, but which in fact is unlikely to work when it is most needed.

TEST PRIORITIZATION

The second organizational issue to tackle in the process of implementing and operating a disaster recovery testing program is usually to determine the relative priorities and sequence of business areas, functions, locations or processing applications to be tested. Theoretically, the earliest test subjects should be those which are deemed most critical. In practice, visibility and the potential for embarrassment are far more likely to be motivating factors for choosing (or avoiding) a functional area than is criticality.

On the other hand, the earliest test participants, if even modestly successful, can serve as valuable role models (if not outright advocates), to encourage other business areas to understand the value and benefits of testing. Therefore, some initial consideration should be given to areas which are likely to benefit significantly and directly from the testing process and to have a positive testing experience, even if these areas are not the most critical. Consideration should also be given to those managers who are "on the fence," likely to be won over and to become enthusiastic supporters of recovery testing.

An additional consideration under the heading of "embarrassment" is that the first few tests are most likely to be the most awkward and cumbersome. In other words, the first areas tested should be aware that they are "guinea pigs." This can be used to advantage: these early participants are, in effect, being asked for their assistance in developing and implementing a workable testing process. Therefore, the pressure on the business area (and potential for embarrassment) is deflected. Table-top exercises and structured walk-throughs are ideal for these first few tests and, with little extra effort, can even be made quite enjoyable for the participants.

Specific, tangible and realistic objectives should always be established for each test cycle. Further, intangible objectives should be considered, which are likely to motivate participants. At the least, the knowledge that their functional area has been tested first and is therefore in better shape to withstand a disruption than other business areas should be appealing.

CONFIDENTIALITY

Especially during the initial rounds of recovery testing, line managers and other test participants are likely to be acutely conscious of the potential to be put on the spot without being sufficiently knowledgeable or prepared. For a testing program to be successful, test participants should feel comfortable being open and uninhibited, especially in identifying weaknesses or shortcomings as well as opportunities for improvement. Clearly, it is inherently uncomfortable for most people to acknowledge their shortcomings. Further, given that these participants probably have had little, if any prior experience conducting disaster recovery tests, this comfort level is likely to be quite low.

One approach to increase this comfort level and thereby increase the productivity of the initial tests, is to assure the participants of some limited degree of confidentiality. With the concurrence of their upper management, the initial recovery testing process can be positioned explicitly as a learning tool (which, of course, it is anyway). If the participants are assured of the confidentiality of the appropriate aspects (i.e., the most potentially embarrassing aspects) of their participation in the testing process, they are far more likely to participate fully and willingly. After the initial round(s) of testing, of course, the need as well as desirability to maintain this level of confidentiality should diminish.

DISCIPLINE

For any disaster recovery testing program to prove effective, it must be ongoing and consistent. The reality of most organizations is that planning and testing for a potential event which may never occur can easily slip down in the priority list when stacked against day-to-day urgencies. Therefore, it is generally advisable to address consistency and discipline early in the disaster recovery testing program. It is a pretty safe bet that management's focus will shift away sooner or later, even if testing starts out as a high priority.

One useful method to at least maintain an ongoing level of awareness and discipline is to document and budget a recovery testing program up front as an ongoing, multi-year program. When presented with a well thought-out, continuing plan, top management (as well as management of affected business or functional areas) are much more likely to stick with the program.

One specific technique which has proved useful in many organizations is to regularly refer to tests or test phases with terms which avoid the inference of completion. Such terms as "interim," "strawman," or "trial" may be used to logically set the stage for the next iteration of testing.

Another technique which works well to focus attention on continuation of the testing process, is to specifically define each test as a step in the overall testing scheme; that is, to spell out a long-term testing program (be aware of the risk of following the approved testing program without periodic reviews and retuning). Alternately, this can be expressed as a percentage of a "complete" testing cycle where the end of one cycle becomes the beginning of the next cycle — the classic analogy of the bridge painter starting over again after reaching the end of the bridge may be appropriate.

CONCLUSION

Continuity / recovery testing is not immune from politics or personalities, and any contingency planner who assumes otherwise will fail — and, as often as not, be out of a job. The failure of many contingency planners is less often in their awareness of politics and personalities than in their willingness to apply the management and interpersonal skills necessary to overcome resistance.

9

CLOSING THE LOOP[1]

by Patrick LaValla, Robert Stoffel and Charles Erwin

IMPROVING PREPAREDNESS, PLANNING, AND RESPONSE

The results obtained from the post-exercise debriefing and evaluation need to be implemented if the exercise is to be of any lasting benefit. The results should be included in the continuing planning and preparedness activities of the jurisdiction.

Exercise planners should initiate efforts to revise existing plans and procedures or develop new ones to reflect the lessons from the exercise. Planners should use the evaluation of the exercise itself to improve future exercises. All other participants (law enforcement, fire, safety, etc.) should take actions appropriate to their roles in the preparedness effort.

Approximately three to six months following the exercise, the contingency plans and procedures should be reviewed to ensure that appropriate changes and revisions have been incorporated.

IMPLEMENTING CHANGE AS A RESULT OF AN EXERCISE

An exercise should focus on evaluating specific components which might include:

Evacuation
Communications
Alert and Warning
Operational Security
Site / Incident Command
Response Decision-Making
Environmental Assessment
Ongoing Accident Reporting
Emergency Service Continuity
Employee and Public Education
Emergency Information Dissemination
Initial Accident Assessment and Notification
Acquisition / Distribution of Emergency Supplies
Emergency Response Management and Coordination

The effort to implement change must focus on three issues:

1. *Are the procedures sufficient?*

2. *Are the resources sufficient to support the procedures?* In other words, do the procedures reflect available resources?

3. *Are personnel adequately trained to use the procedures and resources?*

The changes identified to improve preparedness and response may be difficult to implement because there could be turf problems and other resistance to change. Support for the change effort must come from key people. This must be cultivated prior to the actual need for such support. Discreet use of generalizations can help prevent this problem, such as: "We didn't have the personnel to do the job," may be closer to the truth than: "Joe did it wrong!"

EXERCISE FOLLOW-UP

Just as an exercise without recommendations makes an exercise incomplete, recommendations without follow-up will keep an agency or jurisdiction from getting the full benefit of an exercise.

- According to research, follow-up is the number one most neglected area of exercise programs

There are several techniques to ensure that follow-up occurs in your emergency management system:

- Use the exercise and its goals to establish goals for a long-term exercise development and planning guide.

- All recommended changes and improvements should go through some sort of prioritizing process. In this way, if you are unable to accomplish all of the changes or improvements, at least those identified as being the most important will have been taken care of.

- Assign tasks, schedules, and responsibility for each recommended improvement.

- Monitor the progress of implementing recommended improvements

- Build testing of improvements into the next exercise

The best way to start implementing improvements in an emergency management system is to take advantage of the chief executive's interest in the exercise program.

MONITORING FOLLOW-UP

Monitoring follow-up can be a time-consuming job. Making certain that recommendations are implemented is a task requiring tact and a good working relationship with other department heads. You will know how best to achieve follow-up monitoring for your particular circumstances.

LOOKING TO THE NEXT EXERCISE

Building the recommended improvements into the next exercise is perhaps the surest way to make certain they are implemented. It is probably not necessary to create a re-test of every objective. Rather, pick a few recommendations that would illustrate improvements and include those in a future exercise.

DEVELOPING A SUPPORT SYSTEM

Effective individuals and effective organizations are typically linked by a strong network of support. That is, an informal set of individuals or groups that demonstrate a strong mutual loyalty to their goals and are willing to invest in their attainment.

The process of developing a support system is a critical factor to the success of the emergency preparedness program, especially when the organization and its leaders are called upon to invest considerable resources in an exercise program.

The following checklist of strategies may help develop a support system, or strengthen one already existing:

Strategies for Developing a Support System

Identify people and organizations, within and without the agency or jurisdictional structure that have been supportive of the emergency preparedness activities, including exercises. List the factors that helped generate this support.

- Identify people and organizations that have been either neutral or critical of past activities. Note some of the reasons why this has been so.

- Use the two lists to develop strategies for strengthening the helping factors and reducing the hindering ones.

- Conduct informal interviews with key people to obtain their views on the strengths and weaknesses of the emergency preparedness program.

- Ask for time in a staff meeting to review your findings, identify the critical issues for the organization, and present a responsive program.

- Start with a modest proposal, building on the support that is already there. One success leads to another.

- Develop a progress chart. Note key events from the past. Set reachable milestones and targets for the months and years ahead. Keep a desk journal to mark day-to-day progress.

- Keep senior managers in touch with current estimates of the situation.

- Follow-up on initial interviews to keep everyone involved and to develop effective relationships. Allocate adequate time to those you see as barriers to your program.

The Exercise Design Process

> An exercise program will only add to a jurisdiction's / organization's readiness if there is executive support and a commitment to proactive emergency management.

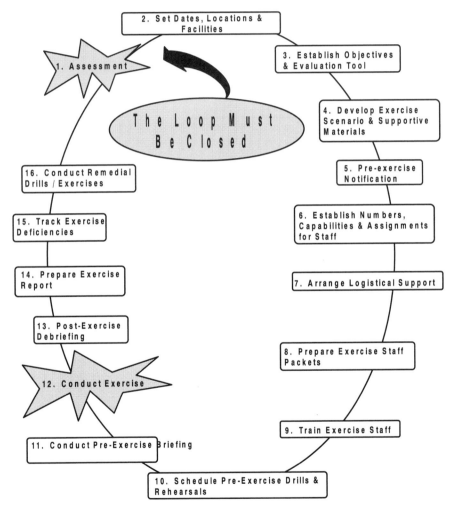

1. Assessment

2. Set Dates, Locations & Facilities

3. Establish Objectives & Evaluation Tool

4. Develop Exercise Scenario & Supportive Materials

The Loop Must Be Closed

5. Pre-exercise Notification

6. Establish Numbers, Capabilities & Assignments for Staff

7. Arrange Logistical Support

8. Prepare Exercise Staff Packets

9. Train Exercise Staff

10. Schedule Pre-Exercise Drills & Rehearsals

11. Conduct Pre-Exercise Briefing

12. Conduct Exercise

13. Post-Exercise Debriefing

14. Prepare Exercise Report

15. Track Exercise Deficiencies

16. Conduct Remedial Drills / Exercises

[1] This chapter has been adapted from the publication *Exercise Planning and Evaluation*, Copyright © 1990, Emergency Response Institute, Inc. Used with permission.

II.

TEST PARTICIPANTS AND RESOURCES

10

THE TEST TEAM
by Michael G. Courton

I have attended countless seminars and conferences which featured presentations from companies that have had to recover from disasters. They usually go into great detail about their planning process, the procedures they implemented, and the tests they performed. However, in summation they all stress that it was their people that invariably saved the day.

One connection that is not emphasized, and it is probably an oversight, is that those individuals who were so instrumental in their recovery were those same individuals who played an important part in the planning and testing process. Development of a disaster recovery plan is done under a small project group. The testing of that plan however, involves a much larger number of personnel and is more important than the development.

In responding to any crisis situation there should be a central core of knowledgeable people who take charge and assists the efforts of all others. Test team members because of their experience, should be a large part of that central core. There are a variety of teams that will be designated to respond to a crisis situation and each of these teams undergo a regular yearly testing cycle. Whether data processing or business, relocation or on-site testing, or even structured walkthroughs, test teams invariably learn things that they can take back to day-to-day operations to benefit the company.

Disaster recovery testing accomplishes three major objectives: first, it trains critical personnel to be able to respond coolly and competently to an emergency; secondly, it assists the planning process by verifying the validity of the plan and by bringing attention to those parts that were either under developed or left out; and third, it provides a way of maintaining the plan by emphasizing those portions that need adjustment and causing the plan to be reviewed prior to each testing cycle.

SELECTION

There are as many possible test teams as there are test scenarios that you could dream up. No book can tell you specifically how to put your teams together, however, there are a few basic guidelines you can follow:

- define the test scenario
- give special consideration to your first test
- involve recovery team members
- determine participation levels
- include senior management
- determine the size of the team
- involve decision makers.

1. Define the test scenario

Needless to say, defining the scenario and its particular objectives as clearly and concisely as possible will greatly reduce the effort it takes to define the test team necessary for accomplishing your task. I will not go into detail here since developed of the scenario was covered in an earlier chapter.

2. Give special consideration to your first test

If you are undertaking your first test, keep it small and simple. Limit the team to no more than 8 people so that a small core begins to develop the working relationship and the confidence in each other's ability that will aid you in reality. For example, it is one thing to believe that the systems support unit can keep the mainframe operating system up and running on a day-to-day basis. But to see them recover it from scratch instills a confidence in everyone else they work with, that will carry over into the performance of every other team not just in their testing but in their recovery planning as well. I have taken part in tests where the ability of a group to accomplish its task in a reasonable amount of time greatly affected the attitude of everyone else taking part in the test.

3. Involve recovery team members

Any person occupying a primary or backup position on the teams listed in your recovery plan should participate regularly. Furthermore these individuals should be rotated so that they are familiar with the roles each will play as well as the roles of the other teams in a real situation.

Also note that in a real crisis you may need two or three teams of a particular type to cover multiple sites during certain phases of your recovery. The Security Team is a good example of this. You will have to provide physical security at the disaster site while concurrently providing security at each of your recovery sites. Coordination of these teams can be accomplished from a central command center. However, leadership of these teams should be under someone who is familiar with operating in recovery mode. That leadership should also be familiar with the major players of the various recovery teams. Participation in the testing cycle is the most logical way to instill this familiarity.

4. Determine participation levels

All attempts should be made to get all personnel in a particular area or that perform a similar task into the testing cycle. In a disaster you never know who you have to call on or who may be available to assist in the recovery. Many recent disasters have been regional in scope and many companies learned the hard way that people will give priority to putting their homes and families back together before the company. If you operate in a metropolitan area, chances are that your employees are geographically dispersed. And it may be necessary to use a senior analyst as a team leader if your primary leadership resides in the disaster zone.

Recovery plans are usually reviewed on an annual basis, consequently if changes need to be made to the plans, then those changes need to be assimilated by the recovery team members. The best way to accomplish that is by testing. Therefore test team members need to be rotated into the testing cycle as often as there are major changes to their portions of the plan.

5. Include Senior Management

I am not advocating that management participate in every test. In my previous experience of coordinating testing cycles, I always made it a point to involve management before a major test. For example, a four-part data processing test cycle went like this:

- First test was a systems test. This is when changes to the basic computer operating system were tested and brought up to date. The DASD administration unit tested new data restoration procedures. Operations tested new operating procedures. Telecommunications tested new network management procedures.

- The second test was to correct any problems encountered in the first. Additionally, major subsystems such as CICS, DB2, and automated job scheduling would be tested. Telecommunications expanded their test to encompass testing telecomm lines. DASD administration expands its objectives to restoring larger amounts of data. Systems support expands to adding more features to the basic operating system.

- At this point we are ready to expand the tests to include applications and internal user areas. Planning for the third test begins with data processing senior management giving the 'troops' a pep talk about the importance of their participation. The third test involves expansion of all prior efforts and inclusion of applications and users. The major application streams would be started, not run to completion. A handful of automated internal user areas would be brought up at their recovery site to test communication lines. All internal and external communications lines would be swung over into disaster mode.

- The final test is a full-blown test of the data processing recovery environment. All applications streams would be run. Several hundred external users would participate to test capacity of the backup network (data and voice lines).

Senior Management from all operational and business areas taking part in the test would visit their respective recovery locations. This serves a dual purpose: It reinforces the commitment of management to the recovery process; but more importantly, it lets them see that recovery is actually possible.

This is important because too often Senior Management steps into a crisis situation and begins to direct specific recovery of functional units when they are unfamiliar with recovery objectives and procedures. If they see it working in a large testing environment then it gives them the confidence to leave functional recovery to the people who know it best. They can then focus on the larger issues of recovery for which they are most qualified.

6. Determine the size of the team

When putting together test teams keep in mind that in times of crisis it will not be business as usual. A functional work unit that regularly employs 20 people does not need to be tested or recovered by all 20 of those people at one time. Do not set yourself up for a logistical nightmare. In the planning process a critical number of personnel needed to recover was estimated. I suggest taking one third of that number as a test team. Then as your test objectives become more or less complicated, vary the number of people. Over the course of one or two testing cycles you should become very familiar with estimating the number of people needed for testing and recovery support. Obviously, if you have small units then the process is simplified.

7. Involve decision makers

This issue seems simpler than it really is likely to be. At first thought you are tempted to start naming middle management positions. Next you expand that train of thought downward to include senior level analysts. But you have to go a little deeper still. In a data processing environment, specifically in the area of operations, 'lowly' computer operators watch your application jobstreams all the time. These jobs display systems messages that require a response, and these messages can get a great deal more complicated than asking for a tape mount. Operators very often know more about application interdependencies than even some of the programmers. Not only that but they know what time of day or night jobstreams run and why.

This type of person should be included in the test team whenever and wherever possible. I am reminded of being in the midst of application testing, only to have a jobstream go berserk and the usual operations personnel familiar with that application not be on duty. The applications support programmer was available but we soon learned that solving those types of problems is a team effort. From that time on, we made sure to schedule applications recovery and operations personnel according to how they worked during a normal work day.

SUMMARY

The personnel involved in disaster recovery planning and testing are a valuable resource to any company, in any industry. Selection and continued education of those individuals should be given some small amount of additional consideration. Many companies have faced crises that could have ended in business failure were it not for some key employees who stepped forward with experience, knowledge and ingenuity to pull them back from "the brink."

11

MANAGEMENT'S ROLE IN TESTING

by Dan W. Muecke

For any disaster recovery / business continuity testing program to be successful, all levels of management must fully support the goals and the activities of the program. This support must be explicit, evident and long term. Management at all levels must recognize that testing for disaster recovery preparedness is an ongoing process — not a single event that is completed and checked off on the corporate "to do" list.

SENIOR MANAGEMENT

Perhaps the most important and most subtle role of senior management with respect to disaster recovery testing is to truly understand why disaster recovery testing is important to the company. Unless senior management is truly appreciative of the need to test and improve the quality of existing disaster recovery plans, the corporate disaster recovery staff will certainly struggle to fulfill its commitment to provide a vital disaster recovery capability.

For senior management to understand the importance of disaster recovery testing, proper communication of the risk involved in not having an adequate testing program is necessary. This must be done in terms management understands and not technical terms. Perhaps the best approach is to frame the discussion in terms of risk and risk avoidance. For some businesses, such as banking, airlines, or mail order companies, the risk of having a disaster occur and being unable to quickly and smoothly recover is obvious.

In most instances, the senior management of these companies will already be predisposed towards supporting disaster recovery testing. In other types of businesses, the need to provide for full disaster recovery testing may be less evident. However, in almost any business, there are certain key issues that will attract senior management's attention. If possible, relating disaster recovery testing to these key issues will allow senior management to properly position disaster recovery testing within the company. Examples of such key issues are:

- the corporation may have covenants or other commitments with investors that require maintenance of specific financial ratios. If a disaster were to occur at a critical time in the reporting cycle, what would be the impact of being unable to provide this information on timely basis? Explicitly quantifying this risk would certainly provide needed information to senior management.

- the extent to which automated procedures have replaced manual procedures in the business process. With the recent trends in corporate re-engineering and downsizing, the resources to move back to a manual processing mode for an interim period often no longer exist — the staff simply does not exist in sufficient numbers or the staff that is present is unlikely to be familiar with the manual process formerly in place.

- the image the company wishes to project. For example, a company that positioned itself as always being able to service its customers would certainly be embarrassed, at best, if it found itself unable to provide customer service due to failure to recover from a disaster. Certainly several prominent mail order companies suffered from just such a failure following the Hinsdale, Illinois switching center fire.

Having understood the relative importance of disaster recovery planning and testing to the overall business strategy of the company, it is now vitally necessary that senior management articulate its understanding to the company's middle managers and employees. This communication must be in terms that are both readily understandable and related to the other similar communications from senior management. An example of a very effective and understandable approach is the theme adopted by one company: "No recovery, no paycheck." This theme instantly makes each employee aware that, for this company, failure to recover from a disaster means that the company is likely to go out of business. This immediately makes successful disaster recovery, including the testing necessary to demonstrate this success, a tangible concern of every employee.

Explicit statements of support must occur on a regular basis. Employees need to be reminded that disaster recovery preparedness is vital to the business. Senior management, of necessity, spends time ensuring that all employees share a common strategic vision of the business. It is through such strategic statement of direction that senior management guides the company and directs the many functions of a modern corporation to work together towards a single goal. The need to maintain company functions in the face of a disaster, whether natural (such as a storm or earthquake), or man-made (such as a fire or terrorist action) must be articulated as part of the basic vision for the company.

Only senior management can make this vision real and communicate its importance to all levels of the company in a credible form. The essence of disaster recovery testing is that it involves multiple groups within the company. The only way that these groups will function to achieve a common goal is if the individual employees and their managers believe that the efforts are in their best interest. This belief can only be established by senior management demonstrating a strong commitment to the need for and the process of disaster recovery testing.

Given that senior management understands the relationship between disaster recovery planning and testing and the continued viability of the company (and has been able to articulate that understanding to its employees), the final role that senior management must fulfill with respect to disaster recovery testing is to be supportive.

The most visible way to demonstrate senior management's support and commitment to disaster recovery testing other than through explicit statements to employees is to provide the resources required to actually carry out the requisite disaster recovery testing. The resources that will be required are many and varied, but will include:

- hardware and software resources required to test the disaster recovery plans for the largest and most critical business functions or applications

- staff (or coverage of overtime costs) to carry out disaster recovery testing at times that are non-critical to normal business processing

- staff dedicated to disaster recovery testing and oversight. In a highly decentralized company, this will likely include the staff in the individual business units needed to actually plan and carry out the tests. In many instances, this resource will come from the existing staff; however, it is critical that senior management explicitly set the priorities of disaster recovery testing high enough to ensure that this function is actually carried out.

- budget resources to enable the business to perform worthwhile disaster recovery testing. If the support of senior management is meaningful, it is likely that these costs will be identified as a specific line item in the budget. The approval of senior management of such a specific line item for disaster recovery testing carries significant weight in establishing disaster recovery testing as a recognized priority.

MIDDLE MANAGEMENT

In the world of the 1990s, the reality of corporate downsizing is likely to be an ongoing theme of the business environment. While corporate downsizing or re-engineering has as its ultimate goal the ability to produce the corporation's products more efficiently, in practice, this often translates into efforts that lead to a thinning of middle management ranks. Disaster recovery testing is one activity where the contributions of middle management are key to the success of the overall effort. It is at the middle management level that these important activities occur:

- the testing plans and associated scenarios are defined

- the testing program is actually managed and carried out

- the process and the results of the disaster recovery testing are reviewed and analyzed

- corrections and necessary revisions to the disaster recovery plan are initiated, closing the feedback loop of which testing is a key component.

If the company chooses to have a disaster recovery planning and testing function at the corporate level or as a resource available to company's business units, it is very likely that this function will be staffed by a small group of middle managers who have demonstrated their competence within the business units. It is this core group that will have oversight responsibility for the corporation to ensure that disaster recovery testing is carried out in accordance with company policy. It will also be this group which certifies the degree of acceptance of each of the tests that are carried out.

Within the company's business units, it will be the responsibility of the senior management of each business unit to ensure that disaster recovery testing is carried out. Whether this function is actually staffed with dedicated staff or is assigned to various middle managers as a part of their day-to-day responsibility will be dependent upon the size of the business units as well as the priority assigned to disaster recovery testing by senior management.

FIRST LINE SUPERVISORS

First line supervisors and their staff will be the people who actually carry out and perform the company's disaster recovery tests. The most important role for these people is to make the test as realistic as possible. In order for this to occur, the following steps must be followed:

- test participants must fully understand the scenario under which the testing is to be conducted. For example, if the test scenario is simulating a major fire at a facility that requires the full evacuation of that facility, this means that no one will be allowed access to the facility in the event that something within the facility is required during the test.

- given that problems are likely to be encountered during the testing process (after all, finding these problems is the major reason tests are conducted), test participants should fully use their resourcefulness to overcome the problems within the constraints of the test scenario. For example, if a critical document was missing where the most readily accessible copy was known to be in the burning building above, in real life it is unlikely that you would simply say that the disaster recovery efforts could not proceed. In a real disaster, people would meet, brainstorm where additional copies might be, and then try everything in their power to obtain a copy of the document. In a testing situation, why should the effort expended be any less?[1]

- in addition to expending the appropriate level of effort to overcome problems, each member of the testing team should note:

  - problems encountered;

  - how the problems were overcome; and,

  - potential changes which could prevent this problem from recurring in a future test or real disaster.

- under no circumstances should problems be hidden. First line supervisors must continually stress that testing is being conducted to find problems. A successful test is not necessarily a test that proceeds to conclusion with no problems — this may simply mean that the test was poorly designed and actually failed to accomplish its purpose.

- first line supervisor must be especially vigilant about identifying undocumented assumptions within the disaster recovery plan, especially with respect to staffing. Examples of undocumented assumptions that may be present include:

  - all personnel are unaffected by the disaster event and available for disaster recovery duty;

  - no key person is traveling or on vacation;

  - all personnel can move freely to the disaster recovery location. There are no impediments to travel due to road conditions, the condition of mass transit, etc.;

  - all individuals are available, when required, for whatever length of time may be required for disaster recovery to be completed;

  - all personnel will be concentrating on completing the disaster recovery efforts and will not be distracted by other concerns.

In most test situations, adequately identifying these hidden assumptions may be difficult. Therefore, each first line supervisor must regularly take time out to ask themselves the question, "Could this effort be sustained in a real situation?"

Following the conclusion of the disaster recovery test, there should certainly be a debriefing by the key individuals involved. It is at this point that first line supervisors must make known:

- their observations about problems;

- actual work-arounds used;

- potential ways to make the disaster recovery process go smoother; and,

- identification of unrealistic assumptions contained in the disaster recovery plans.

To this point, the individual roles of management, from senior management through first line supervisors have been discussed. It would be easy to conclude that as long as each level of management carries out its roles, successful disaster recovery testing will happen. Such is not the situation. The most vital issue for all levels of management with disaster recovery testing responsibility is to function as a team. There are no super-heroes or team super stars in disaster recovery testing; dependence on those super-stars is likely to be hazardous. If disaster recovery testing is to truly be successful and ensure the ultimate success of any disaster recovery efforts when actually needed, it is absolutely necessary that all levels of management contribute effectively and selflessly to the team effort.

---

[1] One difference in a testing situation versus a real life situation is that the test coordinator or referee may allow the use of an "unavailable" resource if the disaster recovery team has uncovered a similar resource somewhere else.

12

PSYCHOLOGICAL ISSUES IN A CRISIS SIMULATION EXERCISE[1]

by David G. Doepel

INTRODUCTION

The group of eight, seven employees and a counselor, were seated in a close circle. Brought together by the events of the previous couple of days they seemed weary, although their conversation had an urgent, intense character to it. One employee voiced concern about a deceased colleague's family, another recounted his lack of effectiveness in the face of the assault, still another, a supervisor, felt she should be strong in the face of this calamity — for the sake of her employees. The group was remarkable in a number of ways: the depth of the feelings was extraordinary, the honesty with which people faced the painful "reality" was commendable and the expression of concern for one another was a true example of the helping spirit that nearly always emerges during a crisis.

Even more remarkable, however, was the setting and occasion of this "debriefing group." These eight individuals were surrounded by approximately seventy-five other people — managers and executives — including a number of senior company officers who had flown in on the company jet for the occasion. The occasion? A disaster that had been in the making for about one year: a meticulously planned, state-wide, thirty-six hour simulation exercise for a national telecommunications company involving hundreds of employees, managers and corporate executives.

This event, the inclusion of psychological issues in a crisis simulation exercise, marks a further stage in the evolution of the role of psychology and traumatic stress theory in corporate emergency preparedness. During the last decade, an enormous amount of research has been conducted on the psychological aspects of the human response to traumatic events and great strides have been taken to incorporate those findings into a company's response plans in the wake of a crisis or crises. Such recent events as Hurricane Andrew and the World Trade Center bombing have shown how a number of major corporations sought out and contracted for "debriefing services" for management and employees. These same events also show that while companies are willing to entertain psychological support for their staff when the need is palpable and immediate, few had incorporated the need for such actions into prior plans even when those plans were thoroughly developed.

THEORETICAL CONSIDERATIONS

Prompt psychological interventions with managers and employees post-trauma have been employed in many workplace settings in Europe, North America Australia and Asia. Such procedures are indicated by the traumatic nature of many workplace crises and are directed at mitigating the long-term debilitating effects of post traumatic reactions through peer support, education and professional mental health counseling.

PRACTICAL CONSIDERATIONS

Any sound corporate crisis management approach will include: the development of crisis plans and procedures; training of employees and managers; testing plans and procedures; and, in the event of an actual crisis, implementation of a mechanism for thorough evaluation. It is possible given this "recipe" of good crisis management to "fold" in the "ingredients" outlined above in a number of creative ways. And by so doing a company will enhance the overall effectiveness of its crisis management activities.

PLANNING

In this phase any company, as it develops new plans or revises existing ones, can pay attention to the psychological aspects of crises in two ways. First, those persons in departments directly involved and responsible for employee well-being can pre-arrange for psychological support in the event of a crisis. Such support could come from an Employee

Assistance Program, a Local Mental Health Center or a specialized psychological services organization that provides emergency mental health services to companies in the wake of traumatic events. Furthermore, those same individuals should also become acquainted with the range of mental health services offered by these various sources as well as their requirements (physical space, level of cooperation from management, clarification of the degree of confidentiality, etc.).

The second level of involvement of the psychological aspects of a crisis is to assist all departments and/or business units that are responsible for creating plans and procedures for their particular group to be aware of the psychological support available (as outlined above) and how it can be accessed in a time of crisis. These same groups should also be educated about the typical kinds of reactions (their intensity as well as their duration) experienced by people in crisis. Such information can prove invaluable in determining staffing levels and in developing activation protocols and realistic work schedules. For example, individuals in a crisis situation will typically be highly motivated to "pitch in," to do "whatever it takes" to get things going again. Managers may be glad for the enthusiasm but will also face the two-fold problem of there sometimes not being enough work to go around (as well as a lack of staff to coordinate "volunteers") or the situation of a crisis lasting longer than 24 - 36 hours and having no "fresh" employees to work a rotation.

The important exception to this rule is a crisis situation that threatens an individual's family or private property. In such situations people find themselves with conflicting loyalties. Clearly in the majority of cases a family's immediate needs will come first. A number of companies during the Hurricane Hugo disaster responded to this situation by providing on-site day care for employee's children.

Information on the psychology of crisis can also be extremely beneficial to those charged with the task of internal corporate communications. Creating and disseminating messages that provide helpful information, particularly around safety issues, is an excellent strategy for addressing employee concerns. Traumatized individuals regularly report that they fear a repeat event and that they generally feel less safe than before, even if the crisis has passed, i.e., they require more reassurance than usual as well as accurate, factual information that can help them feel in control of the situation. Also helpful are the development of strategies that can minimize the potential impact of traumatic news.

Overall the goal is to infuse the entire crisis plan with an appreciation for the direct psychological needs of employees and managers and to use this same information so that the plan anticipates real situations with regard to staff capabilities during crises.

TRAINING AND TESTING

An integral component of any effective crisis management approach is to train employees and managers about crisis plans and their role in a crisis situation. Such training will vary in sophistication depending on the level of responsibility of the trainees. However, it is appropriate in the context of this article to suggest that any person in a management position would benefit from at least a brief overview of the psychological aspects of crises. Such material would be best taught as part of a larger training curriculum that addresses other essentials of crisis theory and practice. Again it is my belief and experience that if a manager is required to be a part of business resumption and business recovery activities, and if they are trained accordingly, then they should know how to interact with their staff and how to work with them appropriately during a crisis and in the post-crisis environment. The goal of such training should be to "learn how people perform under crisis conditions, how they might react during and after a traumatic event, what they need to hear from their managers, and what they will need to see their managers do." Such training should be practically oriented, with a significant amount of case material.

Without exception such training, while touching on sometimes difficult subject matter, should remain educational and not be turned into "group therapy." At the same time the trainer needs to be cognizant of the fact that a significant minority of any audience will know of traumatic experiences first hand and the trainer will need to address sensitive issues in an extremely careful manner. (In one series of training with a total audience of 150 at least 10 participants indicated by their comments in the class or by mentioning to the instructor in private that they had undergone experiences similar to those talked about in the training — murder of a loves one, arson, assault, natural disaster and industrial accidents). In some cases it may be necessary to provide a mechanism for referral for persons who feel the need to talk more personally about their experiences.

Training managers in this way increases their level of competency during a crisis, reducing at least one area in which feelings of helplessness could be generated while at the same time allowing managers to offer timely and appropriate help to their employees and fellow managers. However, unless it is incorporated into one's working world, any kind of training is soon forgotten, and because of the infrequency (hopefully) of traumatic events managers will have limited or no opportunity to practice these skills. (In fact, one introduction to a management training on traumatic stress led with the comment that the presenter hoped the material would never be useful!) Furthermore, not all situations can be anticipated and the uniqueness of every crisis, even those crises that are anticipated, requires creative and novel thinking on the part of employees and managers, creative and novel thinking that cannot always be "taught". These facts have led to the development of simulation exercises that test plans, rehearse skills and procedures, and introduce people to creative problem solving. Fortunately, skills and procedures related to the psychological aspects can also be incorporated into simulation exercises.

SIMULATION EXERCISES

FIGURE 1 - *SIMULATION EXERCISE OPENING SEGMENT*

One of your work colleagues has just called you and said: "Quick, turn on the T.V. - we're on the news... M.I. is burning!"

ANCHOR: Good morning, I'm Lynn Jolicoeur. During the night a four-alarm fire engulfed the offices of Middleton Investments in the Financial District. At this time the fire continues to burn although fire officials say that it should be under control by the time most commuters reach the downtown area. Sandra Harding was on the scene earlier this morning and filed this report.

HARDING: Middleton Investments erupted in a ball of flames at 2:00 a.m. this morning, summoning firefighters from four precincts to battle the blaze that quickly spread throughout the offices on the 27th floor of the Middleton Enterprises building. Since then, fire officials say they have been hampered in their efforts

	to control the flames by low water pressure. Standing with me is Jack Wilson, Chief of the Second Precinct. Chief Wilson, can you tell us how this fire started?
WILSON:	We won't know for sure until we can examine the area, but we've had reports from people who happened to be in the area that they heard a loud explosion. One individual reported seeing glass shatter on the twenty-seventh floor.
HARDING:	Any fatalities?
WILSON:	We understand that a number of individuals in the data processing unit were in the building at the time of the explosion. That's about as much as I can say.
ANCHOR:	We can tell you now that two Middleton Investment employees have died as a result of the fire and three others are still unaccounted for. One firefighter was also killed when a portion of the ceiling collapsed. Commuters are advised that the Middleton Enterprises Building is closed and the area within a two-block radius has been cordoned off. We will continue to bring you more information on this story as it becomes available.

When we come back, a look at today's weather with Bob. |

The fictional newscast (*see Figure 1*) was used to begin a three hour simulation exercise for disaster recovery professionals. Clearly, from this news report, the fictitious company is faced with a disaster of massive proportions that will require crisis management of all critical business functions and extensive use of public relations, human resource and activation of the corporate-level emergency operations center. One of the significant aspects of the Middleton simulation exercise is that it was purposefully designed to test all levels of a company's crisis management activities including those that require dealing with the traumatic stress of employees and managers. In the Middleton simulation, the purpose of including material dealing with stress was two-fold:

- it added legitimacy to the issue by including it along with other "more traditional" crisis issues (*see Figure 2*)

- it gives those participating in the simulation a chance to understand how serious the human response to traumatic events can be.

FIGURE 2: *INJECTS FOR MIDDLETON SIMULATION EXERCISE*

9:41a.m.	**Telecom** Staff answering calls, which have been forwarded to a small number of phones at the hotel, are being flooded with calls regarding option contracts and T-bills as well as people inquiring about the crisis. Can we reroute to Chicago office?
9:45 a.m.	**Data Processing** Plane landed, data recovery team and tapes proceeding to hot site
9:50 a.m.	**Human Resource** One of your managers calls from a nearby hospital to say that another employee has died. The next of kin have not been notified. What should he do?
9:55 a.m.	**Facilities** Receives copy of space available in Boston by courier, as requested, begin selection process.

Using simulated newscasts increases the level of realism and, by inviting participants to face what they would do if a colleague was killed (again fictitious names were used), the simulation assists participants in realizing the importance of the issue and gives them an opportunity to "try out" a number of strategies. One note of caution: in simulations there is a level of realism that is inappropriate and that can have an actual traumatizing effect on players. Great care was taken in this case to not over sensationalize the scenario or provide footage that was traumatizing. In other contexts, screening players or supplying potential players with accurate descriptions of the content of a simulation so that they may be able to self-select out of the game if it is "too close to home" may be appropriate.

In another simulation exercise (which included the scenario introducing this article) of the 132 issues and events injected into the play over a 36-hour period eight were specifically designed to raise the question of psychological trauma and appropriate responses from managers (see *Figure 3*). The integrated nature of that particular company's approach to crisis management also meant that the injects were related to specific elements of the corporate plan and the training program, resulting in a reinforcement of the learning that occurred during the training. It should also be noted that this reinforcement applied to other areas of training as well (i.e., corporate communications).

FIGURE 3: *INJECT FROM TELECOMMUNICATIONS SIMULATION*

MESSAGE AT 1 HOUR 45 MINUTES POST CRITICAL EVENT:

Approximately 200 employees are in the vicinity of the main company building. This number includes people who were on shift when the first explosion occurred but who refused medical treatment, those who were arriving to go on shift, and others who arrived later. Additional employees unable to reach anyone by phone, but hearing about the incident on radio and TV, have also arrived. Some employees followed departing ambulances to the hospitals to check on people who had received treatment, and to determine who the injured and dead were. Throughout the group there is strong evidence of concern about what they should do, how they can help, and clamor over what had caused the explosions. Some talk about going to ——————— to find out where they should report for work, but most stay to find out what will happen next.

Perhaps the most positive aspect of the use of the issue of psychological trauma in corporate crisis simulation exercises is that the issue is present at all. It is also significant that such material was well received and, as reported anecdotally, led to a manager involving mental health professionals to support traumatized employees during a real crisis situation. An involvement, according to the manager that would not have occurred had he not participated in a simulation exercise that raised the issue of psychological trauma.

CONCLUSION

In the 1980s considerable progress was made in applying insights from traumatic stress theory and practice to the area of crisis management. In an earlier article it was proposed that these insights could be developed into models of intervention to be employed in the post-crisis phase. This article argues that the task in the 1990s is to incorporate these practices and insights into the larger activity of crisis management, specifically in planning, training and testing. Experiences in all three of these activities indicate that such a task is not only reason able but is necessary if a company wishes to be fully prepared when disaster strikes. Furthermore, such preparedness empowers managers and companies in the face of traumatic situations, and allows individuals to be recipients of care and providers of it.

It is also possible that these principles could be applied to stakeholders other than those referred to in this article (managers and employees). Any crisis, even those that primarily affect a company, are systemic in nature and the many stakeholders, particularly those at the community level, should be included in this model.

[1] Adapted from an article in Industrial and Environmental Crisis Quarterly, 7 (1993): Doepel, D. G.: *"Psychological Preparedness and Crisis Management: Theory and Practice."* Used with permission.

13
THE CONSULTANT'S ROLE IN DISASTER RECOVERY TESTING
by Marvin S. Wainschel

Testing the Disaster Recovery Plan or Business Continuity Plan requires a variety of skills, many of which may be readily available within a given organization. Sometimes, however, it may be expedient to hire a consultant. The consultant's expertise and experience will vary depending upon the task at hand. There are management consultants and technical contractors. A consultant may be used to provide guidance, train test participants, assist in planning, perform test functions, audit the test, and/or help to correct problems uncovered in the process of testing.

THE TESTING PROCESS

The process of testing is defined in some detail in other parts of this book. Following are those elements of the process in which consultants can play a role:

✔ Identify "customer" (for the testing process) and users (of the tested systems)

✔ Set testing objectives

✔ Establish a test planning team

✔ Coordinate team activities

✔ Run team meetings

Prepare for the test:

- ✔ Contact vendors
- ✔ Establish contact with management whose support is required
- ✔ Create test schedule and logistics
- ✔ Provide team members with contact information peculiar to the test
- ✔ Determine how test results will be measured and prepare methodology for collecting data
- ✔ Prepare test software and data (e.g., system and network gens)
- ✔ Prepare pull-lists for off-site materials such as backups
- ✔ Notify affected groups of the test
- ✔ Arrange for physical and data security

Test:

- ✔ Coordinate
- ✔ Audit
- ✔ Participate (as equipment monitor/operator, scribe, gofer, user liaison, observer/technical assistant, network technician)
- ✔ Analyze results / report results / recommend changes to the recovery plan
- ✔ Track and/or assist in corrective action to meet next test objectives

Despite the diversity of skills for which a consultant could be useful, . . .

DO YOU REALLY NEED OUTSIDE HELP?

Why would you hire a consultant? Summarizing from our opening statement, the reasons are to perform guidance, training, planning, doing, auditing, and/or correcting. Let's examine which of these consulting skills can be applied to consulting tasks as defined above:

CONSULTING TASKS ▼ VS. SKILLS →	GUIDE	TRAIN	PLAN	DO	AUDIT	CORRECT
Identify "customer" (for the testing process) and users (of the tested systems)	✓		✓			
Set testing objectives	✓		✓			
Establish a test planning team	✓	✓	✓			
Coordinate team activities	✓			✓		
Run team meetings				✓		
Prepare for the test:						
• Contact vendors				✓		
• Establish contact with management whose support is required				✓		
• Create a test schedule and logistics			✓	✓		
• Provide team members with contact information peculiar to the test				✓		
• Determine how test results will be measured and prepare methodology for collecting data			✓			
• Prepare test software and data (e.g., system and network gens)		✓		✓		
• Prepare pull-lists for off-site materials such as backups		✓	✓	✓		

CONSULTING TASKS ↓ VS. SKILLS →	GUIDE	TRAIN	PLAN	DO	AUDIT	CORRECT
• Notify affected groups of the test				✓		
• Arrange for physical and data security				✓		
Test:						
• Coordinate				✓		
• Audit				✓	✓	
• Participate (as equipment monitor/operator, scribe, go-fer, user liaison, observer/technical assistant, network technician)				✓		
Analyze results / Report results / Recommend changes to the Disaster Recovery Plan					✓	
Track and/or assist in corrective action to meet next test objective	✓			✓		✓

If you count the check marks, you'll find thirty ways to use a consultant for disaster recovery testing. The question remains, "Do you need a consultant for any one of them?" Each of these tasks can be handled in-house if you have the time and the skills, but do you need the objectivity of a consultant or the diverse experience? Can you obtain management backing to hire outside help for this particular task? That may depend upon a proper definition of the task. Taken one at a time, then . . .

Identify "customer" and users

We are not talking here about the Customer of the corporation's products or services, but the internal customer who is most interested in knowing the outcome of the test and whether objectives were met. It may well be the person whose budget is funding the test. Users use the system(s) whose recoverability is being tested. These people are not likely to be the customer. Confusing users with customers can affect the entire test, because success indicators are derived from customer specifications. It may be worth your while to assure that this step is done correctly by hiring an expert management consultant for just a couple of hours to guide you through the process of identifying the customer, even if the consultant is used for nothing else. This requirement may be a tough pill for a recovery planner to swallow. Typically, planners ignore this step, thinking they know who the customer is — or not caring. However, tests must satisfy the customer, so if you are not absolutely sure who that is, you may not be able to set reasonable test objectives.

The process of identifying the customer is not necessarily trivial, depending upon the complexity and size of the organization and the systems being tested. In a large organization, it is often necessary to chart the business processes which are supported by the systems being tested. Because this task involves some knowledge of the business and how it may be impacted by a functional loss, it may be necessary to query subject-matter experts, and the logistics of achieving consensus among the experts is a planning function that may require outside help.

Set testing objectives

If you solicit outside assistance to set testing objectives, the astute consultant will want to know first who the customer is. That brings us back to step one, so be sure you take things in order. If you must bypass the formal approach to customer identification, you can arrive at an intuitive assessment of "who" and proceed to "what." You need to understand, however, that if your assessment is incorrect, your test may be successful but signify nothing to the real customer.

Objectives are important to the testing program as a whole as well as to each individual test. Consultants with wide experience in disparate organizations can provide a perspective and guidelines for setting up a successful program, which leads to establishing a testing team that sets individual test objectives. Setting objectives is part of an overall planning process, and consultants can help you plan or simply guide you through the process.

Establish a test planning team

There may already be a steering committee for recovery planning, but the testing team will consist of people who are more operationally oriented. Consultants can provide advice about team structure, assist in your plans to bring the team together and define goals, and orient new team members to the mission as well as their responsibilities in achieving that mission.

Coordinate team activities / Run team meetings

For teams to be effective, they need leadership. Management consultants generally excel in this area. Choosing a consultant who is a "people" person and who understands the quality process of team building and facilitation will carry your testing program a long way towards success. The consultant may simply provide advice to the team leader or may be the team leader.

Prepare for the test

The nature of test preparations will vary according to the type of test. A notification test may require only minor preparation, whereas a complete disaster simulation may require detailed scripting, even for a test that is a surprise to most participants. Whatever test preparations are required, consultants occasionally can provide valuable assistance to:

- **Contact vendors** — Vendors who might be involved in testing and test preparation include providers of recovery-site facilities, communications lines and equipment, off-site storage, transportation, hotels, meals, etc. Most experienced disaster recovery consultants have a rapport with at least a few vendors in their field. Whether or not that rapport is with your vendors, the consultant may have a strong basis for negotiating services for which your company might otherwise have to pay a premium.

- **Establish contact with management whose support is required** — Some consultants demonstrate an ability to work well with senior level people and can represent your interests well towards accomplishing a superior test.

- **Create a test schedule and logistics** — This planning needs to be thorough and accurate. What do you expect to happen each hour from the time materials arrive at the recovery-site to the final cleanup activity? Who's responsible for each major objective and what are the milestones leading up to the test? This planning may demand a concentrated effort that regular staff may not be able to work into a busy schedule.

- **Provide team members with contact information peculiar to the test** — For a long or complex test that demands a great deal of coordination, this administrative responsibility needs to key off the larger task of scheduling, coordination, and logistical planning (Refer to previous point).

- **Determine how test results will be measured and prepare the methodology for collecting data** — There is a need here to interview both users and applications systems analysts to determine the base data configuration, how updates will be applied during the test, batch-wise and interactively, and when reports will be generated to compare to the pre-test reports. An experienced consultant will know the right questions to ask, will be quick to understand the implications of the responses upon the testing scenario, and will be able to construct a test scenario including pre-test data collection, that will satisfy the need to measure results, report successes, and, where necessary, take corrective action.

- **Prepare test software and data** — Frequently, recovery-site machines, while compatible to the production machines, are not running the same operating systems. In the least, it is likely that the addresses of peripheral devices will be different. A systems programmer is needed to make the appropriate changes, and sometimes specific telecommunications expertise is required to manage the reconfiguration of front-end processors at the recovery-site. Often, systems and telecommunications personnel on staff are not easily refocused to these tasks, and consultants with this specific kind of expertise are called in.

Even so, consultants will need to be briefed by your own personnel and will need access to technical information. One of the benefits of this exercise is that an external consultant will recognize documentation gaps more readily than the internal expert who knows what belongs in the gaps and in the course of day-to-day operations no longer recognizes the lack of information.

In addition to the need for systems software, sometimes application software and/or "job control" software requires modification to conform to test scenarios. Also, because of time constraints anticipated at the time of the test, it may be desirable to prepare special test data that is a subset of normal production data. Applications programmers faced with this need may also be grappling with their own time constraints and may be convinced that the full database is "good enough" for this test. Yet, time constraints for testing may be unavoidable, whether imposed by the recovery-site provider or determined by the test coordinator. Sometimes, allocating a smaller timeframe for each application to be tested will allow testing of a greater number of applications per test, thereby reducing the number of tests. An external programmer whose focus is to complete testing objectives within the time frames allocated for testing may be more sensitive than an internal programmer to meeting these pre-test objectives, and the additional expense of a consultant for a given test may be balanced against the cost savings of reduced test time.

- **Prepare pull-lists for off-site materials such as backups** — The details of this process are best handled by your own clerical staff or tape-management staff using your tape-management system and/or other tracking and inventory systems. However, a methodology to verify pull-list generation instructions will greatly strengthen the validity of the list. Recovery-site vendors and disaster recovery consultants generally agree that the prime obstacle to successful hot site testing is a missing backup tape, and that circumstance is caused far more often by an inaccurate pull-list than by a clerical error in pulling the wrong tape. A consultant can help to develop a methodology for assuring that the pull-lists are correct as well as algorithms for efficient and verifiable pull-list generation.

- **Notify affected groups of the test** — Ideally, recovery testing is non-disruptive, but this is not always possible. For example, active communications lines sometimes need to be switched or disabled, and people who are not part of the test may be affected.

- **Arrange for physical and data security** — Physical security is primarily an issue when using an external facility for testing. Typically, recovery-site vendors require identification of participants to restrict access within their facility. Some coordination with the vendor is required in this case. More important is the assurance that data is protected before, during, and after the test, just as it must be protected at time of disaster. Since the data used in testing is restored from backups, we would not be overly concerned about unintentional destruction or unauthorized modification. However, unauthorized access (disclosure) of sensitive data is still a concern. Data security systems should be in place during a test not only to protect the confidentiality of the data but to test the data security system at the foreign site.

Test

Consultants can coordinate, audit, or participate in actual testing, as follows:

- **Coordinate** — It may sound strange to have a consultant run your test rather than merely provide guidance for the on-staff disaster recovery coordinator. However, many a successful test has been coordinated by a competent consultant with leadership abilities and a thorough knowledge of testing requirements. A conscientious consultant may help to keep the on-staff coordinator "honest" by avoiding short-cuts in the testing process. Testing can be a simple, useless exercise or it can be a valuable part of the planning for recovery preparedness. Whereas the on-staff coordinator may ask, "How do we assure successful testing?", the consultant is more likely to ask, "Why are we testing and how do we get the most out of it?"

The experience that a consultant brings to the testing scene is likely to produce additional or enhanced accomplishments. For example, it is typical in testing to have secondary objectives, should circumstances allow. An experienced and conscientious consultant will know just how hard to push for the secondary objectives and will usually achieve those objectives — often to the delight and amazement of the other participants.

If you decide to have a consultant coordinate the actual testing, that person should be given the opportunity to run pre-test planning sessions as well and should have ultimate responsibility to create the test schedule and to plan logistics.

- **Audit** — A consultant who has a good deal of testing experience may be the best auditor for a disaster recovery test. For one thing, the consultant has no ax to grind with participants and can view events positively and negatively, but always objectively. Even corporate EDP auditors tend not to be totally objective and there is a tendency for them to be negative. Auditors do not habitually look for what is right with the world; it is not their job. But we need to find what's right with the test as well as its downfalls. Teams consist of people, and people need positive reinforcement. If you want your next test to be a success, consider the needs of the test participants and secure an auditor with a positive outlook. You may need to look outside the company.

  Another reason an outsider may be preferred over an internal auditor is that disaster recovery consultants typically understand disaster recovery and will not have to disrupt testing activities unnecessarily in order to clarify what is going on. To further minimize that kind of disruption, make sure the consultant who will audit the test attends the pre-test planning sessions.

- **Participate** — Unlike consultants who coordinate or audit tests, those who participate in specific testing activities are likely to be technical contractors. For example, a contractor local to the recovery-site can be hired as a computer operator where the recovery-site is remote and it does not seem worthwhile to send staff that distance, or you may wish to thoroughly check the documented procedures by having a "stranger" follow them verbatim. Contractors can serve as scribes to document the work performed by others, or contractors can be sophisticated network technicians who assist and share knowledge with the on-staff technicians while working together to test and re-work procedures for network connectivity. Using technical contractors for disaster recovery testing can also be viewed as building backup personnel resources that could be used later in an emergency.

Analyze results / Report results / Recommend changes to the Disaster Recovery Plan

If a consultant is auditing or coordinating the test, that person may be the ideal analyst or reporter of results. Consultant or not, the person should be meticulous in reporting the facts and unbiased in placing responsibility for corrective action. Two reports are necessary: a *chronology report* for review by participants in post-mortem discussion and a *summary report* for management that links symptoms uncovered in testing to problem definition and then to problem resolution and the persons / departments responsible for the correction. The need for unbiased reporting may best be achieved by personnel not on regular staff.

Track and/or assist in corrective action to meet next test objectives

The most useful part of testing is in detecting problems. What is left is for the problems to be resolved. Consultants can provide guidance in tracking the corrective action or can actually ride herd over the personnel who are assigned to resolve the problem. It is also possible to hire a consultant to fix the problem.

CHOOSING THE RIGHT CONSULTANT

Hiring a consultant for any purpose is a team-building exercise. Select a consultant who will enhance your team, if one exists, or who fits into your vision of a competent team. Watch out for sales people who seem to be superstars but are selling some other consultant within their firm. Insist upon talking to the consultant(s) who will do the job. Ask for a proposal and make sure you have at least one face-to-face meeting to review the proposal with a knowledgeable member of the consulting firm. Do not take the proposal at face value. You are buying consulting services to meet a particular objective, so make sure the consultant understands your objective and can do the job. Remember, however, that if you are hiring a consultant for expertise that you do not have, you have the option to discuss your objectives with the consultant and change your views based upon the consultant's suggestions.

In all cases, ask for references and consider the consultant's reputation. However, you would be wise to downplay "credentials" and whatever tendency you may have to cater to the old-boy network. Choose your consultant on the basis of knowledge, experience, and willingness to support your objectives. The goal is to get the work done.

MANAGING THE CONSULTANT PARTNERSHIP

Don't forget why you hired a consultant. The consultant should be regarded as another member of your team, not as a super-hero expected to out-perform or intimidate others. Aside from the fact that such a person might be disruptive to the team, the truth is that most consultants are not super-heros. Maintain realistic expectations, and, if you want your money's worth, make sure the consultant has your cooperation and the tools to do the job.

You'll need to track the consultant's efforts and achievements, but if you feel you've picked the right consultant, trust will go a long way in the success of the test. If at any time you feel that the consultant has lost your trust and you are unable to communicate to get at the root of your uneasiness, then get another consultant. A consultant you cannot trust, just like any employee in whom you've lost faith, will not be successful. On the other hand, you may need to lose a battle or two in order to win the war. Beware of judging every little event; drive towards the objective — a successful test.

14
THE RECOVERY
VENDOR'S PERSPECTIVE
by John Sensenich

The rapidly growing dependence of business on Information Services (IS) has led to the emergence of the disaster recovery industry to protect this important, but fragile, asset. In the past, companies focused primarily on the contingency planning process, developing elaborate plans to recover their primary business functions in the event of a disaster.

Today, with information widely dispersed throughout the organization – much of which is outside the traditional domain of the IS department, the guardians of the "glass house" – a comprehensive approach to testing these disaster recovery plans is essential.

This chapter presents the vendor's perspective on this critical issue and offers guidelines and recommendations for businesses that want to learn more about the importance of testing in ensuring business survival.

SEMANTICS

IS professionals have used the term "testing" for a number of years. As a concept, testing traces its roots to the 1970s and to the beginnings of the commercial hot site business itself. Unfortunately, the term "testing" carries some negative connotations: the pass / fail implication carried over from school days. Such a view when applied to disaster recovery plans is becoming outdated and, in some cases, counter-productive.

A far better approach is to use the terms "exercising" or "rehearsing." These terms give a more accurate picture of the purpose and process of trying out a disaster recovery plan. After all, the purpose of exercising a plan is to determine its weaknesses as well as its strengths, and to look for ways to ensure a successful recovery in the face of disaster. "Exercising" focuses attention on the positive, not the punitive.

Using more precise terminology is key to developing a healthy appreciation for the process itself. This perception will benefit client and vendor alike and help both in building a successful relationship with each other.

WHY EXERCISE?

The surest way to turn a disaster recovery manual into a waste of time and money is failure to exercise the plan. Exercising is critical in the development and maintenance of contingency plans.

There are five specific reasons why plans should be exercised or rehearsed regularly. They include:

- assessing whether the plan works, and whether it meets the business' recovery needs
- identifying weaknesses in the plan prior to an actual disaster situation
- increasing employee awareness and training them for a potential disaster
- compliance with legal necessity and regulatory requirements in the banking or insurance industries and with emerging requirements in many other industries
- protecting both the company and the company's investment in disaster recovery planning.

These principals apply equally to mainframe, mid-range and work group recovery planning.

VARIATIONS IN THE NEED TO EXERCISE

Just as recovery needs differ from one organization to another, not all organizations have the same needs when it comes to the frequency or approach they apply to exercising these plans. The complexity of the recovery plan, as well as the potential business impact of each component of the plan, will influence an organization's plan exercise needs.

Variations will also be found within the organization itself. Some departments (for example, outside sales and long-term strategic planning) are likely to have fairly low risk in recovery, allowing less rigorous exercising to be done. Process-oriented departments, however, may have greater risk and increased recovery complexities, justifying more frequent personnel training and recovery plan exercising.

For work group recovery exercising, the approaches and frequency depend on the complexity of the organization. For ease of testing and awareness, some plans may be separated and exercised by phase (e.g., test alert notification and alternative site restoration).

In general, technical resources (e.g., computer systems or network recovery) require frequent real-time exercising. Work group computing requires only occasional real-time rehearsals to ensure that the recovery strategies work when they are needed.

EXERCISING – A "WHO'S WHO" OF RESPONSIBILITIES

The best way to ensure a win-win relationship for both client and vendor is to explicitly define the responsibilities of each at the outset of the relationship. Knowing where one party's obligations end and the other's begin can make a world of difference. While many of the most important responsibilities are spelled out contractually, other not-so-obvious obligations may not be documented.

An important client obligation that is often overlooked is their own commitment to exercising and the value they place on the concept itself. Without strong commitment from senior management to this important process, even the best contingency plans can quickly become meaningless.

Beyond this on-going commitment, clients are usually responsible for many of the logistics regarding the exercising of their plans. Interestingly, it is the "little details" – like travel or arranging to transport backup tapes to the recovery site – that can trip up even sophisticated client recovery teams. In fact, missing files are the single most common cause of a problematic exercise.

Another key client responsibility is familiarity with the critical application programs. Typically, the client is obligated to understand their own specialized applications.

In all of these areas, the client bears most of the responsibility though, of course, the vendor must be willing and able to assist if needed. So what should the client expect from the vendor? What are the vendor's responsibilities?

Beyond the basic requirements of maintaining equipment and providing regular access to the site for the client's exercise, the vendor has several important duties that the client has every reasonable right to expect. (*See Exhibit 1*, "A Client's Testing Bill of Rights"). In fact, the client should expect these commitments to be clearly defined in the contract.

EXHIBIT 1

A Client's Testing Bill of Rights

Regarding the testing or exercise of a client's recovery plan, the client has the right to:

1) Expect a contractual guarantee of adequate, professional technical support from the vendor for their testing and recovery needs.

2) Audit the vendor's testing and recovery resources on a periodic basis with regard to availability and adequacy.

3) Expect a contractual guarantee from the vendor that an independent, third-party auditor will annually evaluate the vendor's resources.

4) Expect adequate pre-testing of the client's operating system, network control programs and communications circuits prior to the actual test and outside of the client's contracted test shifts.

5) Expect the vendor to actively document the testing process via both pre-and post-testing records or evaluations.

6) Receive from the vendor user's guides or manuals as an orientation to the vendor's facilities, products and services.

7) Expect to be notified of any changes in equipment or software that may affect the testing of their recovery plan.

8) Expect a clear definition of multiple disaster approaches.

9) Expect the vendor to bring a proactive Crisis Management Approach to the testing process as well as actual recoveries.

10) Expect to be notified quickly when recovery plan tests will be disrupted by actual disaster recoveries underway.

One of the most important is providing adequate, specialized technical support for all elements of the client's recovery plan. Some vendors may offer this level of support only in a disaster situation, ignoring the benefits gained by this support in the exercising process. Many vendors will provide only their facilities to the client for the purposes of an exercise; that is not enough. Often, the client recovery team will be unfamiliar with the layout of the facility or with other details that could impede the exercise.

The vendor must make available professional recovery specialists familiar with the systems and platforms which will be used; they should also be familiar with the details of the client's plan and their expectations regarding the exercise. This duty, in particular, should be spelled out in the form of a contractual guarantee.

Another important vendor duty is contractually committing to an independent, third-party audit of any vendor facilities that will be used when exercising the plan as well as in the event of actual recoveries. The availability of all appropriate resources should be evaluated periodically by the client as well. Allowing and encouraging both types of auditing should be a vendor priority.

The vendor should also take responsibility for continuous improvement of the process. This quality control approach is possible only if a vendor follows up the exercise with an honest evaluation of the results. Strengths, weaknesses and suggestions should all be recorded for future reference to aid both vendor and client in preparing for the next exercise as well as for a real recovery.

Finally, the vendor has an obligation to assist in a "pre-test" before the real exercise. Pre-testing is a thorough check-out of a client's operating system, network control programs and communications circuits outside of the client's contracted test shifts. This helps ensure a smoother, more productive exercise.

ANATOMY OF AN EXERCISE PROGRAM

An effective exercise program requires different types of exercises to evaluate all components of a recovery plan. One type, the *Component Exercise* isolates individual elements of a plan and evaluates the adequacy of each. In a *Systems Exercise*, the components are evaluated based on how well they work together. A third type, the *Corporate Plan Exercise*, tests the recoverability of work groups.

There are differing approaches as well:

- *Auditing or desk checking:*
  Validating the availability of required recovery resources on a periodic basis. Unfortunately, this is often limited to confirming the existence of the resources with little regard to identifying their adequacy.

- *Plan walkthrough:*
  A hypothetical scenario is presented, and the recovery team jointly reviews the recovery procedures without actually invoking the plans. This approach is inexpensive and easy to conduct. Just as important, it helps train recovery team personnel.

- *Real-time exercise:*
  This is frequently done for mainframe or hot site backup plans, but is gaining popularity in work group recovery planning as well. It provides the greatest degree of assurance but it is likely to be the most time consuming and expensive approach.

- *Mock disaster / surprise exercise:*
  A variation on the other three approaches but with the added advantage of being unanticipated. It is generally the least-used approach due to its potentially disruptive effect on client personnel and business operations. However, by carefully controlling the process, clients can reduce the possibility of cheating during exercises.

DEVELOPING AN EXERCISE PROGRAM

There are a few important ground rules that should be followed when developing a program to exercise your recovery plans.

- *Limit exercise preparation:*
  Preparation should be limited to developing a disaster scenario, scheduling exercise dates and times, and defining any exceptions to the plan. Actual exercising should follow the documented recovery procedures.

- *Resist the temptation to cheat:*
  An independent observer should be identified for each recovery exercise. Controls should be put in place to ensure that only resources identified in the recovery plans are used for the recovery effort. The reason for eliminating cheating is not to be punitive, but to ensure that all activities and resources have been identified and will be available at time of disaster.

- *Document and communicate results:*
  The results of the recovery exercise should always be documented, including follow up activities. Corrective actions should be identified, responsibilities defined and dates set. The relevant results should be communicated to all participants (including vendors) and to management in a constructive manner. Successes and problems should be clearly stated with an emphasis on continuous improvement. Ideally, the vendor should take a proactive role in performing both pre- and post-exercise evaluations.

- *Test information reconstruction:*
  Difficulties in data restoration and re-creation are usually discovered only through real-time exercising. The off-site storage facility should be audited periodically to ensure that backups are securely stored. The ability to restore should be exercised using the actual off-site backup media. When information re-creation depends on other facilities, the ability to access this information should be verified as well.

THE CHALLENGE FOR VENDORS AND CLIENTS

While developing an effective and comprehensive business resumption plan is important, companies must focus more effort on recovery plan exercising, looking for ways to improve recovery strategies and minimize risk. Exercising offers the most cost-effective method to maintain and improve recovery plans and to train employees for disaster preparedness. It is, indeed, a "dress rehearsal for disaster."

In the exercising process, the vendor has a unique opportunity to demonstrate the value of outside recovery services, before those services are actually needed. Often, the disaster recovery vendor is viewed merely as an alternate site, a place to recover. This approach is short-sighted and ultimately self-defeating.

It is the human factor that is almost always the most important, in both exercising and recovery situations. The caliber and commitment provided by a vendor's technical support staff is every bit as important as the hardware on the floor. The challenge for both parties is to build a recovery process that works, a process founded on a carefully crafted exercise program and a mutual understanding of shared goals and responsibilities.

15
CLIENT PARTICIPATION IN TESTING
by Michael G. Courton

INTRODUCTION

Over the past five years there have been volumes of information written about the United States becoming a service economy. As companies we are asked to provide more and more services and as consumers we have come to expect more complicated services. These services fall into the category of 'tangible' or 'intangible'. On the intangible side these services are increasingly taking the form of access to information, customer support for manufactured goods, and electronic services such as bank automated teller machines.

In this new model of the service corporation it is impossible to operate efficiently and competitively without the use of computers and advanced telecommunications. This same proliferation of computers and advanced telecommunications has allowed companies to locate separate departments and divisions in widely dispersed geographical locations, in turn causing them to rely more heavily on communications technology to manage their businesses. Thus we have increased our dependence and exposure by propagating an entirely new class of 'internal clients.'

Many communications intensive businesses like public utilities, reservations processing, and point-of-sale processing which rely on information accessibility, retrieval and modification have centralized customer support into national and regional service centers. Some companies have even gone so far as to outsource these vital computer resources to service firms.

In this section we will discuss 'client' participation in disaster recovery testing. In the preceding introduction the word client can be substituted for customer anywhere it appears. Throughout the remainder of this section the two terms, namely client and customer, will be used interchangeably.

BACKGROUND

Client participation in recovery testing is achieved via telecommunications. Because data and voice communications testing will be covered in later chapters of this book, I will not detail them here. Instead, we will discuss it from the viewpoint of being a hypothetical company in the process of planning a test. Further, we will make a few assumptions about our working environment to aid us in developing a recovery scenario, then proceed from there.

Assumptions:

- We are a decentralized service firm

- Technical customer support for our voice and data network is centralized into one department called "communications" with separate units

- Our clients are able to access information via our computers and supporting network

- We will have some means of verifying test success

- Our client services department provides customer support for service requests and non-technical issues

- Our communications units have the capability to switch voice and data lines to alternate locations.

Coordination and design of recovery testing to include customer participation is a multi-divisional responsibility. It is also the most complicated test you should ever attempt to run. I would not suggest attempting it until late in a progressive test cycle, meaning not until after full systems, applications, and telecommunications have been tested successfully. We will approach the process by answering some basic questions:

- **WHY** even include clients, and **WHY** would they participate?
- **WHO** should participate?
- **WHAT** should you and possibly they be testing?
- **WHEN** should they be participating?
- **HOW** should they participate and **HOW** should their participation be coordinated?

SCENARIO

At this point in our testing cycle, we have accomplished the following tasks: Systems staff are able to bring up the base operating system along with the major subsystems that are relevant to doing a client participation test (for instance, communications software such as VTAM, NETVIEW, and CICS). The reconfiguration of the telecommunications front-end computers has been tested. A handful of various types of data lines have been swung over. Switching of voice communications lines to recovery locations via PBXs, and the local telephone company central office has been tested.

On the applications side, operations along with applications support personnel has tested recovery to point of failure as well as automatic job scheduling submission. The database systems have also successfully recovered to point of failure.

Note that the software mentioned above is particular to IBM and IBM-type mainframes. However, the information is general and can be applied to any class of machine running any type of operating system software. Also note that in the author's opinion it typically takes at least three years of regular testing through progressively more complex scenarios before you are ready to attempt a test of this magnitude.

PRE-TEST PLANNING

For many companies telecommunications testing simply means swinging some lines and verifying that the connection was achieved. This is only half of the solution. Once the lines have been swung over how do you know whether the timing between your backup modems and other boxes is in sync with your clients on the other end? Moreover you could suffer from a regional disaster, in which case some of your geographically closer clients would also be recovering at their backup sites. Now you have two backup systems that have to be synchronized. For firms that are data intensive I suggest some means of not only transmitting and capturing data, but also of validating the data during recovery testing. This is most easily accomplished by having clients participate.

One option is to limit participation to either external or internal clients, thus lessening the complexity of the coordination needed in the planning stage. Because of the visibility and the increased attention that many firms are paying to disaster recoverability, I recommend limiting early participation to internal clients only. That way when you make mistakes (and you will, no matter how good you think your planning is) the exposure will be internal to the company and the problem will be easier to locate and fix. After we have successfully and repeatedly recovered internal clients then we will open testing to include a handful of our 'most dear' external clients.

Limiting the participants will also have the effect of reducing the size of the environment we have to recreate since excluding either class of user means that those applications run for their support could be suspended. Furthermore, the coordination of participation by internal customers should not be a task that is beyond the capabilities of your regular planning staff.

A good argument for including external clients at some point is that demonstrating your capability to continue operations under adverse conditions is a very powerful marketing tool. Also, in industries like financial services which are heavily computerized and interconnected it would do your company no good to recover without the firms on the other end being there as well. For example, if you are a large regional bank it would be of little use to recover if you could not reestablish connections to the Federal Reserve and other money center banks.

To lessen the confusion and coordination on the core planning team, all contact with external users should be accomplished via the customer support and client services teams. Think about it: customer support is already familiar with the technical service requirements of all your clients. Client services already has the personal contacts necessary to persuade your clients that it is in their own best interest to participate in your test. It is a regular part of their recovery plan that they be able to relocate and reestablish links to all your customers. Additionally, client services will be integral to disseminating information to the external world in a real disaster situation. Get them to buy in, by giving them the opportunity to practice NOW.

However, these departments do not have the expertise to coordinate disaster recovery tests. What you will have to do is to designate one or two people within their departments to act as liaison between you and them. These individuals will have the responsibility of coordinating the recruitment, testing support, and test follow-up with all your clients. These liaisons should most logically be the project leader and alternate who have been identified as critical personnel for their sections in the company disaster recovery plan.

Client participation then serves as not only a test of reestablishing connection to user areas but also as a test of your ability to recover the departments necessary to support those critical business functions.

As an aside, it has been my experience that external clients often expect to be able to verify the results of their participation. When you are recruiting clients to participate in your testing be very clear as to whether the data they transmit will be used to run applications, which will generate results they can see online. Don't forget — other firms do disaster recovery planning as well, and they also want to show the success of their planning and testing to their upper management.

TESTING

In deciding what our test objectives might be, we have already touched on the fact that we want to have clients transmit data and access information online. Is that enough or do we want more depth?

Our recovery plan calls for the capability of relocating many user areas such as client services to alternate recovery sites. Since we will already have them participating in the test we might as well have one or two of them go to their alternate site. Remember again that no one likes to look bad when reporting test results. As you are selecting what areas to relocate, try to select areas with plans that are comprehensive enough to show successes while simultaneously pointing out problem areas in their plans that may need further development.

Reestablishing voice communications between recovery sites, support areas, departments, and clients is key to the success of any recovery. If you can't coordinate logistics, disseminate information, and make communication as easy as possible, you can forget about a successful recovery. Our recovery plan calls for a communications command center, connections to the data center recovery site and also to the user area recovery sites, all controlled through this facility. There are a couple of options for reconfiguring communications. One calls for areas such as client services to refer to their copies of the disaster recovery plan which hold the new numbers for all of our emergency recovery sites.

The more preferable option is to make the recovery as transparent to all users as possible. From a communications standpoint this means taking advantage of the latest technology for switching lines and circuits. By actively involving your local telephone companies you can switch private networks without changing the numbers. Of course, the planning that goes into this option is much more involved, not to mention the added costs. If you want to consider this option be sure to talk to your carriers first, because the level of technology needed to implement it is not widely available, although that is rapidly changing.

CONCLUSION

It is certainly possible for recovery testing to be productive without client participation. Clearly, the advantages from including clients far outweigh the disadvantages.

16

RECOVERY PLANNING SOFTWARE'S ROLE IN TESTING

by Kenneth J. Bauman

One statement frequently heard in the world of business recovery planning is: "There is no such thing as a failed disaster recovery plan test!" This is certainly true in terms of the lessons learned from the rehearsal of recovery plans, regardless of whether the "recovery" was actually successful or not. These lessons prove invaluable in identifying the aspects of recovery plans that need to be modified to ensure their viability. To reduce the impact on the business operations of an organization, most tests of recovery plans are pre-arranged (as opposed to unannounced tests).

Yet, even with the luxury of knowing when a test will occur, many recovery planners do not properly prepare for the test. The primary purpose of a recovery plan test is to determine the viability of the recovery plan, and to identify weaknesses that can be corrected before an actual disaster happens. This objective is difficult to achieve if the test is not documented in detail. Therefore, if a test is not carefully planned for in advance, or when test results are inadequately documented, it is indeed possible to have a FAILED TEST!

Computer software products can be very helpful in planning and tracking the execution of your recovery tests. The three categories of software that can be useful for plan testing are:

- **Project management software products.** Certainly, general-purpose commercial project management systems such as Microsoft Project, Timeline from Symantec, CA-SuperProject and others can be effective tools for a disaster recovery planner proficient in the use of these products.

- **Recovery testing software.** Although there are relatively few of this type of product available, they are normally designed as project management tools specific to recovery testing. This type of software can automate the development, implementation and management of the testing process, and can facilitate the documentation of test results.

- **Business recovery planning software.** Among the many products of this type available in today's marketplace, a few offer features useful in recovery plan testing. Some of these products that supply such testing modules incorporate this capability by offering an interface to some of the popular commercial project management software systems, such as those mentioned above. Again, this is very helpful to the recovery planner who happens to be familiar with the project management system that is used, and can skillfully make effective use of the powerful planning and reporting capabilities these products have to offer. While using a product that incorporates this type of interface, recovery plan information that is resident in the recovery planning software must be frequently ported to the commercial system through the interface.

  Other business recovery planning products address plan testing by providing project planning modules as an integral part of the software package. One advantage of this integrated approach is that the project planning and test tracking modules can be tightly meshed with the actual recovery task schedules developed by the recovery planner in the same software. Another benefit to this integration is a reduced learning curve, since the test planning and tracking modules usually incorporate a menu system and user interface common to the other modules of the recovery planning tool. Therefore, the recovery planner does not have to take the time to become knowledgeable about a separate project management system. Also, if the recovery planning software is a true relational database product, the test planning and tracking modules should have relational access and linkage to the product's recovery resource data tables (e.g., personnel, locations, etc.).

Recovery planning software is a natural vehicle for coordinating recovery plan tests. The remainder of this chapter will focus on recovery planning products which address recovery plan testing and how they can aid in the three stages of a test: pre-test, testing, and post-test; or, before, during, and after.

PRE-TEST

The most logical method of preparing for a recovery test is to treat the test like any other complex business project. Tasks, or steps, must be taken to coordinate and establish the groundwork for the test. The test objectives, test scenario and benchmarks must be clear and well defined. Someone must ensure that the right resources such as people, equipment, and facilities are available for the plan rehearsal. Someone must be assigned to maintain written logs of events and issues. The recovery planner needs to assign individuals to the responsibility of completing each of the tasks, estimate a duration for each task, and track the progress of the plan test preparation project. A recovery planning software tool with the right features can be an enormous help to the recovery planner in defining and tracking the steps necessary to accomplish the test.

As mentioned previously, some of the recovery planning products provide features to guide the recovery planner in this preparation, either through an interface to a third party project management system, or with an integrated project management module. Some of these tools take this a step further by providing expert guidance, in the form of sample project task lists or testing methodologies. This information is especially helpful to the novice planner who is beginning to plan for their first test. The more sophisticated products provide the ability to assign personnel, duration, location and even costs to each task in the test-preparation project, and track the progress as the steps are executed. *Figure 1* exhibits a sample screen that accommodates the input of such information:

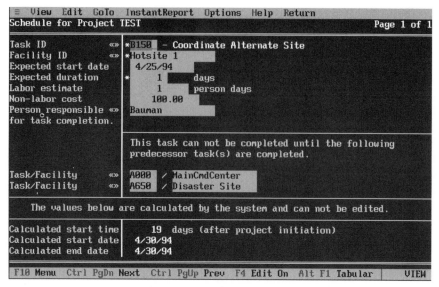

Figure 1 Sample Input Screen

In these more advanced products, project schedules, project variances, cost variances and even Gantt charts can be printed to assist in documenting the planned test and it's performance results. This information is very useful in streamlining the preparation for future tests as well as to better estimate the funds required to conduct a test.

Using recovery planning software to prepare for a disaster recovery test can increase the likelihood of having a smooth rehearsal of your plan by reducing the chance of encountering avoidable complications during your test.

TESTING

As in the Pre-Test stage of a recovery plan test, some of the recovery planning products provide features that assist the recovery planner in the documentation and monitoring of the actual test. Again, this is accomplished either through the use of external third-party software, or with an integrated plan activation module. The former approach typically requires that the recovery plan task information be exported to the external project management system. The latter solution usually interfaces to the development module of the software to prepare the actual recovery plan schedule for testing.

For example, in the test tracking module, the recovery tasks of the plan being tested are presented on the screen (or hardcopy report) in the order of execution. Some recovery planning products allow the planner to record information about actual events during the test, such as start and stop time-stamps, person-hours required to accomplish the particular recovery task, and costs involved with execution of the task.

Figure 2 illustrates a sample screen that provides an area to record information about actual test events, including a section for notes that can be used to describe circumstances that have occurred in the test execution of the recovery plan that have not been anticipated during the initial development of the plan. To the right of this area, information about the recovery task that was projected, or estimated, during the plan development phase is displayed to facilitate an immediate performance analysis.

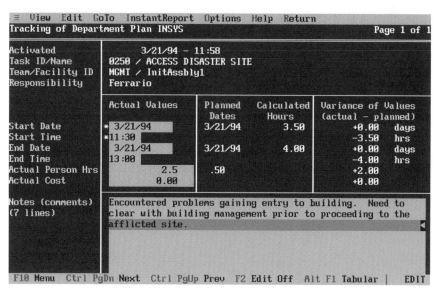

Figure 2 Sample Screen to Record Actual Test Events

This module of the software can be used during all phases and types of testing - whether a "walk-through" or a full test. If a software product is equipped with this type of integrated sub-system, it can be quite useful while plan execution is in progress, either during a test or an actual disaster. The business recovery planning software can then serve as a "quick-access" command center for reviewing the progress of the recovery, and obtaining information from the product's database files that may assist and support decisions that may be required during plan execution.

A word of caution: Since a disaster recovery test is an event the recovery coordinator can prepare for in advance, the software can be quite helpful for test coordination and monitoring. However, do not rely on this software being available during a real disaster. In other words, do not substitute software for an accessible, printed copy of the recovery plan. Remember, you have no knowledge of the extent of the disaster ahead of time. Access to the software and the presence of communication between a command center and the recovery teams is not guaranteed!

To ensure access to the plan, all recovery teams and members should have printed copies of the relevant portions of the recovery plan that document their recovery responsibilities. Software vendors may lead you to believe that their products will run your recovery operation automatically with a push of a button. Do not fall into the trap of being lulled into a false sense of security with this sales pitch. Recovery planning tools were designed for plan development and maintenance, and these should be the only tasks they should be counted on to perform. By all means, if the software is available, it can be extremely useful for analysis, decision support and if equipped, plan execution tracking and monitoring. In the real world, management of a test or an actual recovery will still be performed by people making decisions and taking action.

POST-TEST

Following the completion of the test, an evaluation is usually conducted to assess that the test objectives have been met; the plan has thoroughly covered all the necessary items or considerations; and, missing items or deficiencies have been identified.

Obviously, the actual statistics and notes documented in the recovery planning software during the test will be used to compare against the figures estimated during plan development, to assist in identifying areas of the plan which require refinement. Ideally, a library of reports that will provide an analysis of the recovery plan schedule and cost variances will be resident in the software. A Gantt chart can be particularly useful to graphically depict recovery plan task schedule variances, as illustrated in *Figure 3*.

The planning software may also provide the ability to accumulate and save test results for future comparison and analysis. As plan testing evolves from walkthroughs to component testing to full operational tests, the test results can be useful to examine the effect

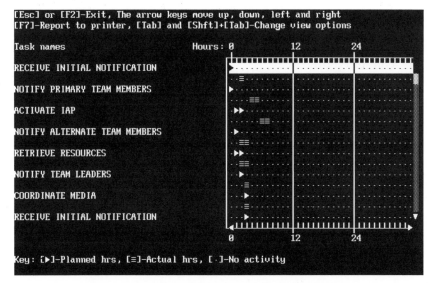

```
[Esc] or [F2]-Exit, The arrow keys move up, down, left and right
[F7]-Report to printer, [Tab] and [Shft]+[Tab]-Change view options

Task names                        Hours: 0        12        24

RECEIVE INITIAL NOTIFICATION

NOTIFY PRIMARY TEAM MEMBERS

ACTIVATE IAP

NOTIFY ALTERNATE TEAM MEMBERS

RETRIEVE RESOURCES

NOTIFY TEAM LEADERS

COORDINATE MEDIA

RECEIVE INITIAL NOTIFICATION
                                         0        12        24

Key: [►]-Planned hrs, [≡]-Actual hrs, [·]-No activity
```

Figure 3 Sample GANTT of Test Schedule Variances

of plan refinement on the actual performance of the plan. If you subscribe to component testing of your plan, results of the individual component tests can be compared to the performance of the total operational test to determine if the interaction of the components exposed any unexpected glitches or delays. The ability to compare test results helps to answer questions, such as: "Were more problems uncovered because of the changes made to the plan?" or "How did the plan execute compared to one year ago?"

Examples of reports that the software may include are:

- **Plan status reports**: These reports can provide a summary of the plan execution during a test or during an actual disaster recovery. This information can be used by the recovery management to help make decisions, or to implement ad hoc changes during the plan execution.

- **Cost comparison reports**: These reports provide a comparison of anticipated recovery costs versus actual costs. For testing, this information can be used as a guideline or justification for recovery testing budget requests. For recovery from an actual disaster, these figures can be quite useful for documenting claims filed with the business interruption insurance carrier.

- **Schedule variance reports**: These reports compare the planned versus actual recovery task timing (along with commentary).

This type of report is invaluable at post-test meetings, since it provides specific information that helps the recovery teams formulate plan modifications. *Figure 4* below is an example of this type of report:

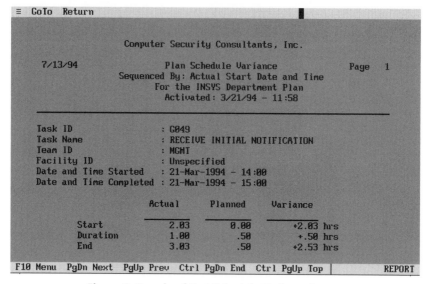

Figure 4 Sample of Test Schedule Variance Report

SUMMARY

As the scope of recovery planning broadens beyond the traditional data center disaster recovery plan to a total organization commitment, recovery plan testing is likely to become far more complex. The sagacious recovery planner carefully prepares for each test in order to minimize inconvenience and disruption to the business. It can be extremely difficult to coordinate and integrate the individual department plans into a test of the total organization's capability to recover without the assistance of some kind of software tool. Implementing recovery planning software to prepare for and document your plan tests may not guarantee a successful test, but it certainly can go a long way in helping the recovery planner avoid the failed test.

17

THE RECOVERY PLAN DOCUMENT IN TESTING

by William J. Krouslis

The test of the business continuation plan is no different than any other test that everyone has been involved with in many different circumstances. We were tested in school to demonstrate our knowledge of a particular subject. We test market a product to determine its capacity to sell. We test a business continuation plan to determine if it is practical. A part of the business continuation plan document is the vehicle which will communicate the test methodologies.

Many contingency planners incorrectly believe that the plan documentation is what they have been charged with creating. Agreeably, the document is one important outcome of the process but it by no means is the process. If the planner's focus is on the generation of a manuscript, the planning project is doomed to failure. It is crucial to understand the rational for establishing a plan document in the first place. Once resolved, we can appreciate the part that the testing component of the plan document play's when we begin to test our plan. In precise terms, the plan document is a communications tool. As a platform for communication, the written document has four primary and vital functions:

1. ***organize*** the strategies that are going to be followed to reclaim a resource

2. *inform* the participants about what their tasks will be after an outage (disaster) occurs

3. *illustrate* to the participants the sequence for these tasks

4. *provide evidence* to second and third parties that a recovery capability exists.

Planning is the task that happens in the pre-disaster world. Planning maps out a group of ideas that theoretically yield the recovery of the tools which enable a business to function. The plan document is the link that will connect these pre-disaster theories to post-disaster actions. Nevertheless, the written document is only an illusion of capability. It is the test that moves documented opinions (i.e., planning theories) into reality. Consequently, the testing component of the plan document should act as a similar bridge when the ideas that we have chronicled are put to the test. The test component of the document should functionally communicate the test agenda so that the planner is reasonably assured that their ideas are usable and achievable in the post disaster world. In this capacity it should:

1. *organize* the procedures that are going to be followed to test a component of the plan

2. *communicate* to the participants what tasks they need try to complete for a valid test to occur

3. *illustrate* the test sequence

4. *provide evidence* to second and third parties that a test occurred.

It is important to remember that the documentation which the planner produces is an instrument of communications. Grandiloquent, pretentious and ostentatious language have no place in the document. We are not trying to fascinate our counterparts with our knowledge; we are trying to get our ideas across so that our business can reclaim the functionality it had prior to the outage.

The preeminent contingency plan document would be the one that could be transcribed onto the back of a business card. To employ the document in the test as the communications tool it is intended to be, the document should contain only information that is specific to the task at hand, i.e., testing the ideas that have been communicated via the written word. No matter what your test strategy, the plan document will be an effective contributor to the trial if it communicates the following:

- *What is your test schedule?* The individuals managing a particular business segment as well as the test participants need to know what is going to happen and when. The testing documentation should communicate the specific dates of testing activities. This information will permit the necessary and affected individuals to allocate time to the task of testing.

- *What is being tested?* No, it is not the contingency plan. It is the functionality of the specific concepts that have been written. For example, a component of your plan may deal with recovering electrical power. Once power is on, offices are illuminated, machinery is humming and the planner's job is secured. This discrete component of the plan is what you are testing. A test procedure for each discrete plan component which the planner intends to test should be explicitly described in the plan test document.

- *What constitutes a successful test and what is a failure?* The planner needs to make this clear. For example, a very simple test to recover electrical power may be to ask the team leader of this activity if they know the size (in kVA) of the generator they intend to procure from a generator supply house. If the answer corresponds to the documented size in the plan one could say that the test was successful. Success or failure is defined by the planner. There are no correct or incorrect tests, only successful or failed tests. Your criteria for success and failure should be included in your test document.

- *Who is going to be part of the test?* Test participants need to know what the planner expects and role they play. The testing documentation is the tool to communicate this information.

- *What are the participants expected to do?* If the planner cannot describe explicit expectations or worse, does not know themselves what they are, you can bet the participants will not, either. A compact description of test responsibilities, outside of the obligations in recovery, should be furnished as part of the plan documentation.

- *Do you need the participation of a vendor?* A procedure to secure vendor contribution should be detailed. For example, part of the test may include contacting the power generator vendor and initiating the delivery process. If that vendor has not been briefed on the testing process, they may assume a real order and actually deliver a generator.

- *What do the auditors need in order to verify the integrity of the test?* Both internal and external audit organizations need specific test audit criteria. The contingency planner needs to work with the auditor to determine these criteria and to document a procedure to ensure that the appropriate information is collected and consolidated into a format suitable for the auditors' use.

- *How do you manage the costs of the test?* The planner has a budget for testing, so a mechanism is needed to collect information on specific expenditures to reconcile against budgetary constraints.

The fundamental purpose of a test is to uncover weaknesses in the plan. If something does not happen the way the planner expects, how would one expose this outcome and communicate it back to the planning process? The test document should describe a procedure to accomplish this task.

Tests should be arbitrated. A responsible individual needs to make the final call. The test referee plays a very important role in interpreting the results of the test. The test referee must understand the guidelines which they will follow in the interpretation of the exercise. If this is not done, then perhaps you had better plan for a referee to referee the referee!

Each test will have different goals and objectives. Setting of goals and objectives is a science in itself. However, a structure for measuring the goals and objectives is an essential item communicated by the test document.

18

THE RESTORATION VENDOR'S PERSPECTIVE

by Ronald N. Chamberlain

Congratulations, the Disaster Preparedness and Recovery Plan is now completed. It was proofread, printed and distributed to everyone in the organization. Now the Plan is about ready to take its proper place on the shelf until needed. Don't do it!

Now is the time for the plan to be tested. Management is still high on the thought that they have a plan, co-workers have contributed and are still in the loop regarding a potential disaster. It is a good time to make sure all personnel get a first hand knowledge of their part in the plan. It is a good time to test the recovery plan.

How the plan is tested will depend somewhat on how the organization is structured. For example, the organization is in a building and on one floor or in one building and on multiple floors. Another possible configuration is all on one site in one building or in many different buildings or maybe it is spread out over one or more states. Different organizational structures can make a difference in how to properly test the recovery plan.

A simple test method to use for small organizations or small segments of larger organizations is the desktop method of testing. This is an inexpensive method to make sure that all the key personnel are on track with the program, but it is a theory test only. Briefly, a desktop test works something like this: either an announced or unannounced scenario is called. All the key personnel assemble at the command post and each key person goes through his/her checklist of items to accomplish. This type of testing does not generally include any outside sources or vendors; nor does it include all the organization personnel.

Plan to test the recovery plan so that all aspects can be tested. Whether the test involves only one department, multiple departments or a whole organization, it should include vendors of choice. Also, outside sources such as police, fire and ambulance services as well as electric, gas and water utilities should be included. Any outside services that are included in the recovery plan are an integral part of the success of that recovery. If, after invitation to participate a vendor does not participate as wished or instructed without valid reason, then review that vendor as a valid part of your recovery plan. Do not shy from changing a vendor that does not fit the plan.

During the actual recovery process, time and safety are of utmost importance. With organization personnel involved plus many outside services and vendors, it is easy to envision a very chaotic condition. This is the very reason the recovery plan must be tested and practiced. It is also the most crucial time to practice managing the recovery plan. In managing the recovery plan, the leader must maximize the safety issues and minimize the time element to full recovery. Without managing these two elements carefully, costs and events can escalate beyond one's wildest nightmares.

In order to manage properly the outside vendors of choice, it is imperative that the recovery plan leader interview and become familiar with the vendor's capabilities long before a test and certainly long before an actual need. Record the capabilities as well as what the vendor cannot accomplish.

Changes take place in every organization. The vendors of choice are no exception. The vendor may have changed ownership, may have gone out of business or may have changed how they do business. It is important the recovery plan leader keep abreast of these changes through communications. Periodically check them out by phone, by mail or by visiting.

Another aspect of change comes from within the organization. Perhaps the manufacturing facility has been expanded or another floor has been taken over in the organization's building or a company was purchased elsewhere. These changes must be communicated to the outside services and/or vendors. The outside resources must become familiar with the new needs. Picture a situation where the location of vital paper documents has been changed. Prior to the change of location a vendor had been charged with the responsibility of making sure those documents were preserved, if they were not destroyed. Now the vendor does not know of the new location. If the vendor had not been notified of a new location and had not signed off on the change, the organization cannot hold the vendor responsible.

It is easy to identify outside resources such as police, fire and medical people, but how does one identify a vendor? In interviews with vendors, make sure vendor personnel wear a uniform, company identification or both. Make sure the vendor can meet the plan's needs. Organization personnel should be trained to recognize vendors by those criteria. If an organization employee does not recognize an individual by the obvious means he / she should ask who the individual is and what he / she is doing. If the person(s) in question cannot satisfactorily answer the questions then it is incumbent upon the employee to summon security. By allowing unauthorized entry, it puts "at risk" all those authorized.

Periodic meetings during the recovery phase (daily, every other day, etc.) are a necessity to manage all resources and effect a safe and timely recovery. Include not only key employees but vendors, city inspectors, insurance claims people and anybody having a valid reason to be there. Have each vendor or contractor and subcontractor involved with your recovery appoint an individual to attend these meetings. This will allow priority issues to be transmitted to all parties and also surface any problems or conflicts which can be dealt with so that all are aware of what is going on. It also keeps all resources on track and allows the leader to manage the recovery.

After each test, critique the test with not only employees but with vendors as well. Even if the recovery plan test went very well, the hard questions must still be asked. The hard questions might have to deal with people, vendors, timing, was the situation a worst case, what ifs — and hundreds of other questions. Encourage people to be honest with both the questions and answers.

During the critique, look for glitches in the plan. After an apparent successful test it is hard to look for flaws but it is imperative to do so. An outside vendor or consultant might be used to help critique the plan. Very often an outside facilitator can act as devil's advocate to help point out flaws.

If private insurance is in use, make sure an agent, broker or underwriter is aware of the recovery plan. The underwriter can be asked to assign an adjuster to the critique. These people will also be able to point out how to best accomplish certain aspects of the recovery in accordance with the policy. This step will go a long way to create good working relationships with the adjuster and insurance underwriter in time of real need. Many insured companies do not act when they have insurance coverage. It is usually in the insured's best interest to proceed as if there were no insurance coverage.

There may be a benefit to having the recovery plan written, practiced and critiqued with an insurance broker, adjuster or underwriter in attendance. The benefit may be that the organization will be able to obtain coverage, obtain coverage without paying higher premiums or not be forced into a very high deductible. These and other benefits may accrue to those who actively and periodically show a proactive method of mitigating loss should an occurrence happen.

Keep in mind that actual scenarios are rarely the ones practiced. The key to a viable plan is to be flexible enough to react to the real disaster and recovery by practicing the pretend disaster and recovery and finding the flaws.

The following is a quick checklist of the salient points:

- Interview carefully any and all outside vendors to ensure their capabilities are what you need

- Notify all vendors chosen they are written into your recovery plan

- When you test the recovery plan, also test your vendors

- Ensure you have accurate floor plans; give your vendors a copy. Keep the floor plans updated

- Test your plan as often as you deem necessary but always after major changes or failed tests

- Critique your plan openly and honestly

- Invite an insurance broker, agent, adjuster or underwriter

- Above all, communication is the key, before, during and after the recovery.

19

THE RISK MANAGEMENT PERSPECTIVE

by Melvyn Musson

Risk managers have an integral role to play in the development and continuation of a recovery testing program. Since their charge is the protection of a company's assets through such risk management techniques as risk avoidance, control, transfer and financing, it is essential that business continuation planning be a part of the risk control function. As a result, the development, implementation and maintenance of the testing program to ensure that the business continuity plan is current, viable and applicable to all critical areas of the company's operations should also be an important part of that risk control function.

In addition, as the Risk Manager is also involved in other areas of the risk control function which necessitate testing and exercising such as building evacuation, testing of protection systems, etc., his involvement in testing of business continuity plans may be considered a logical extension of those testing functions.

The Risk Manager may or may not be a member of the group managing the business continuity planning and testing programs but it almost always would be appropriate for him or her to be a member of those groups.

THE RISK MANAGER'S ROLE

A major role in recovery testing for the Risk Manager should be to provide coordination among the various parties in the group. In some instances, these parties may in fact represent conflicting factions and the Risk Manager should be responsible for reducing friction, enhancing coordination and increasing working cooperation.

Risk Managers should also provide as necessary:

- instructions and procedures to notify insurers of the incident

- instructions and procedures to coordinate actions with insurance company personnel, insurance brokers and adjusters appointed by them

- the specific procedures for formulating the insurance claim.

Test programs should specifically cover the actions to be taken by Risk Management and others in defining and supporting the claim.

Unfortunately, the number of Risk Managers presently involved in the business continuity planning or testing groups within their organizations is low, but increasing. We therefore should consider what the Risk Manager's role should or could be in recovery testing rather than the actual experience of many Risk Managers. The Risk Manager must:

- ensure that the scenarios used as the basis of the test are realistic, applicable to the company's operations and viable from a testing standpoint

- ensure that the tests ultimately cover all critical operations as well as their corresponding business functions and support needs. Initial tests may concentrate on specific departments but, over time, the testing program must be expanded to all important departments

- support and enhance the coordination between departments (including both operational and support functions)

- assist in obtaining the resources and finances for the testing program

- coordinate with the physical damage and business interruption insurers to make certain that their requirements are being met.

DIRECTOR AND OFFICER LIABILITY

Another factor to consider is that the Risk Manager must protect Directors and Officers of the company. Directors or Officers may be subject to shareholder lawsuits or other individual or collective liability if a company's results are impacted by an incident, the impact of which could have been minimized with a business continuity plan. This argument for liability can clearly be expanded to include recovery testing. An initial defense to such lawsuits is to have a continuity plan in place. However, if the plan is inadequately (or never) tested and subsequently proves to be ineffective in a real disaster situation, could it not be argued in a court of law that the Directors and Officers failed in their obligation to ensure the viability of the continuity plan? That, by the omission of an adequate and consistent testing program, they are therefore liable due to a lack of due diligence and prudent management?

This author knows of no actual precedent at this time for this argument although attorneys may be debating it for years to come. However, is it worthwhile for a company to risk exposure to such lawsuits, liability claims (with the corresponding expenditures of time, money and adverse public image), by not having an adequate, viable recovery testing program? It is clearly the Risk Manager's responsibility to ensure that the Directors and Officers of the company are aware of the recovery testing program.

REGULATORY AND LEGAL ISSUES

Similar considerations apply to recovery testing in connection with regulatory or other legal requirements for having a recovery plan in place. Compliance with these requirements may mean more than simply having developed or documented a recovery plan. The possibility of management liability because of the lack of a tested plan should be investigated with the appropriate authorities and attorneys, and management apprised of the exposure.

The Risk Manager should play a key role in these investigations in view of the potential liability to the organization. In addition, since Risk Managers are accustomed to dealing with regulatory authorities and attorneys in other areas such as Workers' Compensation and employee safety, their experience is likely to prove quite valuable.

INSURANCE AND RISK FINANCING

Recovery testing and the subsequent debriefing process will highlight not only the validity of the recovery plan, but will also point out weaknesses which may be rectified before an actual disruption. A tested plan can indicate the potential for a major reduction in the physical damage and business interruption loss. This could be used to negotiate with insurers and to assist the Risk Manager in obtaining appropriate insurance coverage at far more competitive terms than if recovery testing was not addressed.

Response and recovery plans and risk financing (usually in the form of insurance) are complementary. Risk financing can provide funds to pay the cost of the procedures implemented to restore the business operations as well as business interruption losses. However, if such procedures are not predefined and tested it is likely to take far longer to develop or revise them after the fact. Moreover, the impact on the company is such that it may not effectively recover from a disruption.

CONCLUSION

The fact that recovery procedures and arrangements have been predefined does not mean that they will work; testing is intended to do this. If there are no tests, the organization is effectively in the same position as having no plan. As a result, the risk financing arrangement may be inadequate.

The Risk Manager should therefore have a vested interest in testing the recovery plan to complement both the risk financing arrangements and the risk control function.

III.

TESTING METHODS
AND PROCESSESS

20

TESTING METHODS[1]

by Geoffrey H Wold
and Robert F. Shriver

OVERVIEW

Without periodic testing, time has a way of eroding a disaster recovery plan's effectiveness for these and other reasons:

- Environmental changes occur as organizations change, new services are introduced, and new policies and procedures are developed. Such changes can render a plan incomplete, or inadequate

- Hardware, software, and other critical equipment change

- The organization may experience personnel turnover

- Personnel may lose interest or forget critical parts of the plan.

Therefore, periodic testing of the recovery plan is necessary. Some benefits from testing include:

- Determining the feasibility of the recovery process

- Verifying the compatibility of backup facilities

- Ensuring the adequacy of procedures relating to the various teams working in the recovery process

- Identifying deficiencies in existing procedures

- Identifying areas of the plan that need modification or enhancement

- Training of various team managers and members

- Demonstrating the ability of the organization to recover

- Providing a mechanism for maintaining and updating the recovery plan.

Training on special and critical skills that may be required in a disaster situation is an important part of the process. These special skills may include: fire extinguishing; evacuation of patients, visitors, assets, and sensitive resources; emergency communications methods; and shutdown procedures for equipment, electricity, water and gas.

Education and training of recovery personnel in special, critical, and multiple skills can weigh significantly on the success of the plan and the time required to execute it.

The authenticity of the test will vary, depending on some of the following factors:

- Physical size of the installation

- Sensitivity of the organization to data processing services

- Level of service required by users

- Time deemed acceptable for contingency processing and recovery

- Number of locations involved

- Cost to perform the test.

Testing the disaster recovery plan should be efficient and cost-effective. It provides a means of continually increasing the level of performance and quality of the plan and of the people who execute it. A carefully tested plan provides the organization with the confidence and experience necessary to respond to a real emergency. Disaster recovery plan testing should consider scheduled and unscheduled tests for both partial and total disasters.

Recovery plans should be tested at least on an annual basis. For an organization with a relatively new plan, a quarterly or semiannual test may be prudent the first year. After the initial period, semiannual or annual tests should be required as a matter of policy.

In order to assure organized testing, procedures for how a test is to be performed as well as the purpose of the test should be thoroughly developed. The procedures include:

- When the test will be performed
- Where the test will be performed
- Who will be involved
- Effect on other areas within the organization
- Anticipated outcome.

The objectives of the tests should be decided upon to assure the extent of the test.

Testing of the plan can be accomplished using different formats. Testing options may include checklist testing, structured walk-through tests, simulation testing and full interruption testing. "Disasters" or problems that occur during the normal course of business should also be documented and included in the testing section of the plan.

CHECKLIST TESTING

A checklist test determines whether adequate supplies are stored at the backup site, telephone number listings are current, quantities of forms are adequate, and a copy of the recovery plan and necessary operational manuals are available. Under this testing technique, the recovery team reviews the plan and identifies key components that should be current and available. The checklist test ensures that the organization is in compliance with the requirements of the disaster recovery plan. A suggested format for checklist testing is presented in *Exhibit 1*.

EXHIBIT 1:   TESTING CHECKLIST

Purpose:

To document methods and procedures for ascertaining that the disaster recovery plan is current and up to date. These procedures do not require a full test and may be used by the internal auditor for investigative purposes. Testing examples may include current telephone numbers, offsite storage inventories, notification procedures, etc.

COLUMN REFERENCE: EXPLANATION:

Item Description*   Item / equipment tested
Plan Cross Reference*   Cross reference of the procedure to the disaster recovery plan
Frequency*   Frequency of testing the item (i.e., monthly, semiannually, yearly)
S / U   S = Successful; U = Unsuccessful
N / A**   Not applicable
Comments**   Testing comments, observations, notations, recommendations for improvements, etc.

* Complete in preparation for the actual test.** Complete during or after the actual test.

Date: _____   Completed by:_____

Item Description	Plan Cross Reference	Frequency	S / U	N / A	Comments

STRUCTURED WALK-THROUGH TESTING

During a structured walk-through test, disaster recovery team members meet to verbally walk through the specific steps of each component of the disaster recovery process as documented in the disaster recovery plan. The purpose of the structured walk-through test is to confirm the effectiveness of the plan and to identify gaps, bottlenecks, or other plan weaknesses.

Initially, a combination of checklist and structured walk-through tests is suggested to determine modifications to the plan prior to more extensive testing.

An example of a structured walk-through test follows:

Participants

Participants should include:

- disaster recovery administrator
- disaster recovery coordinator
- team managers and alternates
- other selected personnel as directed by the administrator or team managers.

Procedures

Prior to performing the structured walk-through test, each team member should be familiar with the plan and should understand the specific team responsibilities documented in the plan.

During the structured walk-through test, the following procedures should be performed:

a. Arrange the group around a central table (e.g., board room table). The individuals on each team should be seated together, and each team should be able to easily communicate with the other teams.

b. The disaster recovery administrator should:
   - explain to all participants the objectives and scope of the test.
   - describe the test scenario, including:
     - a description of the type of disaster
     - the extent of damage to data communications and/or operations, and anticipated period of outage

- the time of day and day of month that the disaster was reported
- the method of discovery of the disaster
- the disaster's effect on ground and air transportation, surrounding geography, voice and data communications, personnel (i.e., injury or death) and other pertinent information

- describe the plan activation criteria and whether the plan is activated.

c. Each team manager, alternate or team member should:

- review as a team the applicable sections of the plan.
- verbally walk through the responsibilities and procedures detailed in the plan, noting:

- How the activity will be accomplished
- Who will specifically perform the task
- Estimate of time required to perform the activity
- Feasibility of successfully completing the activity
- Comments, observations, enhancements.

d. Once each team has reviewed their respective responsibilities and procedures, the team managers should, as a group, verbally walk through the responsibilities and procedures which apply to the team. This should be performed in chronological order.

e. As each team manager describes the team's responsibilities and procedures, all other participants should carefully note how these activities interface with their procedures. Participants should specifically seek to identify areas of overlap and gaps.

f. The ensuing dialogue should be moderated by the disaster recovery administrator. It is the responsibility of the disaster recovery administrator to call attention to areas that require modification or amplifications.

g. During the course of the dialogue, each team should:

- complete the Notification Checklist as notification responsibilities are fulfilled
- complete the Extra Expense Worksheet as imaginary expenses are incurred, noting when management team approval is required

- complete the Telephone Call Log as telephone calls are simulated
- complete the Recovery Status Report following the conclusion of the test.

h. To conclude the structured walk-through test, the disaster recovery administrator or coordinator should conduct the following activities:

  - discuss general observations, ideas and suggestions for enhancing the plan
  - discuss ideas and suggestions for enhancing the future testing environment
  - update the plan, including its revision level and date. Note additions, changes and deletions on a copy of the Plan Maintenance Form
  - maintain a file of updated forms that will provide evidence that the review and test has been performed.

i. The disaster recovery administrator should prepare a memo documenting that the test was performed. The memo should contain the following information:

  - list of participants
  - date that the test was performed
  - list of the successful and unsuccessful activities
  - disaster recovery administrator's signature.

SIMULATION TESTING

During this type of test, the organization simulates a disaster, typically during non-business hours so that normal operations will not be interrupted. A disaster scenario should identify the following:

- purpose of the test
- objectives
- type of test
- timing
- scheduling
- duration
- test participants
- assignments
- constraints
- assumptions
- test steps.

Testing can include notification procedures, temporary operating procedures, and backup and recovery operations. During a simulation test, the following elements should be addressed:

- hardware
- software
- personnel
- data and voice communications
- procedures
- supplies and forms
- documentation
- transportation
- utilities (power, air conditioning, heating, ventilation)
- alternate site processing.

It may not be practical or economically feasible to perform certain tasks during a simulated test (e.g., extensive travel, moving equipment, eliminating voice or data communications). *Exhibit 2* contains a suggested format for a test preparation worksheet.

EXHIBIT 2:   TEST PREPARATION WORKSHEET

Purpose: *To document various considerations in advance of an actual test. The worksheet is used in the planning process for testing the Disaster Recovery Plan.*

Objectives: *A statement of the specific testing goals (e.g., operational areas to be tested, support activities)* _____

_____

Plan Cross Reference: *Cross reference of the procedure in the disaster recovery plan (i.e., section, page number)* _____

_____

Type Of Test: *Identification of the type of test being performed (e.g., checklist test, simulation test, parallel test, etc.)* _____

_____

Timing: *The hypothetical moment of the disaster (e.g., time of day, day of month, etc.)* _____

_____

Schedule: *Scheduling of the test* _____

_____

Participants: *Contingency organization members participating in the test* _____

_____

Duration: *Estimated time required to perform disaster recovery procedures* _____

_____

_____

Constraints: *Definition of the scope of the test. Identification of test elements to be included or excluded* _____

_____

Assumptions: *Hypothetical operating conditions that prevail during the testing process* _____

_____

Steps:

Steps involved in the testing process; Could be both sequential or parallel

Responsibility:

Person responsible for each step

_____	_____
_____	_____
_____	_____
_____	_____
_____	_____
_____	_____

PARALLEL TESTING

A parallel test can be performed in conjunction with the checklist test or simulation test. Under this scenario, historical transactions, such as the prior business day's transactions, are processed against preceding day's backup files at the contingency processing site or hot site. All reports produced at the alternate site for the current business date should agree with those reports produced at the alternate processing site.

FULL-INTERRUPTION TESTING

A full-interruption test activates the total disaster recovery plan. This test is likely to be costly and could disrupt normal operations, and therefore should be approached with caution. Adequate time must be scheduled for the testing. Initially the test should not be scheduled at critical points in the normal processing cycle, e.g., the end of the month. The duration of the test should be predetermined to measure adequate response time.

Various test scenarios could be planned to identify the type of disaster, the extent of damage, recovery capability, staffing and equipment availability, backup resource availability, and time / duration of the test. The test plan should identify the persons responsible and the time they need to perform each activity. However, only part of the plan should be tested initially. This approach identifies the workability of each part before attempting a full test. It may be best, at first, to test the plan after normal business hours or on weekends to minimize disruptions. Eventually, unannounced tests can be performed to emphasize preparedness.

If the organization uses a service center for part or all of its data processing, it is necessary to coordinate the testing activity with the service center. The initial testing should be conducted after hours or when the interruption will not affect the operations of the organization.

EVALUATING TEST RESULTS AND UPDATING THE PLAN

Personnel should log events during the test that will help evaluate the results. The testing process should provide feedback to the disaster recovery team to ensure that the plan is adequate. The recovery team, which normally consists of key management personnel, should assess test results and analyze recommendations from various team leaders regarding improvements or modifications for the plan. It is essential to measure quantitatively the test results, including:

- Elapsed time to perform various activities
- Accuracy of each activity
- Amount of work completed

Exhibits 3 and 4 contain suggested formats for evaluating testing results. The results of the tests will most likely lead to changes in the plan. The changes should enhance the plan and provide a more workable recovery process.

EXHIBIT 3:   TEST RESULTS EVALUATION FORM

Objectives: *A statement of the specific testing goals* ____

_____

_____

Plan Cross: *Cross referece of the tested procedure in*
Reference: *the disaster recovery plan (i.e., section, page*
                     *number)*_____

_____

_____

Type of Test: *Identification of the type of test being per-*
                     formed (e.g., checklist test, simulation test,
                     parallel test, etc.) _____

_____

_____

Responsibility: *Person responsible for each step* _____

_____

_____

Actual Time: *Actual time required to perform the disaster*
                     recovery procedure _____

_____

_____

Successful /
Unsuccessful: *Test results* _____

_____

_____

Comments: *Comments, observations, notations regarding*
                     the test _____

_____

_____

Suggested Plan   *Specific procedures to be modified based*
Modifications: *on the test results*

_____

_____

_____

EXHIBIT 4:   TEST EVALUATION FORM

DATE: _____

Purpose: To document specific testing procedures and to evaluate results by team. Examples may include manual balancing procedures, offline data storage, data transmission, system restoration from backup tapes, etc.

Dis. Rec. Hour	Plan Cross Ref.	Action #	Action	S / P *	Respons-ibility	Actual Time	S / U **	Comments

* S = Sequential, P = Parallel   ** S = Successful, U = Unsuccessful

(continued)

Column Reference:	Explanation:
Disaster Recovery Hour *	*The estimated time required to perform a specific procedure in case of a disaster*
Plan Cross Reference *	*Cross reference to the procedure in the disaster recovery plan (.i.e., section, page number)*
Action Number *	*Sequence number assigned to the testing procedure to perform*
Action *	*Description of the testing procedure to perform*
S / P *	*Designation of whether the action is performed separately (sequentially) or in conjunction with another action (parallel)*
Responsibility *	*Responsible person or team*
Actual TIme **	*Actual time required to complete the specific procedure*
S / U **	*Test results (S = Successful, U = Unsuccessful)*
Comments **	*Testing comments, observations, notations, recommendations for improvement, etc.*

*** Complete in preparation for the actual test**
**** Complete during or after the actual test**

After all sections have been tested and changes have been made, the plan should be presented to senior management for approval.

Testing of the disaster recovery plan is an ongoing process that should not stop once the plan is approved by senior management. Circumstances change in relation to the hardware and software used by the organization. Telephone numbers of employees and vendors, and other critical information is subject to change and should be kept up to date.

---

[1] This chapter has been adapted with permission from the book <u>Disaster Proof Your Business: A Planning Manual for Protecting a Company's Computer, Communications & Records Systems & Facilities</u>, Copyright © 1991, Probus Publishing Company.

21

TESTING LEVELS AND RESOURCES
by William J. Krouslis

After the decisions have been made on what to test, the next factor requiring attention is the type of resource to be applied to the test and the level at which the resource is to be applied. Each specific resource and level will result in a valid test. However, the higher the test level and the more authentic the resource, the more confident the planner is of a test that will confirm an idea that would perform after an actual disaster. *Figure 1* illustrates these points in a situation involving a business which has identified a manufacturing process as the critical business function to be recovered. A test of the plan to recover a manufacturing process could follow any one of the paths shown.

The testing resource is described as the material being input into the test situation to ascertain if the recovery system will function as expected. It is the piece of matter, substance, data or fact that goes in the front end and is recast by the process and comes out the back. In this example, the manufacturer has an important injection molding process that they plan to "recover" on similar machines which are to be made available from a friendly competitor with excess manufacturing capacity. Although the machines are similar, they are not identical. The "resource" that is used to verify machine compatibility is some form of the raw plastic material that is normally used in the process.

Figure 1

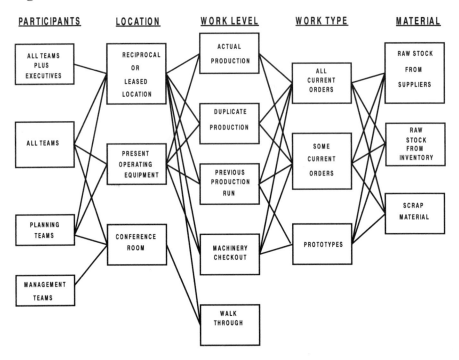

The planner now has a choice on the type of material that will be used in the test: raw stock directly from a supplier, stock in inventory that has been quality controlled and verified to meet current specifications or scrap material that has minimal value to him. Each resource has a different cost and confirms compatibility under different circumstances. Raw material directly from a supplier could be very different from raw stock pulled from inventory.

Using scrap material is again a different situation. The point is that the test results from each resource only "prove" that the compatible machine will work with the tested material. The test with scrap does not empirically confirm a process that will work with vendor supplied raw stock. However, if the raw materials are similar in properties, the alternate source could be used as "proof" that the idea of using the similar machinery is valid. This conclusion is a call only the planner could make with the process manager.

Using the same logic, we can apply the resource and test level model to the recovery of a local area network (*Figure 2*):

Figure 2

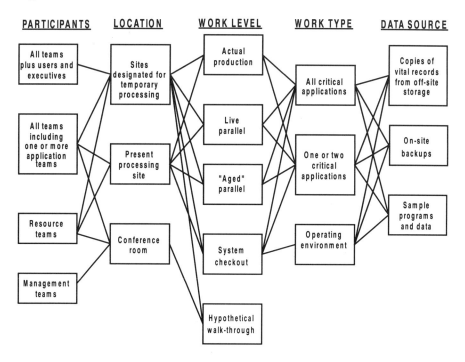

| PARTICIPANTS | LOCATION | WORK LEVEL | WORK TYPE | DATA SOURCE |

In this situation our plan is to recreate the network using the identical LAN topology but with system components that are similar. The servers are not identical in architecture and the workstations will be old 386's that were taken out of service and warehoused for just this purpose. The test resource could be some of the applications and data that the current LAN runs. Should the planner pull current copies of these resources from their off-site depository or should we use on site data or selectively use sample data from a controlled data source? Each test resource will "prove" that the reconfigured LAN will or will not work with that particular resource. Using this particular test to extrapolate the results to all untested applications and data sources is again only a call that can be made by the planner and LAN administrator. The point is that each test level is valid; however, the results would have different absolute conclusions in the overall decision to use this particular test as confirmation of the situation that would exist after a real disaster.

These models can be used by the planner in their own situation by recreating the resources to mirror their particular circumstances.

Each description produces different results, has different costs and involves different risk of confirming the validity of a test.

The resources and test levels are what the planner will use to verify the functionality of the recovery concepts. The test of these ideas are what will move the plan into some form of reality. The gutsy planner would test with an actual production run using real raw material. The conservative one will choose to test at a vastly different level. Both situations are valid. Neither will result in a test that was right or wrong. Both will give a result that "proved" that the test situation either worked or it did not. Unless the test is done at the highest level with real resources it cannot be concluded that the test confirmed the actual circumstances that would exist after the disaster. However, a test at any level is better than no test at all!

22

THE TEST REPORT[1]

by David Sobolow

A Disaster Recovery Test Report will document your test's results and provide the following information about the test:

1. Re-statement of the test's identification information (e.g., its number, dates / times, locations, etc.).

2. Re-statement of the test's logistical objectives.

3. Re-statement of the test's operational objectives.

4. Identity of on-site and remote personnel who supported test activities.

5. A management review of the test and its success level.

6. Observations made during the test and corresponding recommendations. For example, to enhance part of the recovery plan, begin a study to determine or justify a recovery planning issue, to modify a recovery planning procedure, to begin planning for the next test as soon as possible, etc.

A Disaster Recovery Test Event Log may be used to record events during the test. This log would contain event descriptions, by date and time. A sample format for a Disaster Recovery Test Event Log is provided as *Exhibit 1*.

EXHIBIT 1: SAMPLE DISASTER RECOVERY TEST EVENT LOG

Test I.D.: _____ Date:_____

Time	Event Description

In addition, a Disaster Recovery Test Problem Log may be used to record problems encountered during the test. This log would contain problem descriptions and their resolutions, by date and time. A sample Disaster Recovery Test Problem Log is provided as *Exhibit 2*:

EXHIBIT 2: SAMPLE DISASTER RECOVERY TEST PROBLEM LOG

Test I.D.: _____ Date:_____

Time	Event Description	Problem Resolution

To assist you in preparing a test report, a sample Disaster Recovery Test Report is provided as *Exhibit 3*:

EXHIBIT 3: SAMPLE DISASTER RECOVERY TEST REPORT

Test I.D.: _____   Date:_____

[Re-state Logistical Test Objectives:] _____

_____

*[Re-state Operational Test Objectives:]*_____

_____

[Re-state Test Location:] _____

_____

TEST ATTENDEES:

On-site Personnel Names: _____

_____

Remote Personnel Names:_____

_____

TEST DATES AND TIMES:

Scheduled Start Date / Time:_____

Scheduled End Date / Time:_____

Actual Start Date / Time: _____

Actual End Date / Time: _____

Total Elapsed Test Time for this Test: _____ Hrs. and _____ Min.

Test Time   (Hours)

Available at Recovery Facility _____

Used at Recovery Facility _____

Remaining at Recovery Facility_____

MANAGEMENT REVIEW:

On [date], [your organization's name] tested its ability to reestablish and restore [_____] operations at the [_____] recovery facility.

(continued)

On [date], [your organization's name] recovery team personnel arrived to begin this process, and on [date/time] this test was considered successful.

The information presented in this report details this test effort, and describes the items that warrant further investigation and resolution.

TEST OBSERVATIONS AND RECOMMENDATIONS:

OBSERVATION (1):
RECOMMENDATION (1):   *Enhance . . .*

OBSERVATION (2):
RECOMMENDATION (2):   *Begin a study to determine . . .*

OBSERVATION (3):
RECOMMENDATION (3):   *Identify . . .*

OBSERVATION (4):
RECOMMENDATION (4):   *Modify . . .*

OBSERVATION (5):
RECOMMENDATION (5):   *Begin planning for next test . . .*

OBSERVATION (6):
RECOMMENDATION (6):   *Investigate . . .*

---

[1] This chapter has been adapted with permission from the book <u>Recovering Your Business</u>, Copyright © 1993 TAMP Computer Systems Inc., which contains comprehensive 'how to plan' information and tools for business recovery planning.

23
SURPRISE AND UNANNOUNCED TESTING
by James Certoma

INTRODUCTION

Recent events have kept contingency planning professionals extremely busy, either recovering from disasters or reviewing and testing their current plans. Between August, 1992 and August, 1993, many major occurrences — both natural and man-made — have impacted the business operating environment. Hurricane Andrew in 1992 devastated Southern Florida. A major storm during December, 1992 crippled the financial district in Lower Manhattan with excessive flooding. The World Trade Center bombing during February, 1993 brought the harsh realities and destructiveness of terrorism to the United States. A major snowstorm in March, 1993 made transportation impossible in the New York Metropolitan area; fortunately, that event occurred on a weekend when the business impact was lessened, although the computer facility of a major servicer of ATM machines was heavily damaged by the storm. Finally, the Midwestern U.S. was overrun by the flooding Mississippi and Missouri rivers during the summer of 1993 and personal property as well as business were impacted in unprecedented dollar amounts.

Today if polled, most major corporations, and in particular financial services institutions, would confirm that they have data processing recovery plans and business resumption plans developed and implemented. In addition, most firms as part of their contingency planning function routinely test their plans to ensure that they are current and would work in the event of a disaster. Despite such strong feelings of preparedness and ability to handle worst case scenarios, the majority of contingency planning professionals and senior management cringe at the thought of any of the previously mentioned events happening to them. Their reaction is normal and expected. None want to deal with the hard work, long hours, and shortened tempers that are part of recovery. It is a grueling process that interrupts the normal personal and business lives of all employees involved.

In addition to these obvious reasons for being concerned about recovering from a disaster, I would propose that many contingency planners feel that their routine testing programs, while enlightening and helpful to maintaining a strong plan, lack a major ingredient. That element is the "Surprise" aspect of an unannounced test. Disasters are rarely known more than a few hours or possibly days in advance and in most cases they occur with no warning. Yet many of our contingency tests are planned for the year and nicely typed schedules and charts are distributed months before the tests will be conducted.

Given the recent history of disasters, both the wide range of events and that a broad range of geographical areas as well as industries have been impacted, it is time to test our plans in a new way. In the following pages I will describe my personal experiences with the first phase of conducting unannounced or surprise tests. In 1994, we should all realize that the time has arrived for unannounced testing!

DEFINING AN UNANNOUNCED TEST

The concept behind conducting an unannounced or surprise test of your contingency plan is that you are modelling a disaster. The one major difference between this and the real thing is that it is a 'controlled" disaster. Depending on your organization and the status of your current plan you can test individual components of your plan and, in effect, modularize testing in a disaster scenario that is unknown to other members of the organization. The key concept is that an absolute minimum number of people (possibly, only yourself) knows that the plan or a portion of it is going to be tested.

The challenge and therefore the benefit of an unannounced test is that no advanced planning can be conducted by the organizational units, business units or recovery teams that are responsible for executing the contingency plan. In essence, whenever you decide to conduct an unannounced test, all participants will be relying on the validity of their current plan and on the most recent updates.

To understand the significance of a surprise test, consider what happens today. In many organizations, a contingency planning department or individual will publish in January a list or schedule of contingency tests which will be conducted during the year. These tests may include the communication network to contact the critical personnel, the data processing restoration plan and the set-up and relocation of the critical business units to a back-up site for the resumption of their operations. In reality, as soon as that schedule is published, recovery teams typically call a meeting of all personnel. The team leader of the data processing recovery team, for example, distributes the list and informs the members that vacations will not be allowed during the test time periods. In addition, a review of items such as the back-up tape generation and off site delivery procedures will be conducted. Past test shortcomings will be discussed to verify that the necessary corrections were made and will not occur again. Other recovery teams will conduct similar staff meetings. The race is on to be fully prepared when that test date arrives instead of being in a constant state of readiness for any event and knowing that team members must be able to react and improvise to the situation.

An important caveat to any unannounced testing program is that it must be conceived and developed by the planner within the culture of the organization. An unannounced contingency testing program will only be successful if it fits in the organization.

CONTINGENCY PLAN COMPONENTS FOR UNANNOUNCED TESTING

Contingency plans for each organization will differ in their structure and level of detail. Therefore in developing a program of unannounced testing, the parts of the plan to be included will depend on how your plan is currently structured. From my personal planning experiences there are three main pieces which all plans have in common and are prime candidates to be included in a surprise testing program.

The first part is the *Corporate Contingency Communications Network*. Since most disasters seem to occur during the non-business hours when few or no employees are on site with the exception of a security force, the timeliness and efficiency of contacting the critical personnel and of activating the plan may be the most crucial element to an effective recovery.

The second plan component which is routinely and diligently tested by organizations but normally the "most planned" test is the *Data Processing Restoration Plan*. Activation of this plan following a disaster usually occurs with minimal lead time and the current testing programs masks the true effectiveness of the data processing plan.

Finally, the *Business Resumption Plan* for the critical business operations is dependent on the setup of predesignated relocation sites and the movement of critical personnel to these sites to establish a working environment. This is a time-consuming effort in most plans and if organizations test it today, it is rarely done under an unannounced scenario requiring personnel and equipment to be mobilized on short notice.

I will discuss each of these plan components in terms of an unannounced testing program and review some of the issues that I have uncovered and subsequently remedied as a result of these tests.

Corporate Contingency Communications Network

There are three main goals of a corporate contingency communications test:

1) Contact all employees

2) Communicate an accurate and consistent message

3) Perform the communication in a timely and efficient manner.

During a communications test, it is important to not only reach the critical employees, but all employees. Most business areas have a telephone contact tree in place to contact their employees at home during non-business hours. In the event of a disaster, business management may only desire a small crew to show up the next day. If all employees report to work, unnecessary confusion results and recovery is hampered.

One of the key parts of any communications test is to verify whether the message that was passed on was both accurate and consistent across the organization. I will address test monitoring and follow-up in a later section. Above all else, the process of communication must be done in a timely and efficient manner. The recovery cannot begin until the appropriate individuals have been contacted. In this case time is money and every delay is likely to cost the organization both money and customer confidence.

Conducting an unannounced communications test usually starts with a designated individual calling the Security Department outside of normal business hours and after communicating that it is a test, relating a test disaster scenario to the individual. Obviously this cannot be done until appropriate procedures have been developed and all Security personnel have undergone training. The test continues with Security following procedures and, through their chain of command, receiving instructions to contact the designated senior contingency managers in the organization with specific instructions. The communications umbrella begins to unfold and ultimately all employees would be contacted. During a test, the level of contacts attempted is dependent upon the extent of the test goals.

Based on my experiences with this type of test, a wide range of issues can occur. The first result may be that the Security individual receiving the call does not have the appropriate procedures nearby or has not been trained. This most basic issue immediately mandates a review with Security Management of the situation. A common circumstance to be identified is that contact sheets used for the calls to the senior officials are not up to date. The individuals to be contacted may have changed or a simple move may mean the listed phone number is incorrect. Each individual to be contacted must have one or more alternates listed to be assured that the business area is contacted. If an answering machine is encountered during a phone call, a message including date and time of the call should be left, but the alternate should also be called. The rule to be used is typically that an individual from the business area must be reached. Answering machines, spouses, or children do not count as a successful contact.

One other area to be reviewed during the test is the clarity of the message communicated. The initial disaster scenario must be effectively communicated to the individuals called, as well as the next course of action as developed by the Security Management.

The more frequently an unannounced communications test is conducted, the more comfortable the process will become and issues such as those described above will occur less often, with less severity.

Data Processing Restoration Plan

For many organizations which have recognized the need for contingency planning, their first effort has been to develop a data processing restoration plan. As the plan has become reality, a testing program has been created to ensure its validity as well as its currency. To implement an unannounced testing program for the data processing restoration plan the focus should be on the reaction time of the recovery team to the test disaster declaration and the timeliness of the recovery. There are three main goals that should be addressed:

1) Mobilization of the data processing recovery team

2) Movement of personnel to the hot site or recovery location

3) Accurate restoration of the systems within an acceptable timeframe.

Similar to the contingency communications test, the first critical part of the test is being able to reach either the primary of alternate data processing recovery team. Particularly if the disaster occurs during non-business hours and the computer hot site is not a company-owned facility the communication to critical personnel and their movement to the hot site must be done in order to expedite the recovery. The travel arrangements for some, whether automobile, airline or train, must be centrally coordinated quickly or each individual must already be aware of his or her own travel arrangements.

Once all critical team members are on site and the recovery begins, the system must be restored to the most current timeframe without the luxury of prior meetings and strategy sessions. Recovery procedures must be current, personnel (both primary and alternate) must be trained in the latest recovery process and the off site data retrieval process must be timely and complete. This test must also include business user participation to validate the results.

I have initiated an unannounced data processing recovery test program in our organization. Although the organizational management knew that a test was going to be conducted during the year, the day was known only to myself and the hot site vendor. This has helped to ensure that it would be a surprise test. Since this was the first time this type of test was being conducted, I decided to inform the team leader at 3 P.M. that the disaster had occurred and the recovery would begin at 8 A.M. the next morning. Communication of the test during business hours reduced the complexity of the exercise but provided an environment in which the overall goals could be achieved. One aspect of unannounced testing that I continually stress is to crawl before you walk or even think of running.

In summarizing an unannounced data processing recovery test, you quickly realize that all the primary people that always participated in preplanned tests are not available for an unannounced test. As a result, the lack of designation of alternates as well as adequate training is evident. Since people aren't as well trained in the recovery, the shortcomings in the written procedures are noticed. The performance of off-site tape vendors and the promised turnaround times are quickly evaluated. Finally, the ability of the recovery team leader to mobilize a team and give instructions becomes apparent when the test date and time is not known.

Business Resumption Plan

The responsibility for the development and maintenance of business resumption plans almost always resides with the business areas. On the other hand, one planning aspect which is usually coordinated by a central contingency planning group is the assignment of relocation sites and workstations. Within our organization, I have designated these sites and determined both the number and type of workstations that would be set-up during a contingency for the relocating business units. The determinations almost always look great on paper but the underlying question is whether they would work in a real situation and if they could be set up and equipped in a timely manner. Therefore an unannounced test for the business unit relocation site was formulated with the following goals:

1) Verify the accuracy of the layout capacity

2) Mobilize the recovery team and complete the set-up

3) Obtain and install the computer equipment in a timely manner.

During the test, we wanted to be sure that when the required workstations and computer equipment were installed, there would be enough workspace for the critical personnel to operate.

It was important to know that the planned amount of equipment could be borrowed. Our corporate philosophy is to borrow previously designated non-critical equipment from an unaffected facility for the relocation site. This eliminates the dependencies on acquiring large amounts of equipment from third party vendors on short notice. During the test, we wanted to verify that the equipment could be borrowed and returned to the original user. Underlying this effort was the goal to mobilize the necessary personnel to perform the moves and site setup when no advanced planning had taken place.

The test was conducted on a weekend. The recovery team leader was notified on Friday morning that the test was to occur. Friday evening and Saturday were spent setting up the area. Over 300 devices were relocated. On Sunday, management from the relocated units and areas which had given up devices were requested to come to the site and verify that it was workable. A three-day weekend was selected for this test so that Monday could be utilized to break down the site and return the equipment.

The major benefit of the test was the realization that we were short of some devices and would need an additional source of these items. We also realized that the setup of the site was a time-consuming process and additional manpower was necessary to achieve a timely completion. A major benefit of the borrowing of equipment was the awareness by the individuals who normally used that equipment that routine backups are critical to ensure that they would not lose data if their device was moved.

DEVELOPING PARAMETERS FOR UNANNOUNCED TESTS

If an unannounced testing program makes sense for your organization and you plan to develop one, the typical question is, "how far do you go?" One thing that we can all agree upon is the ultimate goal. We want to feel that when a disaster occurs our plan will work and ensure survival of the organization. The difference between your testing program and anyone else's is the road you take to get there. This simply means that you may decide to proceed either slower or faster than others depending on the culture of your firm and the current status and comfort level with your plan.

In deciding how much to test in an unannounced manner, always remember to crawl before you walk and before you run. In devising this plan, stack the deck for success in your favor. In most organizations you may get one or two chances to be successful and if you try to do too much too quickly, the issues arising may hurt the overall plan credibility. In fact, a major goal of an unannounced test is to enhance the program's credibility to management.

A good way to develop the parameters for an unannounced testing program is to avoid extremes while still achieving your goals. As an example, if you are conducting a communications test, there is no need to call people in the middle of night. That will certainly create a surprise but it will probably be a surprise that hurts the program. If you are trying to determine whether critical people can be reached at home and the contact lists have been maintained, a call in the evening or on a weekend will suffice.

Once you have thought out exactly what parts of your plan are to be included in an unannounced program and how extensive the tests will be, you are ready to present and sell your proposal to your management.

SELLING UNANNOUNCED TESTING TO MANAGEMENT

Implementation of an unannounced contingency testing plan MUST be understood and endorsed by senior management. But, before conducting your selling efforts, take note of the fact that you must have a solid plan in place if you are suggesting an unannounced test plan at all. This is a major accomplishment in itself and if your management is aware of the complexity and completeness as well as the success you have had thus far in normal testing, the new program may not be so difficult to sell.

Your best ally in convincing management of the need for this program is your senior contingency committee. Most such committees are comprised of representatives from all major organizational areas who meet routinely to discuss the plan. In your discussions, remind them that recent disasters have not been planned and known in advance. There are enough recent examples to reinforce this point. Also, emphasize that testing in the past has been to validate the written recovery plans and procedures and not necessarily how well people and the plans react in a sudden and unknown situation. This is your next, new goal in testing.

Your biggest challenge is to calm the anxieties of senior management with regard to this new mode of testing. As mentioned in the last section, do not "shoot for the moon" in your unannounced testing plan. Rather, play it conservatively so management does not reject the plan because of a risk of failure. Management must feel that the test will not interfere in any substantive way with normal work. You cannot jeopardize the normal business of the organization by your test program. You can tell them in advance that the tests will be done on weekends when there is no production and you will rule out heavy processing timeframes such as the end of a business quarter. If you remain in contact with the business areas and are aware of new business coming aboard and system conversions, you can assure management that revenue-producing activities will not be adversely impacted. You should also assure management that you will inform employees that unannounced tests will be conducted during the year and address any questions that may arise. Finally, your "ace in the hole" is to state that the test can always be delayed or cancelled if any current business is at risk. You will be telling them that you are creating a disaster scenario to test your plan but the ultimate control of cancelling resides with them.

If you have a well-developed recovery plan and prepare a detailed and convincing argument for unannounced testing, you have an excellent chance of selling it to management.

SURPRISE TEST MONITORING AND FOLLOW-UP

The value of any testing program, whether planned or unannounced, is in monitoring of activities as well as the resolution of any issues raised. It is particularly important to monitor an unannounced test since there will be very few people who are aware of the test and can therefore assist you. If your contingency planning department is typical of most organizations, the staffing may be limited for this effort. Based on that fact, it is important to focus on the surprise elements of your test and not all pieces of the test. For example, if you are declaring an unannounced test of your data processing plan and will restore the system at a backup location, you may want to focus your monitoring primarily on the reaction of the team members and the leader. Since the team has successfully done data processing recoveries as part of your previous testing, you do not need to focus a lot of time and attention on the ordinary recovery tasks. You should want to know that the recovery team members are contacted and successfully reach the backup site, with proper instructions. One other key aspect to observe is the functioning of team member alternates and how familiar they are with the recovery process.

As you observe and record personnel reactions to an unannounced test, the shortcomings must be rigorously followed up and resolved. To help evaluate the test and identify areas of improvement, a valuable source of information is the business user community. As part of unannounced contingency communications tests, I distribute questionnaires to senior management recipients of calls so I can help determine the effectiveness of the communication process. I have also made random calls to a wide base of employees the day after the test to determine whether the telephone communication chains were attempted by the individual business areas. The result of these questionnaires and test observations are reported to the senior contingency management committee.

As previously mentioned, an unannounced contingency test program is a progressive effort with each subsequent test building on the prior one and dependent on proper monitoring and follow-up on the weaknesses. I cannot stress strongly enough the importance of these steps in order to continue a successful test program and someday reach the ultimate test of a full-scale unannounced test of your contingency plan.

THE *"ULTIMATE"* TEST
by James Certoma

Developing, conducting, monitoring and resolving issues for the first unannounced contingency test that you complete is the toughest part of an unannounced testing program. After your first test, you have begun to establish a mind-set in your organization that preplanned tests are to be minimized and real disaster-type testing (unannounced) will become the standard test mode. This change in the perception of contingency testing at an organization may take a fair amount of time or tests to occur but it should develop into a snowball effect whereby people start thinking in that fashion when the subject of contingency testing arises.

The optimal goal is to conduct what I have entitled the "Ultimate Test," where notice is given and all components of your testing plan go into effect at the same time. This includes the communication of the disaster, the restoration of the data processing function in the hot site and the establishment of the relocation site for the business units which are displaced by the disaster. The business aspect of the test includes the movement of critical personnel to their operating areas and validation of the restored data processing systems.

The concluding question to all of us is whether we will ever achieve the "ultimate" test. Most of us cannot at this time honestly answer that. We have a long way to go to reach that point and each day our planning efforts are challenged with new business developments as well as technology changes. This is increasingly an issue with respect to local area networks. Whether we ever conduct the ultimate and complete test of our plans or are forced by circumstances to use our plans following a real disaster, the time has come for us to begin redefining our contingency testing programs by introducing the element of surprise.

24

DISASTER RECOVERY TESTING CYCLES

by Judith A. Hinds

A disaster recovery program must be more than a plan document that sits on a shelf if it is to be of maximum benefit to an organization. One of the premises of this book is that testing helps ensure that procedures, products and people all work together to the same end: a successful recovery from a disruption. For testing to be successful, it is worth spending time and thought not just on single tests, but on the overall design of the testing program itself.

Successful testing is a complex task for a number of reasons, and the concept of the test cycle helps structure the task for best results. A test cycle is a series of increasingly elaborate tests, each one usually longer than the preceding one, and separated by enough time to resolve problems which could prevent completion of testing steps at the next stage. Testing in cycles has a cumulative impact on the organization, infusing disaster recovery preparedness at all levels.

The testing cycle is, above all, a learning environment: an opportunity to solve problems, overcome obstacles and explore new approaches. A pre-planned test cycle reduces some of the variables, thereby increasing the likelihood of success at each stage. In the beginning of a testing program it may almost seem as if activities are progressing in slow-motion. Yet this deliberate approach makes it easier to determine the root of problems. Time trials can come later in the sequence. The goal should not just be to avoid making mistakes but also to hone problem-solving skills, especially since a real disaster is bound to introduce further variables or complications which could not be foreseen.

To give a straight-forward example, a typical, four-part cycle for a data processing recovery test begins with recovery of the operating system. As in a building, if this foundation is solid, then the rest of the structure is likely to proceed with fewer problems. The second step is the data restoration phase, usually involving the validation of file recovery priorities. Missing datasets and file-related problems encountered here need to be resolved before moving on to the recovery of applications in the third phase. When applications are running smoothly, the fourth stage, testing with internal and external users, can be accomplished with best chances for success.

Data processing recovery testing is nearly always carried out in addition to support of the normal production workload. Staying late, coming in early and working weekends on top of the regular job, can all contribute to frustration and burn-out. Team members will not soon forget a Superbowl Sunday afternoon spent fruitlessly waiting for the system to come up. By organizing tests in cycles, the overall task is broken down into more manageable components. Staff with specialized responsibilities can be scheduled more effectively. It is easier to sustain interest when team members feel that their group's performance contributes measurably to the success of the whole.

Several factors contribute to the complexity of disaster recovery testing. The dynamic character of the typical organization's technological environment virtually requires that testing be conducted as an ongoing series of exercises and not just as a one-time or once-a-year occurrence. Evolving hardware platforms, more sophisticated software products, greater integration of application processing and expanding network connectivity all challenge the adequacy of previous recovery procedures. Not only is the technology evolving constantly but most companies are also experiencing dramatic changes in the business itself. New markets, products and services, new service-delivery mechanisms, new customer service goals and new organizational structures contribute to constantly changing priorities for business recovery. Cycles of recovery tests are a mechanism for managing all of this change effectively.

Planning a series of tests as a cycle also helps with another complexity in disaster recovery: coordination of communications. As the cycle evolves, the skillful use of many communications tools helps keep everyone informed about the relationship between his / her part and the larger picture. It is important to recognize that individuals assigned to cover the test may not have been able to attend all of the preparatory meetings. Team members present at the start of a test may leave before those scheduled to complete the work arrive. A person arriving in the middle will want to know what has happened and how far along things are. Senior managers, auditors and external users wishing to observe test activities may require orientation different from that provided to other team members. Simple hand-drawn time-lines can be as useful in their place as output from sophisticated project management software packages. Different types of meetings also serve as vehicles of communication. Conference calls, site visits, vendor liaison meetings, briefings for multiple shifts, "rally-the-troops" talks by senior management — all of these over the course of a test cycle help in decision-making, information dissemination and morale boosting.

The starting point for the design is to build the testing goals. These are laid out in preliminary meetings with management, the test coordinator and representatives of key technical groups. It is particularly important to highlight changes that have occurred since the last test, especially changes in software products, releases, versions, program fixes, enhancements, new user interfaces, new storage devices and media. At the very start it is also important to identify items and issues that may require long lead times, such as telecommunications purchases and installations or major systems migrations. Milestones, target dates, and estimated timeframes will emerge as the process goes forward. Alongside the major goals can be minor objectives which if accomplished independently can contribute to success in a later phase.

The quality of the data backup program needs to be a top priority for successful recovery, and testing cycles help ensure that data recovery procedures are current, constantly updated and fully understood by all involved. Data processing operations is not the only area that carries responsibility for effective backup procedures. It is important to recognize the roles of such disciplines as data storage management, data software management, database administration and capacity planning. When the expertise of staff in many areas is tapped during testing cycles, it drives the awareness of recovery issues deep into the organization.

Identifying resources needed to accomplish recovery goals and assuring their availability make the testing cycle a valuable research project. The short, early tests in a cycle usually raise questions about file selection, data capture, file retention and off site rotation. Questions also come up about software utilities, many of which are taken for granted in normal operations. Which ones should be available for recovery? Automated scheduling software, backup and restore packages, data security software and monitoring programs are some of the tools which may warrant consideration.

Other resources to be researched include data storage devices, special terminals and printers, data feeds from external sources and connectivity to remote users. Special research may also be needed to identify and prepare a range of representative transactions so that all systems and their interconnections can be judged to work satisfactorily in the recovery environment. These kinds of tasks may only move to the foreground in the later stages of a testing cycle.

Documentation benefits from the iterative nature of the test cycle. From test to test, team members refine their scripts and checklists for content as well as clarity. The predecessor-successor relationships among tasks are validated and communicated. Cross-references between documents are added. Maintenance becomes less of a chore as procedures for automatically updating documentation are developed. This is yet another example of a strengthened link between production and recovery.

In a test cycle there is a strong relationship between the end result of one test and the beginning of another. It is all too easy, after many hours of testing, to rush through the final steps and "just get it over with." There are several benefits in paying careful attention to clean-up activities. Most important, no doubt, is to ensure that test data does not inadvertently carry over into production. At least equally important is to be sure that no confidential data remains on storage devices at a remote site. Capturing test output for detective work after the test should not be neglected. System logs, screen prints, copies of disk datasets and even hardcopy output, if not too voluminous, will yield clues to problems and minimize finger-pointing. When it is understood how valuable the test evidence is, it is more likely that the assignment to preserve it will be taken seriously.

Debriefing activities also tie the end of one test to the beginning of the next, with an emphasis on moving ahead. There is an opportunity, once the fatigue is gone, to hear what went well, what needs to be fixed, and what would make things better next time. Some of the best ideas surface when the pressure is off but while the experience is still fresh. It is also the perfect time to offer recognition in whatever form is appropriate.

The concept of testing in cycles has many benefits to an organization. A comprehensive, dynamic recovery capability may enable the company to offer new business services. Employees have new opportunities for job enrichment. Continuous on-the-job training and cross-training occurs quite naturally. Insularity among groups diminishes. Technical staff are exposed more fully to the business of the company. There are new software and other tools to master. There are specific opportunities to develop problem-solving and presentation skills. The learning environment of the testing cycle fosters a greater appreciation for the contributions of each individual. Finally, the permeation of recovery thinking throughout the company has the beneficial side-effect of increasing protective measures in production: quality improves overall.

IV.

WHAT IS
BEING TESTED

25

DATA CENTER RECOVERY TESTING

by Joan Blum

The protection and recovery of data center software, hardware and telecommunications capabilities from unexpected events have become increasingly vital due to the modern corporation's dependency on technology. Development of standards and guidelines for mitigating potential loss and for recovering from the sudden loss of unforeseen events are critical to organizations who leverage technology for competitive advantages.

Data center recovery testing is an integral component of a firm's disaster recovery strategy. In this electronic age most lines of business utilize technology for daily operations. Whether accessing applications from a LAN, minicomputer or mainframe system, businesses need to outline and regularly test the feasibility of their recovery strategies. This chapter specifically addresses the essential elements for data center disaster recovery testing.

THE DATA CENTER PLAYS AN ACTIVE ROLE

Preparing for a data center test can prove both time-consuming and expensive. Experience has proven that preparation is the first step toward complete recovery planning. A test provides an opportunity to exercise pre-designed plans to ensure their integrity and viability. Meetings with recovery team members should occur regularly and include staff from operations support, data center, telecommunications, application development and the "front office" or end user areas.

Prior to an application area turning over its disaster recovery plan to the data center, operations staff need to review and study the plan. Since data centers typically have "ownership" of the equipment on which applications operate, they are generally in the best position to give valuable feedback. For example, all applications may request a small portion of CPU power but on an aggregate basis there may not be sufficient capacity in the recovery environment to accommodate all requirements. If the data center has not reviewed the plans with the application areas within the last six months, there is a good possibility that what was once sufficient will no longer meet today's needs.

By the time test preparation occurs, all test participants should be generally familiar with the recovery plans.

TEST TIMING

To select a date for a test, data center management may consider numerous factors. Determination can be based on the only day(s) when the business line will allow the systems to be non-operational or on telecommunications line transfer requirements for the test. Power shutdowns for maintenance in buildings where data centers reside sometimes offer an optimum testing opportunity. A scenario of limited or no access into the building (from a physical and telecommunications standpoint) can be tested in conjunction with a power shutdown.

Most data centers choose dates well in advance to ensure the feasibility of the exercise. Declaring a disaster with no prior knowledge is theoretically an ideal way to prove recovery capabilities, but surprise testing would generally introduce a host of interruptions and liabilities for most organizations. When using an off-site storage vendor, advance warning is likely to limit the validity of testing the vendor's response time for contingency purposes.

Tests should also simulate failures at various times during the processing cycle, not simply the end of a week, coinciding with the backup schedules.

SCOPE OF THE TEST

The scope of data center testing will probably vary based on corporate standards and audit requirements. Federal standards may apply as well depending on the industry (e.g. banking). Preparation of a basic outline for the test will prove helpful. The outline should address recovery in the context of at least the following variables:

- *Application Selection* - Which applications to test and the extent of testing need to be determined. Designated application criticality may determine whether to test at all. If an application consists of online and batch components, will both be tested? If so, will batch processing run to completion?

- *Minimal Operating Capability* - Due to limited resource availability during recovery, basic service levels may be substantially reduced. Business areas need to define the required service levels and to ensure that there is a basic understanding by all senior management. Items to consider for testing include:

  - *Functionality* - Will all of the application's functionality be tested or only a portion? This should be consistent with end user and management expectations in the recovery environment.

  - *Transaction Volume* - How many transactions will be tested? Again, the answer depends on the expected recovery environment. Testing only 10% of the expected number of transactions may or may not limit the value of the test. Will the processing environment survive when users require 50% or 100% of a day's transactions?

  - *Interfaces* - What internal and external environments will be available in the recovery environment? Without testing the proper lines, interfaces and feeds, the confidence level in the recovery environment may be deceptively high. Many application areas choose to "dummy out" the feed segments of their applications to simplify testing while controlling costs. This method can prove to be counterproductive if a full recovery environment is required following a disaster.

- *Fallback levels* - The point in time at which application data is recovered will vary based on a host of factors such as:
  - the ability to capture a day's lost transactions
  - the financial and legal liabilities involved with lost transactions
  - the time involved to restore the data while being able to service clients.

  For example, a heavily transaction-oriented company facing legal repercussions may choose to recover to the point-of-failure using remote shadowing and mirroring. The fallback level for each application is a strategic business decision that requires careful consideration.

- ***Customer and Staff Involvement*** - Who will participate in the test and what roles will they play? What involvement will customers or end users play? Will they try to log on to the systems and test, or will technologists simulate their testing using scripts?

Prior to any testing exercise, everyone involved needs to have a detailed understanding of what will transpire during the testing period.

KNOW THE ALTERNATE SITE

Chances are that visits to your alternate processing site are limited to infrequent tests with perhaps a few additional, infrequent visits. For data centers using "hot site" vendors, the contractual agreement details when to test and when to visit the backup facility. But what happens if a disaster strikes more than just your facility? If an unforeseen event affects a widespread area there may be many firms attempting to gain access to the "hot site." In these cases of widespread disasters most hot site vendors will make available their other facilities across the country. There is a very good possibility that the relocation site assigned is hundreds or even thousands of miles away, making it unlikely that recovery team members have visited that facility.

It is essential that recovery team members visit the recovery site(s) to gain an understanding of the layout, available equipment, office supplies, logistics, personnel and general building amenities. Data center disaster recovery plans should contain diagrams of the backup facilities. Recovery time during a disaster is not the time to become familiar with the site; recovery testing, on the other hand, presents an ideal opportunity to develop familiarity.

KEEP THEM HONEST!

During any data center disaster recovery testing, components being tested are expected to experience some degree of failure. It would not be a reasonable testing exercise if everything went exactly as planned – i.e., the data center should not be "testing for success." There is often a powerful temptation to sidestep problems and create quick solutions given the limited test time intervals and the amount of work involved.

For instance, after data center staff recalls media from an off-site storage vendor, certain datasets may be missing or unusable. It may be possible that the data was never backed up or taken off-site. Under these circumstances it is very appealing to simply call the primary data center and request that a copy be sent to the backup facility. In a true disaster such as a fire, chances of retrieving data from a primary site may be remote; an alternate means of recovery would be necessary.

If an auditor or independent observer is present during the test, that individual may remind data center staff of real circumstances that could cause the need for (or hinder) recovery. This is especially important because it forces what may seem like an obvious thought process: what would actually be necessary to recover the data if a real disaster had occurred. It may, for example, be necessary to revert back to the prior day's data and inquire of the business area how to recover the lost day's transactions. In other circumstances, the data may be recreated using data files from other applications. The main point is that testing is a learning experience. During the test evaluation, participants can research why the data was not off-site and take appropriate corrective action to head off a future problem.

Documented backup methodologies in the disaster recovery plan require explicit testing. For example, if a data center does full weekly backups of an application's data and then runs daily incremental backups, the recovery process should involve restoring the full backups and then applying the incremental backups. A full image backup of the data for the day chosen as the disaster date should not be taken for disaster recovery testing purposes: the objective of data center testing is to test the normal recovery strategies used regularly, to ensure that in a true disaster applications would genuinely be able to recover.

DATA COMMUNICATIONS INVOLVEMENT

Data communications is an integral component of most any data center, yet all too often telecommunications staff begin the disaster recovery planning process only weeks prior to the testing exercise. Data centers may succeed in recovering and restoring applications, but without user connectivity along with reasonable and appropriate response times, recovery efforts are likely to be worthless. It is common to see very high data center uptime statistics that actually mask system availability issues resulting from telecommunications problems.

Early involvement by the telecommunications group is crucial for recovery. If the recovery plan is clearly documented and regularly reviewed (detailing data line switching, router connections and other telecommunication equipment), test preparation by the telecommunications staff may require only a brief review. Telecommunications should function smoothly as all of the major pieces in the recovery puzzle.

DATABASE TESTING

Many of today's core applications are using relational database technology. Database recovery testing enables areas to test the feasibility of their recovery strategy regardless of the hardware platform. Some strategies may include using a "snapshot" of the database and appropriate transaction log files enabling a roll-forward of the database to the time of day just prior to the disaster. If the database is minimally populated and daily transaction levels are low, areas may choose to rebuild the database rather than attempt to roll forward. The method chosen for recovery must adhere to the acceptable user requirements including availability of views and data. Database testing can be limited to functionality testing with users accessing a limited amount of data. However, if not sufficiently tested, recovery methods including index rebuilding or applications of logs during an actual recovery can cause unexpected delays.

TEST EVALUATION

Auditors, independent consultants and staff who are not intimately involved with the test can provide objective evaluations. Whoever conducts the evaluation should review test accomplishments and compare them to stated goals as outlined in the scope of the test. All recovery team members should review the findings and assist in the preparation of the summary report. Senior management should receive a copy of the findings. Any component, application or communications connection that failed during the test needs to be re-tested within a reasonable timeframe to ensure the viability of the recovery approach. Depending on the nature of the failure, a subset of the original test may be required.

Careful test plan design, good coordination and a well prepared test outline are key elements for conducting successful data center recovery tests. The disaster recovery plan is a guide which should be utilized before and during the testing exercise. Thorough recording of the events which occur during the actual test will provide valuable input towards improving the recovery plans to ensure the existence of a viable data center disaster recovery plan.

26

DATA COMMUNICATIONS RECOVERY TESTING

by Paul F. Kirvan

Data communications has evolved considerably in the past ten years. It has progressed to where it is likely to be the most important communications elements in a company. As businesses depend more today on information systems, data communications has emerged as a strategic business tool. As companies shift operations from the traditional, mainframe-based orientation to enterprise-wide information systems, data communications is the key.

Loss of data communications for almost any duration can devastate a company's information systems, both internal and external. Data communications is usually included in data center disaster plans, and addresses the following situations:

- loss of local network service

- loss of wide area network service

- failure of data communications systems

- loss of communications from mainframes to local and remote terminals

- loss of data communications network internetworking devices

- power system outages

- cable damage.

This chapter will address recovery testing activities for data communications systems and communications services. It will also describe the key elements of these systems and network services that should be included in a disaster plan testing program.

This book advocates regularly scheduled data communications disaster plan tests for the following reasons:

- to validate the plan's effectiveness

- to verify the accuracy of the information contained in the plan

- to ensure that disaster team members are working together during various disaster scenarios

- to identify aspects of the plan that need further refinement.

This philosophy assures the company that its critical data communication systems and network services will be protected in most disaster scenarios.

DATA COMMUNICATIONS SYSTEMS

Data communications systems and products are listed in Table 1. The following paragraphs summarize key functions of each system, and the importance of those functions to an organization. Principal testing strategies are listed after each system description.

Table 1 - Data Communications Systems

MODEMS, MULTIPLEXORS

PROTOCOL CONVERTERS

CHANNEL SERVICE UNITS (CSU)

DATA SERVICE UNITS (DSU)

CHANNEL BANKS

DATA PBXS, MATRIX SWITCHES

FRONT END PROCESSORS

BRIDGES, GATEWAYS, ROUTERS

NETWORK MANAGEMENT SYSTEMS

MINICOMPUTERS

PERSONAL COMPUTERS

The most widely used components in data communications are *modems and multiplexors*. They provide the interface between information systems and the network services that link them together. *Protocol converters* establish communications between networks and/or systems whose communicating protocols are not compatible. *Channel service units (CSU) and data service units (DSU)* also provide important connecting elements in data networks. Loss of modems, multiplexors and CSUs/DSUs can cripple a company, especially if the devices in question support critical business applications.

Testing Strategies - Locate devices in secure equipment areas, with suitable environmental controls and limited access to the area except by authorized personnel. It is not uncommon for these devices to be installed in office environments as well. The same kinds of security precautions should be taken. When possible, configure redundant processing elements, e.g., CPUs and memory, for multiplexors and similar devices. Have available spare circuit boards for CPUs and memory, as well as network interface boards. Keep updated copies of system databases in multiple sites so that multiplexors can be reconfigured quickly after a shutdown. Install air conditioning failure alarms so that systems can be protected from overheating. Make arrangements with system manufacturers or distributors to have emergency access to these products in an emergency.

Channel banks are associated with high-speed digital network services. They provide the interface between multiple customer devices and the high-speed network service. Loss of a channel bank can render a critical network facility useless, unless protective measures are taken.

Testing Strategies - Locate channel banks in secure equipment areas. If this is not possible, locate devices in a closet or suitable room that can be secured. Provide redundant processing elements when possible. Have supplies of spare circuit boards and other key components available. Retain current copies of the system database in multiple locations. Locate and confirm sources of emergency replacement systems and components in an emergency.

Specialized systems used for dynamically connecting data network services in various configurations are known as *data PBXs and matrix switches*. Each system supports both asynchronous and synchronous communications in variable configu.:tions, speeds and protocols, depending on the applications.

Testing Strategies - Locate data PBXs and matrix switches in secure equipment areas. Provide redundant processing elements when possible. Have supplies of spare circuit boards, interface cards, and other key components available. Retain current copies of system databases in multiple locations. Locate and confirm sources of emergency replacement systems and components in an emergency.

Traditionally associated with mainframe computers, **front end processors (FEPs)** provide the communications access point for data streams coming into and departing a mainframe, minicomputer or similar device.

Testing Strategies - Locate front end processors in secure equipment areas. Provide redundant processing elements when possible. Have supplies of spare circuit boards, interface cards, and other key components available. Retain current copies of system databases in multiple locations. Locate and confirm sources of emergency replacement systems and components in an emergency.

Communications across multiple networks are supported by three different products, called *bridges, routers, and gateways*. These devices are typically used in local area networks.

Testing Strategies - Locate bridges, routers, and gateways in secure equipment areas. If located in an office environment, keep devices in protected areas if possible. Provide redundant processing elements when advisable. Have supplies of extra devices, spare circuit boards, interface cards, and other key components available. Retain current copies of system databases, where applicable, in multiple locations. Locate and confirm sources of emergency replacement devices and components in an emergency.

Data communications networks are generally complex, supporting hundreds of devices and different operating environments across multiple locations. Keeping track of network performance, identifying alarm conditions, running diagnostics and troubleshooting programs is the job of the *network management system*. Companies often invest in multiple network management systems, simply because a universal network management system – one that is compatible with all or most network operating environments – has yet to be introduced in the market. Users with extensive data networks must build and test their recovery plans to address the potential loss of one or more network management systems.

Testing Strategies - Locate network management systems and their associated terminals and components in secure equipment areas. If network management user interface terminals are located in an office environment, keep these devices in protected areas if possible. Provide redundant processing elements when possible. Install A/C failure alarms so that systems can be protected from overheating. Keep updated copies of the system database in multiple sites so that the system(s) can be reconfigured quickly after an outage. Arrange for emergency replacement systems and components with the system manufacturer or distributor. Have supplies of spare circuit boards, interface cards, terminals, peripherals and other key components available.

Minicomputers and personal computers are integral components of data communications systems. They are used in data PBXs, matrix switches, front end processors, and network management systems. Loss of these elements can partially or totally disable data communications systems and networks.

Testing Strategies - Locate minicomputers in secure equipment areas, with environmental controls and limited access. Configure redundant processing elements to minimize system downtime. PCs (and some minis) can be located in office areas, and the same guidelines apply for them. Provide spare circuit boards, especially processors, memory, motherboards, and chip sets. Keep updated copies of operating systems, applications, system files and databases in multiple locations so that the system can be quickly reconfigured. Install A/C failure alarms so that systems can be protected from overheating. Arrange for backup systems with system manufacturers or distributors.

DATA COMMUNICATIONS SERVICES

Numerous data communications network services are available, more so than voice communications. These services are provided by long distance carriers, telephone companies, and other specialized operators. Operational integrity of data network services is also maintained by these organizations. As such, these carriers are also responsible for restoring data services in an outage. Data communications professionals are also accountable to management for data network services. That is why procedures must be established to ensure that carrier-provided data network services can be quickly recovered and restored.

Data communications network services are listed in ***Tables 2 and 3***. Table 2 lists the principal switched data services. Table 3 lists the principal private line data services. Testing strategies are also summarized.

Table 2 - *Switched Data Communications Network Services*

LOCAL EXCHANGE SERVICE (DIAL TONE)

INTEREXCHANGE SERVICE

VIRTUAL NETWORK SERVICES

SWITCHED 56 / 64K SERVICE

SWITCHED 384K SERVICE

SWITCHED 1536K SERVICE

PACKET SWITCHED NETWORK SERVICE

VALUE-ADDED NETWORKS (VAN)

INTEGRATED SERVICES DIGITAL NETWORKS (ISDN)

SWITCHED MULTI-MEGABIT DATA SERVICE (SMDS)

FRAME RELAY

ASYNCHRONOUS TRANSFER MODE

Table 3 - *Private Line Data Communications Network Services*

UNDER 1200 BPS

1200 - 9600 BPS

9600-56 / 64K BPS

T1 / T3

FRACTIONAL T1 / T3

Despite the growth of digital network services, most businesses still use ***switched voice communications services*** as one of their principal means of accessing the outside world. Local exchange service is used for modem-based communications to remote databases, bulletin boards, and other data terminals. It is also widely used as a network backup option for digital services. Principal sources of local dial tone are telephone companies. *Interexchange service* supports data communications outside one's local calling area. It is typically provided by AT&T, MCI and Sprint. Loss of local and long distance network services poses a serious threat to businesses, and is a key component of network recovery plans that must be regularly tested.

As in voice communications applications, virtual network services can be used in data applications. These software-defined services take advantage of advanced technologies to define private networks based on switched services. Telephone companies and long distance carriers offer a wide range of virtual network services. Loss of virtual network services, like traditional long distance service, can severely impair a company's ability to conduct business.

Testing Strategies - Clarify and test network recovery service offerings with local telcos and long distance carriers. Most major carriers offer several network recovery options. These must be regularly tested for proper operation. Activate programs for local, long distance, and virtual network services. Use more than one long distance carrier for long distance service and virtual network services. Consider using the growing number of competitive access providers (CAPs) which also offer switched access services. Allocate data communications requirements across the two or more carriers. Establish diverse routing of local exchange access lines from the local telephone company office. Verify that local exchange carriers have diversely routed connections to long distance carriers. Test the use of cellular telephone service as an emergency alternative for wire-based local access facilities.

Switched digital communications are probably the fastest growing segment of the data communications network service industry. Telephone companies and most major inter-exchange operators offer switched digital communications services. Typical services include *switched 56 / 64K service, switched 384K service, frame relay, asynchronous transfer mode, packet switched network service, and integrated services digital networks (ISDN)*. A relatively recent switched digital service, called *switched multi-megabit data service (SMDS)*, is offered exclusively by telephone companies. Each of these services supports a specific range of data transmission speeds. Packet switched service is a highly efficient way of transmitting data, and with recent advances in switching technology, can support data speeds in excess of 100 megabits per second. Value-added networks

(VANs) are specialized networks based on packet switched services. ISDN and SMDS are both advanced packet switched network services. Loss of any of these services can have serious implications for companies that depend extensively on their availability.

Testing Strategies - Confirm and test availability of digital network service recovery offerings with local telcos and long distance carriers. Most major operators offer network recovery options for their digital services as well as analog counterparts. These must be regularly tested for proper operation. Activate programs for all services in use. Use more than one local and / or long distance operator for local and long distance services. Consider using CAPs for switched digital services. Use at least two carriers for digital network service requirements. Establish and test diverse routing of local access lines from the local telephone company office. Verify that local exchange carriers have diversely routed connections to long distance operators. Test the use of cellular phones as an emergency alternative, but only for relatively low-speed (e.g., under 64K bps) applications.

Digital private line services are dedicated to specific customers. Circuits are typically configured as either point-to-point, or point-to-multipoint. Loss of digital private lines can seriously impair information movement, especially for firms that have numerous locations. Circuits are typically selected on their optimum transmission throughput speeds. Digital channels from under 1200 bps to 64K bps are widely used. For higher data throughput requirements, T1 (1.544M bps) and T3 (45M bps) channels are quite popular. More recent developments include fractional T1 and T3 service, which provides bandwidth in 64K-bps multiples (fractional T1) and 1.544M-bps multiples (fractional T3).

Testing Strategies - Similar to switched digital services, identify and test available private line recovery services with local telcos and interexchange carriers. Use more than one long distance operator for wide area digital private lines. Use competitive access providers as another alternative for local digital access line services. Have the ability to dynamically transfer to switched access services (e.g., local access, ISDN, SMDS) if private lines are disabled. Test these capabilities for proper operation. Arrange for diverse routing of private lines. Test these arrangements for proper operation. Confirm that local exchange operators have diversely routed connections to long distance carriers.

POWER SUPPLIES

Clean, uninterrupted power is critical for data communications systems. When testing data communications systems, test power supplies and other ancillary equipment as well. ***Table 4*** summarizes power component associated with data communications systems.

Table 4 - *Power Systems and Related Components*

BACKUP BATTERY

UPS EQUIPMENT

DIESEL / GAS TURBINE GENERATORS

POWER REGULATION

POWER DISTRIBUTION

CIRCUIT BREAKERS

GROUNDING / SHIELDING

POWER CABLES / CORDS

Data communications systems utilize commercial AC power. Depending on the type of system, AC power is either used directly or is converted to DC power to operate the system. This must be tested to ensure that backup power systems provide suitable protection. Data communications systems usually have their own power supplies that convert AC to whatever power is needed for the system. To ensure uninterrupted operation, several options are available. Most data communications equipment vendors offer ***backup batteries*** to provide short-term protection. To provide additional protection, ***uninterruptible power systems (UPS)*** are recommended. For larger system installations, or specialized applications (e.g., hospitals) where power must not be interrupted, ***diesel or gas turbine generators*** are recommended.

To ensure efficient power usage in a data communications system, several important elements should be present. Check with the manufacturer or distributor to identify the optimum power component configuration. Included are ***power regulators*** to ensure that the correct power levels are maintained; ***power distribution systems*** to manage power flow to various datacom devices, and to monitor power levels; circuit breakers and fuses to protect vital electrical circuits from overloads; and **grounding and shielding** to protect users from electrical shocks and other anomalies. In addition to these items, use of the correctly rated *power **cables and cords*** minimizes the chance of electrical damage to datacom systems.

> *Testing Strategies - Work closely with datacom equipment vendors to determine and then test the optimum power configuration. Work with qualified electricians to install wiring and other critical connections prior to testing. Work with electric utility companies to determine their procedures and priorities for power restoration in an outage. Follow National Electric Code (NEC) procedures. Provide backup power systems wherever possible; do not depend solely on commercial power supplies. Test these systems regularly. Keep fuel levels in external power generators full; install low fuel warning gauges. Wire all systems on separately-fused circuits. Invest in diversely routed commercial power feeds from the electric utility. Obtain power sources from different power grids, if possible. Regularly test these operations. Locate power systems in secure areas, with proper environmental management. Provide emergency power shut-off switch. Provide power to datacom system components from more than one power distribution system. Provide alternate wiring of system modules from multiple distributors to minimize loss in the event of a power distributor failure. Test this arrangement regularly. Have a supply of spare components, e.g., wire, connectors, fuses, UPS circuit boards, etc. that can replace damaged units. Identify and confirm at least two local sources of emergency power systems in case of major disaster.*

CABLE AND WIRING

Loss of data communications system cabling through cable cuts, fire, flooding, or vandalism can partially or totally disable systems and networks. Several different elements comprise wiring in a typical datacom system or network. These are listed in **Table 5**. Protection of the wire plant in a data communications system is just as important as the system itself, system software, terminals and power supplies.

Table 5 - Wiring Components

MAIN FEEDER CABLES

CABLE VAULT

RISERS, CONDUITS

MAIN DISTRIBUTION FRAME

INTERMEDIATE DISTRIBUTION FRAME

STATION AND DEVICE WIRING

WIRE AND CONNECTORS

TOOLS, TEST EQUIPMENT

Feeder cables provide service from the outside into a customer's building. These typically enter the building and are terminated in a *cable vault*. Service for individual customers is then brought into their equipment room via a series of *risers and conduits*. Incoming wires are terminated on the *main distribution frame (MDF)*, which is the wiring hub for data communications systems. This is where device and terminal wires are first connected, prior to routing them to individual devices. In most buildings, *intermediate distribution frames (IDFs)* are used to provide efficient routing of cable. The final connection to a device or user terminal is called station wiring. To make sure that all connections are properly made, numerous *wiring connectors* and a wide range of *wire* are used. Verify the proper wiring arrangement with the system manufacturer or wiring contractor. Finally, to ensure that all connections are properly made, and that service is functioning correctly, use the correct *tools and test equipment*. Just installing wires and connectors is not enough. All circuits must be tested for proper operation before outside network services and data terminal devices can be used.

Testing Strategies - Work closely with datacom equipment manufacturers, cable contractors and / or electricians to determine optimum wiring arrangements prior to testing. Make sure that all contractors are suitably qualified to install data wiring and other critical connections. Work with manufacturers, distributors, telephone companies and electric companies when planning and installing wiring. Test all circuits and connections for proper operation. Follow National Electric Code (NEC) procedures. Invest in diversely routed cable distribution arrangements so that a failure of one route will not disable an entire area. Test these arrangements for proper operation. Ensure that cable vaults, MDFs and IDFs are secure. Have a supply of spare components, e.g., wire, connectors, connector blocks, etc. that can replace damaged products. Identify and confirm at least two local sources of emergency wiring components, and installation contractors in case of major disaster.

DATA COMMUNICATIONS RECOVERY TESTING

When conducting a data communications recovery test, start by defining specific test objectives. Next, summarize activities that will be conducted in the actual test. Define successful test criteria, e.g., which systems must be restored, the priority of their recovery, recovery alternatives, and guidelines for evaluating test results. Review test objectives and procedures with equipment manufacturers, distributors, and network service providers. Finally, conduct the test in an environment that maximizes the opportunity to observe 1) the ability of team members to work together, 2) how fast the recovery is likely to be, and 3) how well datacom recovery procedures interact with recovery of other systems. The following lists summarize the parameters for testing data communications recovery plans and procedures:

Objectives of A Data Communications Recovery Testing Program

1. Verify proper system/network service operation.

2. Verify proper operation of backup systems.

3. Verify proper activation and operation of backup network service arrangements.

4. Ensure that recovery procedures are in proper sequence.

5. Ensure that prioritization schedule is realistic and can be accomplished.

6. Identify improperly backed-up systems.

7. Identify improperly backed-up network services and facilities.

8. Identify faulty procedures or processes.

9. Determine corrective measures to ensure successful re-test.

10. Verify that equipment and network services can be recovered.

11. Verify that backup software assets function properly.

12. Verify that vendor/carrier testing activities work properly.

13. Verify that recovery team members understand disaster procedures, and can work effectively with other recovery teams.

14. Identify how the recovery plan should be modified.

Data Communications Disaster Recovery Plan Testing Activities

1. Test disaster plan with primary and alternate team members.

2. Review test procedures with equipment manufacturers and distributors.

3. Review facility testing procedures with local and long distance carriers.

4. Review test procedures with emergency suppliers of components, systems, etc.

5. Set reasonable and reachable objectives for a test.

6. Create reasonable disaster scenarios, especially those which have occurred most frequently over the past 5-10 years.

7. Testing objectives must be sufficiently challenging so as to identify plan deficiencies, but not so rigid as to discourage team members.

8. Regularly test individual recovery plan components; this makes a full-scale plan test more effective.

9. Conduct full-scale plan test at least once a year, in conjunction with test of other critical information systems.

10. Consider different types of plan tests: walkthroughs, simulations, component testing, application tests, mock disasters, etc.

Procedures for Conducting a Data Communications Disaster Recovery Test

1. Select at least one disaster scenario which has occurred in the company.

2. Define parameters and scenario for the test participants.

3. Document all test activities carefully.

4. Ensure that plan documentation is followed.

5. Ensure that security procedures are followed.

6. Encourage team members to role-play; assume scenario is a real disaster.

7. Notify appropriate recovery team members, police, fire, emergency rescue squads of pending tests.

8. Notify vendor/carrier/utility company representatives of pending tests.

9. Schedule appropriate time for the test; secure an area that is free from interruptions.

10. Conduct initial test of critical components and subsystems.

11. Conduct test of critical data network services to ensure their recovery within planned time frames.

12. Require written status reports from each team member.

13. Verify that backup systems, network facilities, emergency equipment areas, command centers can be established in a timely fashion.

14. Conduct full-scale test after tests of critical component recovery are completed.

15. Note procedural problems and adjust procedures to eliminate/minimize problem(s).

16. Note how recovery team works together; how well they work with other recovery teams.

17. Again, verify that all critical data communications systems, analog/digital network services, power systems, wiring elements, and other key components can be recovered as per plan.

18. Note vendor / carrier response activities and adjust procedures to eliminate/minimize problem(s).

19. Develop new and / or revised procedures as required, eliminating inappropriate or unsuccessful procedures.

20. Enact corrective action(s) immediately to correct plan deficiencies.

21. Obtain detailed critiques of test from internal audit, company management, outside consultants, and any other observers.

22. Test plan modifications as soon as possible; report findings to appropriate organizations.

23. Update recovery plan documentation, and distribute as needed.

27

VOICE COMMUNICATIONS RECOVERY TESTING

by Paul F. Kirvan

In most companies voice communications is like a double-edged sword. It is usually the principal way the company communicates with the outside world, and it is usually considered a business overhead expense, nothing more. How unfortunate that many businesses in 1994 still embrace those two facts.

Loss of voice communications for almost any duration could be devastating to a company. Most disaster plans include provisions for data centers and, by extension, data communications. However, precious little is factored into the plan to address the following situations:

- loss of local telephone service

- loss of long distance telephone service

- loss of 800 service

- telephone system failure

- cable facility damage.

This chapter will describe the kinds of systems and communications services usually associated with "voice communications." It will also describe the key elements of these systems and services that should be included in a serious disaster plan testing program.

Throughout this book it is clear that regularly scheduled disaster plan tests must be conducted for the following reasons:

- to validate the plan's effectiveness

- to verify the accuracy of the information contained in the plan

- to ensure that disaster team members are working together during various disaster scenarios

- to identify aspects of the plan that need further refinement.

This same philosophy must apply to voice communications in order to ensure that an organization's critical telecommunications systems and network services will be protected in most disaster scenarios.

VOICE COMMUNICATIONS SYSTEMS

Traditional voice communications systems are listed in *Table 1*. The following paragraphs summarize the key functions of each system, and the importance of each system to a company. Principal testing strategies are listed after each system description.

Table 1 - *Voice Communications Systems*

PBX SYSTEMS

KEY SYSTEMS

CENTREX SERVICE

TELEPHONES

ANSWERING SYSTEMS

HANDS-FREE DEVICES

ACD SYSTEMS

VOICE MAIL SYSTEMS

TELEMANAGEMENT SYSTEMS

FACSIMILE

MINICOMPUTERS

PERSONAL COMPUTERS

MODEMS, MULTIPLEXORS

The cornerstone of business communication systems today is the **PBX system**. Typical systems range in size from under 100 stations to over 10,000 phones. Loss of a PBX system can effectively shut down a company, especially if no contingency plans have been developed and tested.

Testing Strategies - *Depending on the severity of the disaster, several key test strategies can be identified for protecting PBX systems. First, each system should be located in a secure equipment room, with suitable environmental controls and limited access to the area except by authorized personnel. When possible, configure redundant processing elements, e.g., CPUs and memory, to minimize system downtime. Provide supplies of spare circuit boards, including CPUs, memory, station and trunk boards, and switching network boards. Keep updated copies of the system database in multiple sites so that the system can be reconfigured quickly after a shutdown. Install air conditioning failure alarms so that systems can be protected from overheating. Make arrangements with the system manufacturer or distributor to have access to a backup system in an emergency. Make arrangements for relocation of attendant console(s) to handle incoming calls. Make arrangements with the local telephone company to have temporary Centrex service available in an emergency. Make arrangements with local cellular operators to obtain cellular phones.*

Smaller than a PBX (but no less important) is the **key system**. It typically ranges in size from about 2-3 phones to about 100 phones. In many cases, features found in larger and more sophisticated PBXs can also be found in key systems.

Testing Strategies - *Locate systems in a secure equipment room, similar to PBXs. If this is not possible, locate the equipment in a closet or room that can be secured. Provide redundant processing elements when possible. Have supplies of spare circuit boards, telephone sets, and other key components available. Retain current copies of the system database in multiple locations. Secure access to backup systems and components in an emergency. Make arrangements with the local telephone company for temporary Centrex service. Contact cellular telephone operators for emergency cellular phones.*

Centrex service differs from PBXs and key systems in that the switching "engine" is located within a telephone company's central office. All that is located on the customer's site are telephones and other ancillary devices. Loss of Centrex service is often an after-effect of a central office outage, which in itself can affect thousands and even millions of telephone service subscribers.

Testing Strategies - *Discuss telephone company plans to recover Centrex service in an emergency. Determine what the priority of recovery for Centrex service is likely to be in different scenarios. Note that some Centrex users (other than critical organizations like hospitals and police departments) may not be high on priority lists for recovery by telephone companies. Have available supplies of spare telephone sets and other key components. Test arrangements for relocation of attendant console(s) to handle incoming calls. Test access to backup systems (e.g., PBXs and / or key systems) and components in an emergency. Contact cellular telephone operators for emergency cellular phones.*

In a serious voice communications outage, the switching system is not the only item that can be damaged. All the many different devices that connect to a PBX, Centrex or key system are vulnerable. These include **telephones, answering systems, headsets, external displays, and hands-free speaker-phones**. Suppose just the telephones in a work area are damaged by a leaking roof. The PBX is unaffected. The company's ability to conduct business is just as much at risk here, as it is with a PBX disruption.

Testing Strategies - *Have available supplies of spare telephone sets and other key components. Secure access to at least two suppliers of these components. Buy reconditioned or refurbished telephones and related devices. They work the same as brand new products, and the savings can be significant.*

As companies develop more efficient ways to sell products and services, the use of **automatic call distributors (ACDs)** has also grown steadily. ACDs efficiently process large numbers of incoming calls to specially trained people, usually referred to as agents. ACDs can be used for outbound telemarketing activities as well. Loss of an ACD could seriously impair a company's ability to generate revenues.

Testing Strategies - *ACD recovery testing strategies are similar to PBXs. Locate ACDs in secure equipment areas, with environmental and access controls. In most cases, redundant processing elements are absolutely essential to minimize system downtime. Provide supplies of spare circuit boards, including CPUs, memory, station and trunk boards, and switching network boards. Keep updated copies of the system database and all administrative support systems in multiple sites. Install air conditioning failure alarms so that ACDs can be protected from overheating. Make arrangements with the system manufacturer or distributor to obtain backup systems in an emergency. Make arrangements for relocation of agent terminals for handling incoming calls. Make arrangements with the local telephone company to have temporary Centrex service available in an emergency.*

Fifteen years ago, when **voice mail systems** first appeared, people thought they were just expensive answering machines. Today, voice mail has become an accepted (and often essential) business tool. Loss of voice mail, while not necessarily as serious as the loss of a PBX, Centrex, ACD or key system, can still impair a firm's ability to communicate. Voice mail functions are frequently integrated with PBXs, ACDs, Centrex and key systems. In those situations, the same testing strategies apply for voice mail as for their respective phone systems. However, voice mail products are often installed as adjuncts to existing telephone systems. In that situation, specific testing strategies can be defined.

Testing Strategies - *As with the associated phone system, each voice mail system should be located in a secure equipment room, with environmental controls and limited access. Configure redundant processing elements to minimize system downtime. Provide supplies of spare circuit boards. Install A/C failure alarms so that systems can be protected from overheating. Keep updated copies of the system database in multiple sites so that the system can be reconfigured quickly after an outage. Arrange for backup systems with the system manufacturer or distributor.*

Voice communications system performance is usually enhanced through the use of **telemanagement systems.** These products typically link to special data ports in a PBX, ACD, Centrex or key system. Call detail records (e.g., calling number, called number, date/time of call, duration of call) generated by the phone system are processed into management reports by the telemanagement system. Loss of a telemanagement system – by itself – will not impair a company's ability to conduct business. But telemanagement systems ensure that the associated phone system is performing at its best. They also provide valuable audit trails to identify any unauthorized calling or system misuse. Typical telemanagement systems include a personal computer or minicomputer, a device (data buffer) that accumulates call detail records, operating software, system database, and a printer.

Testing Strategies - Locate telemanagement system components in secure equipment areas. Have access to spare components, such as modems. Keep updated copies of the system database in multiple locations; test each copy for proper operation. Arrange for access to emergency PCs or minicomputers if those components should be disabled.

Few companies today can survive without **facsimile terminals.** They provide record communications virtually anywhere in the world. Rapid market growth has helped drive prices downward to where almost anyone can afford a fax machine, or a fax board that installs into a PC.

Testing Strategies - As much as possible, locate facsimile terminals in secure areas, although most are in general office areas. Since many companies have more than one fax unit, the loss of one terminal is not necessarily serious. Replacements are generally easy to obtain, as they can be purchased at a wide variety of outlets. Identify both primary and alternate suppliers.

Minicomputers and personal computers are likely to be integral components of voice communications systems. They are used for special applications, such as telemanagement systems, voice mail systems, and (in the case of minicomputers) are the processing elements in PBXs and ACDs. Loss of these elements can partially or totally disable voice communications systems.

Testing Strategies - Minicomputers should be located in a secure equipment area, with environmental controls and limited access. Configure and test redundant processing elements to minimize system downtime. PCs (and some minis) can be located in office areas, and the same guidelines apply for them. Provide spare circuit boards, especially processors, memory, motherboards, and chip-sets. Test these for proper operation. Keep updated copies of operating systems, appli-

cations, system files and databases in multiple locations so that the system can be quickly reconfigured. Test these for correct operation. Install and test A/C failure alarms so that systems can be protected from overheating. Arrange for backup systems with system manufacturers or distributors.

Linking voice communications systems to various communications network services are **modems and multiplexors**. While these critical components are largely commodity products, their continued operation is essential.

Testing Strategies - *As with other components, locate modems and multiplexors in areas where they are protected from damage, vandalism, or other events. Provide spare circuit boards (e.g., for multiplexors) as well as an inventory of modems. Test these for proper operation. Keep updated backup copies of operating systems, applications, and databases as needed. Test these for proper operation. Arrange for at least two sources of replacement devices.*

VOICE COMMUNICATIONS SERVICES

Numerous voice communications services are available from a growing number of organizations. These services are under the control of long distance carriers, telephone companies, and other specialized operators. It is generally the responsibility of these organizations to keep their services operational. And it follows that they are also responsible for restoring service in an outage. But telecommunications professionals are also accountable to their management for voice communications. Users need to establish procedures to ensure that carrier-provided services can be quickly recovered and restored.

Voice communications services are listed in **Tables 2** and **3**. **Table 2** lists the principal switched voice services.

Table 2 - *Switched Voice Communications Services*

LOCAL EXCHANGE SERVICE (DIAL TONE)

INTEREXCHANGE SERVICE

VIRTUAL NETWORK SERVICES

Table 3 lists the principal private line voice services. Testing strategies are also summarized.

Table 3 - *Private Line Voice Communications Services*

EXTENSIONS OFF PREMISE

FOREIGN EXCHANGE

TIE TRUNKS

Most businesses use **switched voice services** as the primary access to the outside world. Virtually every business uses **local exchange service** as its principal communications access service. Principal sources of local dial tone are telephone companies. Telco dominance of local service is being challenged by specialized operators, known collectively as competitive access providers (CAPs). Based on recent regulatory developments, the day is not far off when business executives will be able to obtain dial tone from someone other than the telephone company. Regardless of the source, however, loss of local dial tone almost always places businesses in serious jeopardy.

Next in importance is **interexchange service**, which provides long distance communications outside one's local calling area. It also provides connections for international long distance service. Companies like AT&T, MCI and Sprint provide domestic and international long distance voice communications. Loss of long distance service also poses a serious threat to businesses, since most companies communicate regularly with other firms outside their local area.

Virtual network services take advantage of advanced computer technologies to create networks based on switched services that operate like private lines. Telephone companies and long distance carriers offer a wide range of virtual network services. Loss of virtual network services, like traditional long distance service, can severely impair a company's ability to conduct business.

Testing Strategies - *Discuss tests of network recovery service offerings with local telcos and long distance carriers. Just about every major operator today offers several network recovery options. Test programs for local, long distance, and virtual network services. Use more than one long distance carrier for long distance service and virtual network services. When CAPs are authorized to offer switched access service, consider using their services as well. Divide service requirements across two or more carriers, and test recovery capabilities of each. Establish and test diverse routing of local* *exchange access lines from local telephone company offices. Confirm the local exchange carrier has diversely routed connections to long distance carriers. Test cellular telephone service as an emergency alternative for wire-based local exchange service.*

Private line services differ from switched services in that they are dedicated to a specific customer and provide a dedicated, wire-based connection between two or more locations. Loss of private lines can seriously impact a company, especially one that has numerous locations, each connected by one or more private line circuits. An **extension off premise** is simply a circuit that locates basic communications service at another site, either on the same property or across the country. **Foreign exchange (FX)** service is actually a hybrid of switched access plus a private line. Companies that desire local switched service from an area other than where their local service originates can subscribe to FX service. Arrangements are made with a long distance operator (e.g., AT&T, MCI) to obtain dial tone from another telco exchange office. The long distance carrier provides a dedicated circuit between the distant central office and the customer's premises. Special private lines that connect two or more PBX systems are called **tie trunks**. They provide direct communications without using the telephone switching network.

Testing Strategies - As with switched services, identify and test available network recovery services with local telcos and long distance carriers. Use more than one long distance carrier for long distance private lines. Use competitive access providers as another alternative for local private line services. Test availability and quality of services. Have the ability to dynamically transfer to switched access services (e.g., standard long distance) if private lines are disabled. Test these capabilities. Arrange and test for diverse routing of private lines. Verify that local exchange carriers have diversely routed connections to long distance operators.

POWER SUPPLIES

Provision of clean, uninterrupted power is critical to smooth operation of voice communications systems. When testing voice communications systems, their associated power supplies and other ancillary equipment must also be tested. *Table 4* summarizes the key power elements associated with voice communications systems.

Table 4 - *Power Systems and Related Components*

BACKUP BATTERY

UPS EQUIPMENT

DIESEL / GAS TURBINE GENERATORS

POWER REGULATION

POWER DISTRIBUTION

CIRCUIT BREAKERS

GROUNDING / SHIELDING

POWER CABLES / CORDS

Voice communications systems utilize commercial AC power. Depending on the type of system, AC power is either used directly or is converted to DC power to operate the system. This must be tested to ensure that backup power systems provide suitable protection. Voice systems usually have their own power supplies that convert AC to whatever power is needed for the system. To ensure uninterrupted operation, several options are available. Most vendors offer **backup batteries** to provide short-term protection. To provide additional protection, **uninterruptible power systems** (UPS) are recommended. For larger system installations, or specialized applications (e.g., hospitals) where power must not be interrupted, **diesel or turbine generators** are recommended.

To make sure power is properly managed (and subsequently tested) in a voice communications system, several important elements should be present. Check with the manufacturer or distributor to identify the optimum arrangement. Included are **power regulators** to ensure that the correct power levels are maintained; **power distribution systems** to manage power flow to various devices and to monitor power levels; **circuit breakers and fuses** to protect vital circuits from overloads; and, **grounding and shielding** to protect users from electrical shocks and other anomalies. In addition to these items, use of the correctly rated **power cables and cords** minimizes the chance of electrical damage to voice systems.

Testing Strategies - *Work closely with equipment manufacturers to determine the optimum power system configuration before testing. Work with qualified electricians to install and test wiring and other critical connections. Work with electric utility companies to determine their procedures and priorities for power restoration in an outage. Follow National Electric*

Code (NEC) procedures. Provide power backup systems wherever possible; do not depend solely on commercial power supplies. Keep fuel levels in external power generators full; install low fuel warning gauges and test them regularly. Wire all systems on separately-fused circuits. Invest in diversely routed commercial power feeds from the electric utility. Obtain power sources from different power grids, if possible. Locate power systems in secure areas, with proper environmental management. Provide emergency power shut-off switch. Provide power to system components from more than one power distribution system. Provide alternate wiring of system modules from multiple distributors to minimize loss in the event of a power distributor failure. Have supply of spare components, e.g., wire, connectors, fuses, UPS circuit boards, etc. that can replace damaged units. Identify and confirm at least two local sources of emergency power systems in case of major disaster.

CABLE AND WIRING

Loss of voice communications system cabling through cable cuts, fire, flooding, or vandalism can partially or totally disable a system. Several different elements comprise the wire infrastructure in a typical voice system. These are listed in **Table 5**. Protection of the wire plant in a voice communications system is just as important as the system itself, system software, terminals and power supplies.

Table 5 - *Wiring Components*

MAIN FEEDER CABLES

CABLE VAULT

RISERS, CONDUITS

MAIN DISTRIBUTION FRAME

INTERMEDIATE DISTRIBUTION FRAME

STATION WIRING

WIRE AND CONNECTORS

TOOLS, TEST EQUIPMENT

The **main feeder cables** provide service from the outside into a customer's building. These typically enter the building and are terminated in a **cable vault**. Service for individual customers is then brought into their equipment room via a series of **risers and con-**

duits. Incoming wires are terminated on the **main distribution frame (MDF)**, which is the wiring hub for voice communications systems. This is where station wires are initially connected, prior to routing them to individual station terminals. In most buildings, **intermediate distribution frames (IDFs)** are used to provide efficient routing of cable. The final connection to a user terminal is called **station wiring**. To make sure that all connections are properly made, numerous wiring connectors and a wide range of wire are used. Verify the proper wiring arrangement with the system manufacturer or wiring contractor. Finally, to ensure that all connections are properly made, and that service is functioning correctly, use the correct **tools and test equipment.** Just installing wires and connectors is not enough. All circuits must be tested for proper operation before outside lines and station terminal devices can be used.

Testing Strategies - Work closely with equipment manufacturers, cable contractors and/or electricians to determine the optimum wiring arrangements prior to testing. Make sure that all contractors are suitably qualified to install wiring and other critical connections. Work with telephone companies and electric companies when planning and installing wiring. Follow National Electric Code (NEC) procedures. Implement diversely routed cable distribution arrangements so that a failure of one route will not disable an entire area. Test security for cable vaults, MDFs and IDFs. Have a supply of spare components, e.g., wire, connectors, connector blocks, etc. that can replace damaged products. Identify and confirm at least two local sources of emergency wiring, components, and installation contractors in case of major disaster.

VOICE COMMUNICATIONS RECOVERY TESTING

When conducting a voice communications recovery test, begin by outlining the objectives of the test. Next, define the activities that will be conducted in the actual test. Define criteria for a successful test, e.g., which systems must be restored, priority of their recovery, recovery alternatives, and the guidelines for evaluating the test's results. Review test objectives and procedures with equipment manufacturers and distributors. Finally, conduct the test in an environment that provides maximum opportunity to examine:

- the ability of team members to work together

- how fast the recovery is likely to be

- how well voice system testing procedures interact with testing of other systems.

Objectives of Voice Recovery Testing Programs

The following lists summarize the parameters for testing voice communications recovery plans and procedures.

1. Verify proper system / network service operation.

2. Verify proper operation of backup systems.

3. Verify proper activation and operation of backup network service arrangements.

4. Ensure that testing procedures are in proper sequence.

5. Ensure that the prioritization schedule is realistic and can be accomplished.

6. Identify improperly backed-up systems

7. Identify improperly backed-up network services and facilities.

8. Identify faulty procedures or processes.

9. Determine corrective measures to ensure successful re-test.

10. Verify that equipment and network services can be recovered.

11. Verify that backup software assets function properly.

12. Verify that vendor/carrier testing activities work properly.

13. Verify that recovery team members understand disaster procedures, and can work effectively with other recovery teams.

14. Identify how the testing plan should be modified.

Voice Communications Disaster Recovery Plan Testing Activities

1. Test disaster plan with primary and alternate team members.

2. Review test procedures with equipment manufacturers and distributors.

3. Review facility testing procedures with local and long distance carriers.

4. Review test procedures with emergency suppliers of components, systems, etc.

5. Set reasonable and reachable objectives for a test.

6. Create reasonable disaster scenarios, especially those which have occurred most frequently over the past 5 - 10 years.

7. Testing objectives must be sufficiently challenging so as to identify plan deficiencies, but not so rigid as to discourage team members.

8. Regularly test individual recovery plan components; this makes a full-scale plan test more effective.

9. Conduct a full-scale plan test at least once a year.

10. Consider different types of plan tests: walk-throughs, simulations, component testing, application tests, mock disasters, etc.

Procedures for Conducting a Voice Communications Disaster Recovery Test

1. Select at least one disaster scenario which has occurred in the company.

2. Define parameters and scenario for the test participants.

3. Document all test activities carefully.

4. Ensure that plan documentation is followed.

5. Ensure that security procedures are followed.

6. Encourage team members to role-play; assume the scenario is a real disaster.

7. Notify appropriate recovery team members, police, fire, emergency rescue squads of pending tests.

8. Notify vendor/carrier/utility company representatives of pending tests.

9. Schedule appropriate time for the test; secure an area that is free from interruptions.

10. Conduct initial test of critical components and subsystems.

11. Conduct test of critical network services to ensure their recovery within planned time frames.

12. Require written status reports from each team member.

13. Verify that backup systems, network facilities, emergency equipment areas, command centers can be established in a timely fashion.

14. Conduct full-scale test after tests of critical component recovery are completed.

15. Note procedural problems and adjust procedures to eliminate/minimize problem(s).

16. Note how recovery team works together; how well they work with other recovery teams.

17. Again, verify that all critical systems, network services, power systems, wiring elements, and other key components can be recovered as per plan.

18. Note vendor / carrier response activities and adjust procedures to eliminate / minimize problem(s).

19. Develop new and/or revised procedures as required, eliminating inappropriate or unsuccessful procedures.

20. Enact corrective action(s) immediately to correct plan deficiencies.

21. Obtain detailed critiques of test from internal audit, company management, outside consultants, and any other observers.

22. Test plan modifications as soon as possible; report findings to appropriate organizations.

23. Update recovery plan documentation, and redistribute as needed.

28

LOCAL AREA NETWORK RECOVERY TESTING
by Paul F. Kirvan and Philip Jan Rothstein

Local area networks (LANs) exhibit several characteristics which cause them to be potentially difficult to recover, as well as challenging to test for recoverability:

- LAN components are physically dispersed

- Interconnection of components is generally at least as important as the components themselves

- Technical settings such as jumpers, DIP switch settings, BIOS levels, cable configurations, control files, software release levels, etc., can be volatile. As such, LAN usability can be highly sensitive to these technical settings and/or components

- Numerous individual components and interconnections, e.g., cables or circuit boards, that can be difficult to inventory or monitor, may affect recoverability

- LAN components frequently are housed in office areas instead of secure computer centers

- The value of a LAN to a company is often a function of its accessibility to end users. Indeed, recovery is typically a function of where end users are located.

With these considerations in mind, the development of a disaster recovery testing program for LANs is likely to be more complex, in many ways, then for mainframe or mid-range system environments. Moreover, communications issues are likely to be very sensitive with LANs.

Based in part on the relative newness and rapid growth in LAN technology and deployment, LAN disaster recovery expertise and tools are just beginning to become significant. Recovery testing resources and expertise for LANs have generally lagged behind efforts for mainframes and mid-range systems. LAN administrators frequently do not have the time nor expertise to develop and implement disaster recovery plans and/or capabilities, much less test them. Nevertheless, it should still be possible to implement an effective LAN recovery testing strategy in most cases without a sizeable investment.

Loss of local area network communications for almost any duration can seriously compromise a company's internal information systems. Recovery of LAN technology is a response to one or more of the following scenarios:

- Loss of one or more servers
- Loss of operating systems, applications, user files, or other critical data
- Loss of end user workstations
- Loss of connectivity between servers and workstations
- Loss of connectivity between LANs, e.g., using bridges, routers, gateways, etc
- Loss of connectivity between LANs and other computing environments, e.g., host-based communications
- Loss of data communications networks and related systems connecting LANs
- Corruption of system software through viruses, worms, etc.
- Unauthorized access to a network through hacking, stolen passwords, etc.
- Physical damage to critical components through vandalism, fire, smoke, flooding, etc.
- Power system outages
- Cable damage.

This chapter will discuss local area network recovery testing activities. It will also describe the key elements of the systems and network services that should be included in a LAN disaster plan testing program.

LAN COMPONENTS

Principal local area network systems and products are listed in *Table 1.* The following paragraphs summarize key functions of each system, and its importance to a company. Principal testing strategies are listed after each system description.

Table 1 - *LAN Components*

SERVERS

BRIDGES, GATEWAYS, ROUTERS

NETWORK MANAGEMENT SYSTEMS

WORKSTATIONS

Servers are the engines of local area networks. They provide the means for users to access business applications running in the server. Loss of a server can shut down a LAN, which can seriously affect the firm's ability to conduct business. This is particularly important if the server's applications are considered mission-critical.

Testing Strategies - Aside from locating servers in secure equipment areas, arrange for additional servers that can "mirror" production servers. This ensures that in a server failure, another unit is ready to take over immediately. Also arrange for duplexed server channels to key peripherals, e.g., disk drives, so that communications to those peripherals is assured if a primary channel fails. Further, arrange for mirrored disk drives so that every time data is written to disk, it is written to two disks simultaneously. The mirrored disk drive should also be located in a different area than the primary disk drive. Suitable environmental controls and limited access to server areas should be enacted. Have available spare server circuit boards, network interface boards, power supplies, disk drives, tape drives, etc. Keep updated copies of network operating systems (NOS), databases, applications, and files in multiple sites. Identify emergency sources of servers, workstations, and other pertinent systems in an emergency.

LAN interoperability is key to the growing acceptance of LAN technology. Using **bridges, routers, and gateways,** the total number of users on a LAN can easily get into the hundreds.

> *Testing Strategies - As with servers, locate bridges, routers, and gateways in secure equipment areas, if possible. If devices are located in office areas, keep the units in protected areas. Provide redundant processing elements when possible. Obtain spare devices, extra circuit boards, interface cards, and other key components. Retain current copies of system databases, where applicable, in multiple locations. Locate and confirm sources of emergency replacement devices and components in an emergency.*

LANs today are highly complex. They support hundreds of devices and different operating environments in multiple locations. **Network management systems** keep track of network performance, identify alarm conditions, and run diagnostics and troubleshooting programs. NOS manufacturers usually incorporate extensive diagnostic routines in their products, simply because those diagnostics will probably operate more efficiently in a "native" environment.

> *Testing Strategies - Operate network management and diagnostic routines as standard operating procedures. If separate devices are required for network management activities, locate those elements in secure equipment areas. If network management user interface terminals are located in an office environment, keep these devices in protected areas if possible. Provide redundant processing elements when possible. Keep updated copies of system databases in multiple sites so that the system(s) can be reconfigured quickly after an outage. Arrange for emergency replacement software and components with manufacturers or distributors.*

Workstations are the human interface for LANs. They can be standard personal computers with suitable network interface cards, or diskless workstations / personal computers that derive all their functionality from the network. Loss of workstations can seriously hamper business activities.

> *Testing Strategies - As much as possible, locate workstations in office areas, with sufficient security and environmental controls. Have available spare circuit boards, especially CPUs, memory, motherboards, and chipsets. Keep updated copies of*

operating systems, applications, system files and databases in multiple locations so that workstations can be quickly reconfigured. Arrange for rapid shipment of replacement systems with manufacturers or distributors.

POWER SUPPLIES

Like most other information systems, LANs require clean, uninterrupted power. When testing LAN disaster plans, test power supplies and other ancillary systems as well. *Table 2* summarizes LAN power components.

Table 2 - *Power Systems and Related Components*

UPS EQUIPMENT

POWER REGULATION

POWER DISTRIBUTION

CIRCUIT BREAKERS

GROUNDING/SHIELDING

POWER CABLES/CORDS

LANs generally use commercial AC power. Servers, disk / tape drives, and workstations usually have their own power supplies that convert AC to whatever power is needed for the device. To ensure uninterrupted operation, several options are available. Start by installing individual power management devices for each component. These units help minimize the effect of power surges and sags. More protection can be provided by ***uninterruptible power systems*** (UPS). Building power supplies should be backed up with storage batteries, UPS equipment and standby diesel and/or gas turbine generators.

To ensure clean, uninterrupted power for LANs, several important elements should be present. Check with server manufacturers or distributors to identify the optimum power component configuration. Install ***power regulators*** to ensure that correct power levels are maintained. Install power distribution systems to manage power flow to multiple servers and workstations. Monitor power levels. Install ***circuit breakers and fuses*** to protect vital electrical circuits from overloading. Ensure that critical circuits are ***grounded and shielded*** to protect users from electrical shocks. Use the recommended ***power cables*** and cords to minimize electrical damage to LAN components.

Testing Strategies - *Work closely with LAN vendors to establish and test optimum power configurations. Use qualified electricians to install wiring and other critical connections. Check connections prior to testing the disaster plan. Work with electric utility companies to determine their procedures and priorities for testing as well as power restoration in an outage. Follow National Electric Code (NEC) procedures. Provide backup power wherever possible; do not depend solely on commercial power supplies. Test backup power systems regularly according to the manufacturers' recommendations. Ensure that fuel levels in external power generators are full; install low fuel warning gauges. Wire servers and critical storage devices on separately-fused circuits. Provide emergency power shut-off switches. Provide power to LAN components from more than one power distribution system. Provide alternate wiring of LAN components from multiple power distributors to minimize loss in the event of a power distributor failure. Test this arrangement regularly. Have spare components, e.g., wire, connectors, fuses, UPS circuit boards, etc. that can replace damaged units. Simulate disaster scenarios, and check whether this inventory is adequate. Identify and confirm at least two local sources of emergency power systems in case of major disaster.*

CABLE AND WIRING

Loss of cabling through cable cuts, fire, flooding, or vandalism can partially or totally disable LANs. Several different elements comprise wiring in a typical LAN. These are listed in ***Table 3***. Protection of LAN wiring is just as important as the servers, storage devices, workstations, software, and power supplies.

Table 3 - *LAN Wiring Components*

WIRING HUBS

PATCH PANELS

MULTISYSTEM ACCESS UNITS

NETWORK ACCESS DEVICES

RISERS, CONDUITS

DEVICE WIRING

WIRE AND CONNECTORS

TOOLS, TEST EQUIPMENT

LAN wiring comprises several key elements besides the cables themselves. ***Wiring hubs and patch panels*** are used to connect LAN terminals in various configurations. They are essential for establishing a LAN's overall topology. ***Multisystem access units (MAUs)*** are used in token ring LANs to connect several workstations onto a ring. ***Network access devices*** connect servers, workstations and other peripherals to LANs, typically Ethernet. Verify the proper wiring arrangement with system manufacturers or wiring contractors. Finally, to ensure that all connections are properly made, and that service is functioning correctly, use the correct ***tools and test equipment***. Just installing wires and connectors is not enough — all circuits must be tested for proper operation before turning up the LAN.

Testing Strategies - Work closely with LAN equipment manu-facturers, cable contractors and/or electricians to determine optimum wiring arrangements, and type of cables to be used, prior to testing. Make sure that all contractors are suitably qualified to install LAN wiring and other critical connections. Work with manufacturers, distributors, and electric companies when planning and installing wiring. Test all circuits and con-nections for proper operation. Follow National Electric Code (NEC) standards. Invest in diversely routed cable distribution arrangements so that a failure of one route will not disable an entire area. Test these arrangements for proper operation. Ensure that cable areas are secure. Have an appropriate sup-ply of spare components, e.g., wire, connectors, connector blocks, etc. which can replace damaged products. Identify and confirm at least two local sources of emergency wiring, compo-nents, and installation contractors in case of major disaster.

LAN RECOVERY STRATEGIES

The testing approach for LAN disaster recovery is heavily depen-dent on the overall recovery strategy selected. Most LAN disaster recovery strategies typically fall into the following three categories:

- Mirrored, asynchronously updated or redundant servers with fault-tolerant communications links

- Standby or fallback servers and communications links, ready to be reconfigured and reloaded upon disruption of the primary servers/links

- On-the-fly acquisition of components, either from inventory, from preempted, non-critical use elsewhere, or from an exter-nal vendor.

LAN RECOVERY TESTING STRATEGIES

As in other environments, LAN recovery testing should utilize specific, clearly defined scenarios. These scenarios can be physical, such as fires, flooding, server failure or power failure; or non-physical, such as data corruption, communications breakdown, hacker or virus penetration. It is particularly important that the identified test scenarios address concurrent disruption of end users, since many (if not all) of the physical LAN components may be located in the same office area. Specifically, both the LAN recovery plans and LAN recovery testing plans should be designed as components of a departmental or organizational business continuity (and business continuity testing) plan.

LAN recovery testing depends on whether the LAN recovery approach assumes 1) an in-place restoration or relocation of the end users and/or LAN components to a different location, and, 2) as discussed in a previous section, the availability of "hot standby" or fallback components. Whether in-place recovery or physical relocation is assumed, LAN recovery tests can be designed through one of two approaches: 1) disruptive or 2) non-disruptive to the production LAN environment. A disruptive test, involving shutdown (actual or simulated) of the live, production LAN is sometimes the best way to identify the likelihood of a failed recovery. Naturally, the company may have to pay a price for this knowledge, in terms of reduced or impaired productivity from the disruptive test. And unfortunately, the risk also exists that a disruptive test could become truly disruptive, causing a real disaster.

Non-disruptive testing assumes that a production LAN is not physically or logically impacted by a test. An example of a non-disruptive test might be a "paper walkthrough." In this case, certain employees are selected to be recovery test "volunteers." The recovery test committee decides a date and time, and announces the specific event to the selected players. The volunteers are then expected to follow steps outlined in the plan to complete the "recovery." Additional individuals are selected to audit and analyze how well the recovery plan — and the staff — handle the disaster.

Should an entire production LAN be tested? Perhaps more can be accomplished by selectively testing specific LAN recovery elements (as well as by testing the ability to avoid a LAN disaster), short of a full-scale LAN recovery test. Moreover, these subtests are likely to be more realistic to plan and execute in a busy organization, as well as less intrusive. Some examples include:

✔ Restoration of LAN data from backups to a replacement server or disk module in a specific time frame

✔ Recall of data backups from off-site storage

✔ Restoration of electrical power after an outage

✔ Repair of cable or network link failures

✔ Restoration of damaged or corrupted critical data bases

✔ Replacement of servers in real-time, e.g., on-the-fly swap-outs

✔ Simulated destruction or inaccessibility of a production server

✔ Validation of hardware, communications, and software vendor responsiveness.

One recent example serves to highlight the importance of selective process testing. An organization with a rigorous server backup program in place, including nightly off-site storage of backups, tested their data restoration process for an entire LAN server. Nightly backups only took two or three hours, and selective file restores were frequently completed in less than an hour. However, restoration of the entire server required close to forty hours. As a result, a new backup methodology was required to significantly reduce the time needed for data restoration. If not for this test, the company could have suffered a sizeable loss from a server failure because of the excessive time required for data recovery.

FREQUENCY OF LAN TESTING

Where mainframe disaster recovery tests may take place as infrequently as once every year or two, LAN recovery tests should be required much more frequently — monthly if possible. This is a function of the volatility of a typical LAN environment. At the least, checklist testing should be performed frequently. The checklist test is a particularly valuable, yet inexpensive method to discover changes which might impair LAN recovery. As a minimum, a checklist test or walkthrough test should be scheduled whenever:

✔ New hardware is installed or existing hardware is modified

✔ Technology changes are implemented

✔ Applications or systems software is modified or upgraded

✔ Significant changes in personnel, procedures, volume or usage occurs

✔ Workstations, servers, and related components are added (or removed)

✔ Locations or connections are changed.

CONDUCTING A LAN RECOVERY TEST

When conducting a LAN recovery test, begin by defining test objectives. Next, summarize the test activities. Define test criteria, e.g., which servers, applications, and data files must be recovered, the priority of their recovery, recovery alternatives, and guidelines for evaluating test results. Review test objectives and procedures with hardware / software manufacturers and distributors, as well as with external network service providers. Conduct the test so that the company can observe (1) the ability of team members to work together, (2) how fast the recovery is likely to be, and (3) how well LAN recovery procedures interact with recovery of other systems. The following lists summarize the parameters for testing LAN recovery plans and procedures:

OBJECTIVES OF LOCAL AREA NETWORK DISASTER RECOVERY TESTING PROGRAMS

1. Verify proper LAN operation.

2. Verify proper operation of LAN backup systems.

3. Verify proper activation and operation of backup LAN network service, off-site data recovery arrangements.

4. Ensure that sequence of recovery procedures is logical and workable.

5. Ensure that LAN recovery priorities are realistic.

6. Identify improperly backed-up systems.

7. Identify improperly backed-up network services and facilities.

8. Identify faulty procedures or processes.

9. Determine corrective measures to ensure successful re-test.

10. Verify that equipment, Network operating systems (NOS), applications, data files and network services can be recovered.

11. Verify that emergency recovery site can support a disaster.

12. Verify that recovery team members understand plan procedures, and can work with other recovery teams.

13. Identify modifications or changes to the recovery plan.

PLAN TESTING ACTIVITIES

1. Form a Disaster Plan Test Committee that will:

    *   Define objectives of the test

    *   Define content of the test, e.g., the type of test

    *   Determine date and time of the test

    *   Identify test observers and critics

    *   Determine who will advise appropriate outside parties (e.g., recovery site, carriers, equipment vendors) that a test will occur with a certain time frame, (e.g., 48 hours.)

    *   Advise internal user departments of the planned test, especially those whose LAN components will be included in the test

    *   Announce the test

    *   Coordinate the test through to completion and evaluation

    *   Ensure that the LAN disaster plan is updated following the test

    *   Provide results of the test to company management, recovery center management, carriers, vendors, etc.

2. Test LAN disaster plan with both primary and alternate team members.

3. Review test procedures with equipment manufacturers and distributors.

4. Review facility testing procedures with network service providers, e.g., telephone companies and long distance carriers.

5. Review LAN test procedures with emergency suppliers of components, systems, etc.

6. Set reasonable and reachable test objectives.

7. Create reasonable disaster scenarios.

8. Make testing objectives sufficiently challenging so as to identify flaws, but not so rigid as to seriously disrupt business operations.

9. Regularly test individual LAN recovery plan components.

10. Conduct full-scale plan tests at least annually, particularly in conjunction with disaster plan tests for other critical information systems.

11. Require that all mission-critical systems and applications have tested disaster plans in place before going into production.

12. Consider different types of plan tests: walk-throughs, simulations, component testing, application tests, mock disasters, etc.

PROCEDURES FOR CONDUCTING A TEST

1. Select at least one disaster scenario which has occurred in the company.

2. Define parameters and scenario for the LAN test participants.

3. Document all LAN test activities carefully.

4. Ensure that plan documentation is followed.

5. Ensure that LAN security procedures are followed.

6. Notify appropriate LAN recovery team members, police, fire, emergency rescue squads of pending tests.

7. Notify vendor/carrier/utility company representatives of pending tests.

8. Schedule appropriate time for the test; secure an area that is free from interruptions.

9. Conduct initial test of critical components and subsystems.

10. Conduct test of critical data network services to ensure their recovery within planned time frames.

11. Require written status reports from each team member.

12. Verify that LAN backup systems, network facilities, emergency equipment areas, help desks, command centers can be established in a timely fashion.

13. Conduct full-scale LAN test after tests of critical recovery components are completed.

14. Note procedural problems and adjust procedures to eliminate/minimize problem(s).

15. Note how LAN recovery team works together; how well they work with other recovery teams.

16. Again, verify that all critical LAN systems, power systems, wiring elements, and other key components can be recovered as per plan.

17. Note vendor/carrier response activities and adjust procedures to eliminate/minimize problem(s).

18. Develop new and/or revised procedures as required, eliminating inappropriate or unsuccessful procedures.

19. Enact corrective action(s) immediately to correct plan deficiencies.

20. Obtain detailed critiques of LAN recovery test from internal audit, company management, outside consultants, and any other observers.

21. Test LAN recovery plan modifications as soon as possible; report findings as required.

22. Update recovery plan documentation, and distribute as needed.

CONCLUSION

LAN disaster recovery testing, while potentially more challenging in some ways than mainframe or mid-range computing environments, is usually achievable with a reasonable level of effort and investment. The key to effective recovery testing in LAN environments, more so than in large computer environments, is the design of the recovery testing program concurrent with the recovery program, ideally along with the initial design and implementation of the LAN environment.

29
TRADING FLOOR RECOVERY TESTING
by James N. Loizides

The need for Trading Floor Recovery Testing is obvious to those who are associated with support or management of a Trading Room operation. As in all areas of an organization, technology has impacted the functions required to perform the associated tasks, but the effect of technology in a Trading Room has created a dependency second to none. This fact, and the large dollar amounts associated with this volatile function, demands a testing plan that encompasses every area of detail.

The components included in Trading Floor Recovery Testing can be grouped under the following categories:

- recovery facility
- communication requirements
- information providers and market data
- data processing requirements and interfaces
- support services and personnel.

Each of these main categories requires detail planning and testing procedures. The complexity depends on the size of the Trading Department and the timeframe required for recovery. In all cases, a Master Inventory System associated with a detailed plan is required.

TESTING THE COMPONENTS

The **Recovery Facility** is the first area which requires testing. This backup facility can either use in-house space in a different location which is made available when requested or an outsourced facility provided by a hot site vendor. In either case the backup facility must be able to house the traders as well as their support staff, along with all of the necessary equipment which makes them effective. Testing of the facility must take place at least twice a year. These test must insure that all the services that are needed by the traders are functioning at this secondary facility. Key areas of concern include:

- all forms and required documents are stored at the back-up site

- calculators and miscellaneous equipment are at the site

- the facility has all the appropriate support services such as faxes, copiers, Telex and personal computers

- security at the facility must be tested to ensure a safe working area, at least as secure as the principal trading floor

- space requirements are flexible enough to accommodate change at the time of an emergency

- all of the trader services can be tested down to the workstation level.

Since the back-up facility will be the place from which you resume your business operation, don't overlook all the little things traders require to perform their functions. Remember, if they can't trade, the company is losing money.

Communications is the lifeline for the trading department. Every trader has their own way of doing business; this makes keeping track of the communications requirements a never-ending job. The market is a fast moving operation, with new instruments being announced or new products being tested every day. This causes changes to the trader's environment on a frequent basis. How do we maintain all of this activity? The answer is to have a structured system that keeps track of each individual trader's profile. This becomes the 'bible' of what each trader needs to operate under normal conditions and can be modified to show what is the minimum requirements during a emergency.

The trader profile also becomes the vehicle which we use for testing the trader communications requirements. The trader profile must include at least the following:

- private lines: carrier information, circuit number and the name of the person or company at the other end

- dial tone lines: how many are required and what they are used for (dial out, fax, etc.)

- call forwarding requirements

- speed dial requirements

- '800' number requirements

- long distance and international calling requirements

- speakers: quantity, and how they are used

- voice recording requirements.

These important pieces of information give the communications manager the means to track what is required by each trader. Testing this information must be done in coordination with the recovery facility. A method must be developed which allows you to test these services and insure they will work at the recovery site. Once this is developed, then those procedures must be part of your semi-annual test at the recovery site.

Information Providers and Market Data Services are as crucial to the trader as their telephone lines. The accuracy and timeliness of local and worldwide news and information is the lifeblood of the trader's decision-making process. While there are some seventy or more different market data providers and news services available, the trader must identify those services which are the minimum required at the recovery facility. In most cases, the trader must recognize that they cannot have all the services at the recovery site that they have in their primary location.

Testing of Market Data Services is required at each trader's desk at the recovery facility. During the semi-annual test the delivery service that provides the requested market data must be live, with all the optional services at each of the desks requested. This is the only way that the traders can test the effectiveness of the services they will have available to them in an emergency.

Data Processing Requirements and Systems Interfaces allow the trader the ability to connect to the back-office systems or the support local-area networks which are needed for trading. This function is unique to each company. The trading group is normally supported by a group of data processing professionals who are responsible for systems integration and trading software. The difficulty usually lies in providing all of the required services at a recovery facility. Specific interface software or backup systems must generally be put in place at the recovery facility in order to provide this capability. Communications software and data lines must be acquired to allow the systems to communicate. The following test procedures should be used as a guide:

- maintain backups of all local area network file server data at the recovery site (daily if possible)

- keep backup software at the recovery site

- test all equipment at the hot site, preferably at least monthly

- establish update criteria for new software releases

- list in the trader profile all the software need at the trader desk

- connect to the back-up computer at least twice a year

- ensure all gateways are tested and kept current

- test all data lines and modems for compatibility as well as functionality.

Testing data processing requirements for trading floor disaster recovery is likely to be more complex than mainframe recovery testing. Traders maintain their own software as well as software maintained by others. To fully test all of the services and software required by the traders can be a full-time task. The recovery facility must provide adequate personnel to accomplish this task. There are no shortcuts to thorough testing – frequent, planned tests are the only way to maintain the accuracy of the information required by the traders.

Support Services and Personnel are the final components in trading floor disaster recovery testing. These include the basics, like the proper calculators or time-stamp machine at the recovery facility.

Many traders process a high volume of transactions per day, and all of this information must be captured and processed by the end of the day. This means that support staff are required along with a work area for them to operate at the recovery facility. This should include telephones, personal computers and access to all the forms or documents they need to do their jobs.

The testing of the support services should coincide with the semi-annual testing performed by the traders. Key members of the support staff should work from the recovery facility to insure that all that is required is present and operational. In addition, a profile of the support staff requirements should be maintained in the master inventory system along with the traders' profiles and requirements.

If there was one lesson we learned recovering trading floor operations for clients following the World Trade Center bombing in February, 1993, it was that more frequent and thorough testing of recovery plans and procedures would have saved those companies both time and money, as well as reduced their risk considerably.

30

TESTING PUBLIC AND INTERNAL COMMUNICATION[1]

by James E. Lukaszewski

There is a common management bias against communicating in times of stress, disaster and difficulty. Communicating about bad news is a problem that literally bedevils management. Nobody wants to talk much when the news is not good or when there are many unknowns. Familiar, though foolish, excuses abound:

- *"The fewer people that know about this, the less likely it will become a serious problem."*

- *"It's none of their business. When it is, we'll tell them about it."*

- *"What gives outsiders the right to ask questions about what we believe to be a strictly internal situation?"*

- *"If our employees spent more time worrying about doing their jobs better, rather than asking us embarrassing questions or talking to the media, situations like this might not happen."*

These excuses reflect attitudes that make public and internal communication one of the most neglected areas of disaster preparation, not to mention testing.

The lack of aggressive, realistic and appropriate communication can turn a serious operating problem into a public relations nightmare. For the manager whose people and property are involved, lack of empathetic, relevant communication and openness can transform a manageable problem into a career-defining moment.

In reality, no matter how good your strategic, technical or response preparations are, even if they are executed with excellence, if your public and internal communications do not work, the perception will be that you did not do the right thing, that you stalled or that you were stonewalling. If reputation and credibility mean something to your organization, preparing to communicate when problems arise will have a very high priority.

In assessing the successes and failures in handling adverse situations, the most common criticisms revolve around communications which worked or failed. Increasingly, accountability to community, to neighbors, to government, to those most directly affected by your actions has come to mean timely, if not aggressive, internal and external communication. Almost without exception, when communication is handled properly and executed aggressively — and in the absence of something truly stupid, horrendous or criminal — the media and the public lose interest because they have the perception that you are in control and can fix the problem so that it will not happen again.

There is a useful checklist of crucial, appropriate behaviors which should form the basis for your crisis response:

RESPOND QUICKLY

TAKE APPROPRIATE RESPONSIBILITY

ASK FOR HELP AND UNDERSTANDING

INFORM EMPLOYEES IMMEDIATELY. SHOW CONCERN

BE OPEN TO SUGGESTION

REHEARSE ALL STATEMENTS AND MESSAGES

EXPLAIN TO THE COMMUNITY AS SOON AS POSSIBLE

INVITE LOCAL OFFICIALS IN TO HELP WITH EXPLANATIONS, WHERE APPROPRIATE

SEEK OUT AND TALK TO AFFECTED GROUPS

SEEK OUT AND TALK TO AFFECTED AGENCIES

USE SIMPLE, DIRECT, POSITIVE MESSAGES

STICK TO THE FACTS AND COMPANY POLICY

USE COMMON SENSE

REALISTIC SIMULATIONS ARE CRUCIAL

Two questions face crisis planners. First, how can they best help a reluctant management be ready to respond verbally as well as administratively and physically? Second, once an approach is suggested, how can management be assured that their participation will mitigate potential reputation damage?

The technique The Lukaszewski Group increasingly uses involves effective, dramatic, participant-involving simulations. Here are the guidelines we follow for developing excellent communication simulation experiences:

Take a positive approach and deal only with the most serious scenarios.

Use a dramatic story or problem which is both plausible and directly relevant to an existing business issue.

Set specific learning objectives.

Provide specific instructions to players for role playing.

Use a skilled facilitator.

Establish positive goals for the exercise which demonstrate what participants do correctly. Show them how they can improve, on the spot.

Hold an interactive, verbal assessment session later the same day for the specific purpose of making your points about preparation — in an extremely positive and productive fashion.

Have only two or three specific, positive recommendations at that meeting. (No boss cares enough about these problems to absorb many more.)

Be prepared to provide participants with single-sheet scenarios containing action checklists and outlines of their duties during a particular operating or non operating problem.

There are several approaches which tend to kill management participation and interest and must be avoided:

- **Finding fault** - telling participants what they did wrong after putting them through a brief (perhaps even humiliating) exercise.

- **Preparing a negative follow-up report** - which documents errors without effectively pointing out actions for improvement.

- **Teaching crisis management** - apparently on the assumption that management really wants to know all about what you are being paid to know how to do.

CRISIS RESPONSE AND COMMUNICATIONS PRINCIPLES

Headquarters and field operations should together develop a series of pragmatic principle statements against which both staff and operating portions of the company will be measured when emergency responses have concluded, or are reviewed or tested.

They should be similar to these sample principle statements:

1. **Responsiveness:** When problems occur we will be prepared to talk about them internally and externally as aggressively as we respond to them operationally.

2. **Openness:** If the public should know about a problem we are having, or about to have, which could affect them or our credibility, we will voluntarily talk about it as quickly and as completely as we can.

3. **Concern:** When business problems occur, we will keep the community and those most directly affected posted on a schedule they set until the problem is thoroughly explained or resolved.

4. **Respect:** We will answer any questions the community may have and suggest and volunteer additional information in the event the community does not ask enough questions. We will respect and seek to work with those who oppose us.

5. **Cooperation:** We will be cooperative with the news media as far as possible, but our major responsibility is to communicate compassionately and completely with those most directly affected by our problems, as soon as possible.

6. **Responsibility:** Unless incapacitated or inappropriate, the senior executive on-site is the spokesperson during emergencies.

7. **Sensitivity:** At the earliest possible moment we will step back and analyze the impact of the problems we are having in the determination to communicate with all appropriate audiences, both to inform and to alert.

8. **Ethics:** If we are at fault, we will admit and explain the mistakes as quickly as possible.

9. **Compassion:** We will always show concern, empathy, sympathy and remorse.

10. **Generosity:** We will find a way to go beyond what is required and to "do penance" where appropriate.

11. **Commitment:** We will learn from our mistakes, talk publicly about what we've learned, and renew our commitment to keeping errors, mistakes and problems from re-occurring. Our goal is zero errors, zero defects and zero mistakes.

A MODEL SIMULATION

One of the more interesting simulations The Lukaszewski Group uses, because it teaches so many of the communications lessons today's corporations are concerned about, is The Peppermill Scenario. This simulation can be adapted to involve participants in public meetings; in solving internal communications issues, media relations problems and issues, and litigation and legal issues; in dealing with angry neighbors, competitors and disgruntled employees; and in resolving the chaos which crisis situations often generate.

The lessons the Peppermill Scenario teaches can be applied broadly across your organization to a variety of potential threat circumstances. These lessons directly reflect the checklist of appropriate crucial behaviors described earlier in this chapter. Remember, somewhere, somehow, victim, community, employee and government questions will be answered, and quickly. If you are not ready, the response will come from outside your organization or in ways you neither like nor can control.

Why are simulations so important? It is because the last time you want to get ready for solving a problem for the first time is when that problem is actually occurring.

THE PEPPERMILL SCENARIO

Peppermill Background Information

SK Industries, known as SKI, is preparing to propose a new operational site for its chemical recycling division on 18 acres of land known as the Peppermill property. The first of a series of public meetings, sponsored by the county, will be held later today.

The Peppermill site carries the name of Cyrus W. Peppermill, an entrepreneur who operated a number of industrially-related businesses on this site in the past. While a variety of chemicals including inorganic and organic acids and some volatile solvents were used, there has never been any indication that these materials were improperly disposed of, until yesterday.

Yesterday's local newspaper carried a front page story alleging that contamination from the Peppermill site, which could contain lead and various halomethanes, had leaked into Pitchfork Creek, a principal drinking water source for many farm animals up and down stream from the site. In the article a state environmental quality official called allegations, "very troubling." He estimates that it will cost millions to clean up the problem, and he will in all likelihood speak against siting the new facility at the public meeting.

A spokesperson for the Federal Environmental Protection Agency said as much but was not quoted directly in the article. Former employees at Peppermill said that while some chemicals were disposed of in various places on the site, "None of the disposal pits ever filled up, so there must not have been any pollution."

In this morning's newspaper the local city councilman representing the district in which the facility would be constructed said, "My phone is ringing off the hook. I've got farmers who are concerned about their animals, and fearful parents whose children play on the site." The councilman is expected to lead a group of angry neighbors against the proposed project at today's meeting.

The group called CASKET (Citizens Against SK's Environmental Terrorism) has hired a former SK Industries employee who, according to Tom Williams, spokesman for CASKET, "has very damaging inside information on just how this company operates here and around the U.S." Williams also said, "They'll only get to use this land over our dead bodies."

Among those who have also indicated they plan to testify are a potential new neighbor, a former SKI employee and a local business leader who is president of the Chamber of Commerce.

You will have approximately 60 minutes to complete developing the messages which will fit your role in the cast for this simulation. Some participants will need to prepare for significant media interest.

Remember no matter which role you have in the cast, the meeting will be very intense for each cast member. As a part of your preparation you should try to prepare to respond to questions and issues which reporters and others at the meeting may raise about you and the role you will play.

Some individuals and groups will receive specific instructions unknown to the rest of the players.

SK INDUSTRIES BACKGROUND INFORMATION

SK Industries (known as SKI) is a medium-sized, diversified, international chemical company. It has many small plants scattered across the United States and in 31 countries.

The problem facing the company today is the relocation of a chemical recycling plant which was destroyed by a hurricane.

The chemical recycling to be done involves chemical compounds collected from all U.S. SKI facilities and brought to this site for re-refining or proper disposal.

SKI, like most large companies in the United States, has had environmental and legal problems in the past. The company has suffered substantial fines and adverse legislation in California, Florida, Louisiana, Minnesota, New York, Ohio, Oregon and Texas. The company is awaiting trial on federal criminal charges of environmental pollution in the state of Utah.

In many communities in which it operates, the company has no standing record of community participation, including matching educational programs for its employees, support for changes and improvements in local education. Employees do volunteer aggressively throughout the communities in which they live, some serving as elected and appointed public officials.

Until recently, SKI employees could count on life-time employment. However, due to changes in the economy and competitive problems, the company has embarked in the last 14 months on an aggressive downsizing, reconfiguration and re-engineering of the corporation. Four months ago the first wave of employee layoffs and dismissals was announced. Approximately seven percent of the company's 31,000 U.S. employees were released. Many of those dismissed had worked for the company since its founding almost 25 years ago.

The Wall Street Journal has characterized this company "as being in a stall . . . unable to pull itself out . . . perhaps it will crash."

PEPPERMILL SCENARIO SUPPLEMENT #1

Confidential Instructions to the Local City Councilman:

You are in a tough spot. You are up for re-election this year and the last thing you need is a bunch of constituents angry about this project.

Although you originally endorsed the project, your position now is wait and see. For the moment, however, you are siding with the important and urgent concerns of your constituents. You are reasonably comfortable with SK Industries and would really like to see something done with the Cyrus W. Peppermill property. But, if you had to vote today, you would vote against siting this facility.

Fortunately you do not have to vote today, but you do have to express really serious reservations about the project until the company answers some important questions raised by fearful residents and neighbors.

You will be asked to speak early in the proceedings because you are an elected official, representing the people most directly effected. And, you will be asked to speak last at the meeting for the same reason; you represent the neighbors.

Note, if your constituents become noisy and rowdy you will have little choice but to attempt to lead them for fear of alienating them in the upcoming election cycle. Or, you could be courageous and oppose them. It is up to you.

The meeting is run by appointed officials. You outrank all of the public officials in the room because you are an elected representative; therefore, you may get your way on almost any issue that is raised if you choose to challenge those in charge.

Peppermill Scenario Supplement #2

Confidential Guidance to the State Environmental Quality Official:

As far as you are concerned, old Cyrus Peppermill did not care about the environment — no matter how much people love him around here.

You have been with the state for many years. SKI's purchase plus its failure to be aware of the contamination on this property make for one of the dumber corporate decisions you have ever witnessed.

You are troubled by what you have heard about SKI's reputation for past mistakes. Frankly, you do not understand why a company would come to a site like this and spend what you estimate to be several million dollars to clean up the site before even being able to put up a building or begin operations. To assure yourself that the company is serious, you may want to suggest that the company put up a bond — perhaps amounting to two or three times your cost estimate — to remediate the site and to make it usable.

Peppermill Scenario Supplement #3
Confidential Guidance to Angry Neighbors:

This is something you absolutely do not want. You cannot be convinced. That is why you formed a neighborhood group called CASKET to stop it.

You have a chant and a slogan. The chant is simply, "CASKET, CASKET, BURY SKI," and your slogan is, "We'll remember in November," if public officials actually do approve this site.

You are also angry at public officials for even considering SK Industries' proposal, since it is so obviously something the community does not need and probably will be harmed by.

You may wish to try and build some coalitions with other angry individuals who will be attending the meeting. You may also wish to demonstrate loudly and by other means your displeasure with what appears to be going on.

The former SK Industries employee you have hired to give surprise testimony at this meeting left the company on extremely good terms, with an employment recommendation from his immediate supervisor and letters of recommendation from other senior company officials with whom he had worked. His testimony will be devastating.

Special note to Tom Williams, spokesman for CASKET: You will plainly reflect the feelings of your group and will be the vocal champion for your people, leading whatever demonstrations or other efforts you may agree to undertake to make your positions and feelings as clear as possible to the powers that be.

Peppermill Scenario Supplement #4
Confidential Information to the Former SK Industries Employee:

Your credentials are impeccable. You left SK Industries with a recommendation letter from your supervisor for a better job with a competitor. You also have other letters from other SKI managers who have appreciated your work style and working skills over the years.

You left the company out of frustration and anger. The branch you worked in (which the current Peppermill site manager previously managed for four years) had one of the worst spill records and manifest error rates in your division, perhaps in the company. In your time at SK Industries you saw spills that went unreported, manifests that were falsified and covered up by management. You saw several people set up illegal side businesses selling SKI recycled chemicals with the blessing of the local manager. You know there are many SKI branches that operate as well as they can under the circumstances and within the law, but from your perspective SK Industries has a lot further to go, and it has to make some pretty tall promises for this community to be comfortable with having it both remediate and operate at the Peppermill site.

Peppermill Scenario Supplement #5
Confidential Guidance to the Former Employee at Peppermill:

Basically, you liked Cyrus Peppermill. He was a great entrepreneur. At the time you worked at Peppermill, you did everything according to existing rules. In fact, years ago Pitchfork Creek was more like a river. You and everyone else in the area went swimming in it, your children went swimming in it and your grandchildren went swimming in it as recently as this past summer.

You do not know anyone who has had any ill effects from being in contact with it.

Sure, Peppermill employees dumped lots of stuff in the Creek everyday. It was always gone by morning.

What is this big hullabaloo all about? It is just a bunch of newcomers who never speak up about anything positive. They are always complaining and want to tear down the community.

Peppermill Scenario Supplement #6
Confidential Advisory to Farmers:

Your farm animals have been drinking the water and moving in and out of Pitchfork Creek for decades, but only over the past two years have they really seemed to do less well. They get ill more often and the birth weight of new calves has dropped up to 20 percent. Until now, you could not figure it out.

You wonder whether it is the government's fault or the Peppermill Company's fault. Will it now be SK Industries' obligation to pay for injury to your animals, even if it never operates a branch from this site?

Your brother and sister-in-law own an adjoining farm through which Pitchfork Creek also runs. They are in Bermuda on vacation, but really wanted to be there to voice the same concerns. They wonder who is going to pay for the damage to their herd and for the potential loss of their livelihood.

Will SK Industries assume this responsibility?

Peppermill Scenario Supplement #7
Confidential Guide to Fearful Parents:

You have all the concerns of parents who have just discovered their children have been playing on a site that contains very dangerous, even toxic, chemicals. You worry about rashes the children have had, which you now believe came from hazardous chemicals rather than simply from scrapes on the playground or some other cause. You recall that the children suffered headaches and sleeplessness from time-to-time. You now have a reason for why these things you did not understand before occurred.

You are extremely concerned about how a site like this could ever be cleaned up enough to allow a business to operate from it, let alone what the ongoing effects of your children's exposure could be.

You spoke to an attorney today after the news story appeared. He advised you to be very cautious about what you say, but to remain very aggressive in your position. He would like you to ask really tough questions about the chemicals that are there.

You might wish to talk to some of the angry neighbors to see if you can link up resources and really take a shot at defeating any further movement on this proposed land use by SK Industries.

For sure, you want to be a part of CASKET.

Peppermill Scenario Supplement #8
Private Instructions to Local Business Leader, the president of the Chamber of Commerce:

You have been in business in the town near Peppermill for thirty years. If there is one thing this town needs, it is more business and employees. You enthusiastically support what SK Industries is trying to do; however, you have some serious reservations because you own some property not far from the Peppermill site. The news of the pollution is very disturbing.

It may be the first time in the ten years that you have been president of the Chamber of Commerce that you actually may have to oppose a business expansion in the area because of the questions raised about the site. You need some answers.

For the present you are not going to align yourself with the angry neighbors or other people who are vocally antagonistic to SK Industries.

You might even want to talk to SKI people before the hearing to find out just what the situation is, and whether the company can actually tell the truth about such a potentially serious problem.

Peppermill Scenario Supplement #9
Confidential Guidance to Potential New Neighbor:

You think that many people will refuse to move into this area once they find out how serious the contamination seems to be at the Peppermill site. You are certainly reconsidering your own move.

You have a sister who lives near a Superfund site in California. She no longer sleeps nights wondering what might actually be under the ground near her house and what her family has been exposed to.

You are demanding assurances from SK Industries and from the government that there is no danger. Can they absolutely guarantee that there will be no ill effects from these chemicals either now or as the clean up process proceeds?

Peppermill Scenario Supplement #10
Confidential Instructions to the County Siting and Environmental Committee Chairman and Deputy Chairman:

Your job is to serve as meeting chair and run this first public meeting on an impartial basis. This is an informational meeting, meaning no decision will be made on SK Industries' proposal today. The purpose of the meeting is to enable everyone to have a say who wants to have one, and for SKI to have the opportunity to lay out its plan and to respond to those who have questions. There will be more meetings on this siting question.

The forty-five-minute meeting will begin promptly with your explanation of the purpose of the meeting and procedures that will be followed. Here are the ground rules:

1. All presentations will last no longer than two minutes

2. There may be questions from the audience. Questions should be directed to the meeting chair, who will then direct the questions to the individual testifying

3. The meeting chair will close the meeting with a one minute wrap up.

There may be strong emotions at this meeting. You will simply have to gavel them down and move along. The actual hearing portion is limited to forty five minutes. You have no Sergeant-At-Arms or any means of throwing people out who are rowdy. You will simply have to manage the meeting as best as you can.

Here is the order of the meeting:

X:00 p.m.   SK Industries makes an opening description of its proposal (2 minutes).

X:02 p.m.   City councilman makes an opening presentation on behalf of his constituents (2 minutes).

X:04 p.m.   State environmental quality official testifies (2 minutes).

X:06 p.m.   SK Industries testifies and responds (2 minutes).

X:08 p.m.   CASKET spokesperson, Tom Williams, testifies (2 minutes).

X:10 p.m.   SK Industries testifies and responds (2 minutes).

X:12 p.m.   Former employee at SK Industries testifies (2 minutes).

X:14 p.m.   SK Industries testifies and responds (2 minutes).

X:16 p.m.   Former employee at Peppermill testifies (2 minutes).

X:18 p.m.   SK Industries testifies and responds (2 minutes).

X:20 p.m.   Farmers testify (2 minutes).

X:22 p.m.   SK Industries testifies (2 minutes).

X:24 p.m.   Fearful parents testify (2 minutes).

X:26 p.m.   SK Industries testifies and responds (2 minutes).

X:28 p.m.   Local business leader (and president of the Chamber of Commerce) speaks (2 minutes).

X:30 p.m.   SK Industries testifies and responds (2 minutes).

X:32 p.m.   Potential new neighbors testify (2 minutes).

X:34 p.m.   SK Industries testifies and responds (2 minutes).

X:36 p.m.   CASKET's second opportunity to speak (2 minutes).

X:38 p.m.   SK Industries responds (2 minutes).

X:40 p.m.   SK Industries' closing presentation (2 minutes).

X:42 p.m.   Local city councilman makes closing comments (2 minutes).

X:44 p.m.   County chairman wraps up meeting (1 minute).

Peppermill Scenario Supplement #11
Confidential Instructions to the SK Industries Team:

Here are some important facts:

1. You bought this site. You knew it was contaminated. It was the only way the county would ever consider letting you start up there. You have an urgent need for this site because the hurricane knocked out your only facility in this part of the United States. You have no choice but to do something with it, whether you ultimately operate a branch from it or not.

2. The former SKI employee hired by CASKET has a excellent employment history at SK Industries. One of the reasons he left the company was that his supervisor gave him an excellent recommendation for another job with a competing firm. His credentials are unimpeachable. You did not know he was angry.

3. You are not coming to a pleasant environment, so a word to the wise. Keep your cool and focus on the goal which is getting your proposition well explained and heard during this meeting. Listen.

No decision will be made at this meeting. It is an informational meeting held both for the company to express its plans and ideas and for the community to voice its concerns and questions.

You will probably want to rotate your spokespersons, assigning a specific task to each. One person should deal with environmental questions, another with siting issues and perhaps another, the new manager who will actually be on the site permanently until it is either fully remediated and operational or simply fully remediated, to answer other questions.

You will get to talk more than anyone else. The meeting will be structured so that you get to present your information and answer questions in between every presentation. All other presenters with the exception of city councilman will present only one time. The councilman will make an opening presentation and a final presentation at the end.

Regardless of what happens at the meeting, be sure that you aggressively cover your agenda, making sure that your entire story gets told and that you respond to those issues and concerns raised by neighbors and others who will be talking.

There may be some surprises; be prepared.

You will call and hold a news conference immediately following the public meeting.

Instructions to Simulation Facilitators:

1. After reading and explaining the situation, allow one hour for preparation.

2. After handing out the private instructions to various participants (Peppermill Scenario supplements 1 through 11), have a brief, private discussion with each to make sure that they understand their role thoroughly.

3. Encourage aggressive, creative participation.

4. Enforce the two-minute presentation rule at the public meeting.

5. Following the public meeting, allow a maximum of ten minutes for a news conference.

Adaptation of the Peppermill Simulation

The Peppermill Scenario is fairly complicated. The more sophisticated the problem you choose to test using simulation, the more skilled your facilitator must be. If you plan to use simulations without professional facilitation, we recommend that you keep the scenario simple with few interruptions or distractions.

The most common interruptions and distractions involve producing or providing news bulletins intermittently during the planning and preparation stages which change the bases of the problem, and subtracting key players at critical times. For example, you might put the leader of the SKI presentation team on an airplane to handle another urgent, far-away problem, thus depriving the SKI team of its principal spokesperson at a crucial moment.

Other useful interruptions include:

- the secret memo (with the damning handwritten note in the margin)
- surprise admission of guilt by key employee, vendor or manager
- political attack
- employee complaints or grievances
- comments by high government officials given without attribution

The keys to simulation success are keeping the lessons the simulation should teach in mind as the scenario is developed. Remember, keep it real and keep it practical.

31

THE EMERGENCY MANAGEMENT EXERCISE PROCESS: A STEP-BY-STEP BLUEPRINT[1]

by Patrick LaValla, Robert Stoffel and Charles Erwin

. . . here's another success story . . .

The emergency operations plans were not thick with dust or unfamiliar territory for key officials. Those in charge and those helping them knew what to do because such vital operations as alert and notification, traffic control, and evacuation had been taught in county sponsored training and practiced repeatedly during field exercises. This experience paid off in a big way on March 24 as one after the other emergency worker reported that he or she knew instinctively what to do — their actions were like second nature.

Another benefit that was realized from the training and practice exercises was that volunteers responded naturally to their role and were well-prepared. Because the emergency management volunteers had been called regularly to participate in classroom and field training and to assist with other disasters over the years, they perceived their volunteer "jobs" as vital, took them seriously, and were accustomed to emergency operations. They had been kept active and involved and were ready to perform.

Evacuation of Nanticoke, Pennsylvania, due to a metal processing plant fire (March 24, 1987), U.S.F.A. Fire Investigation, Technical Report Series.

The steps (tasks) presented in this chapter have been developed for use not only by an exercise team representing a community, but also by a single unit such as a fire department or a rescue unit with the need to practice their response capabilities.

GUIDELINES FOR A GOOD EXERCISE

A basic premise of exercise development is that exercises must meet the needs of the local jurisdiction. Exercises must be tailored to fit the community. There cannot be, therefore, a cookbook to exercises. No guide can prescribe a little bit of this and a lot of that and guarantee a successful exercise.

The goal of this chapter is to distill a lot of experience into a few pages in order to suggest some techniques that have been successful elsewhere and alert you to potential pitfalls and failures.

Basic assumptions that must be established in the development of any effective exercise program include:

- exercises are local jurisdiction's affairs
- exercises are fundamentally good, beneficial, and worth the effort
- not all jurisdictions have equal emergency capabilities; therefore, emergency exercises must meet varying needs
- exercises are not one-time shows. They are part of a jurisdiction's commitment to improving the emergency response system
- an exercise development program begins with a single exercise but is a progressive commitment to improvement throughout the future.

WHAT IS AN EMERGENCY MANAGEMENT EXERCISE?

Exercising consists of the performance of duties, tasks, or operations very similarly to the way they would be performed in a real emergency. However, the exercise performance is in response to a simulated event. Exercises require a simulated input to emergency personnel that motivates a realistic action.

The exercises you conduct will practice, develop, and improve skills in operational procedures and decision-making. Exercises are management tools that are useful for informing or training personnel and evaluating personnel performance or procedures.

Simulation is a tool to create an artificial situation to which participants in an exercise respond. The situation attempts to approximate reality by using symbols, maps, drawings, scripts, or in more elaborate exercises, films, videotapes, or computer graphics. The purpose of the simulation is to evoke responses that are very similar to those that a real emergency would prompt. Therefore, realism is the key to simulation.

EXERCISE TASKS

Each jurisdiction or organization will follow the path to an exercise best suited to its resources and needs.

The following steps, or tasks, are given to better help you organize your approach to developing an emergency management exercise to test your community's response capabilities.

THE EXERCISE DESIGN PROCESS

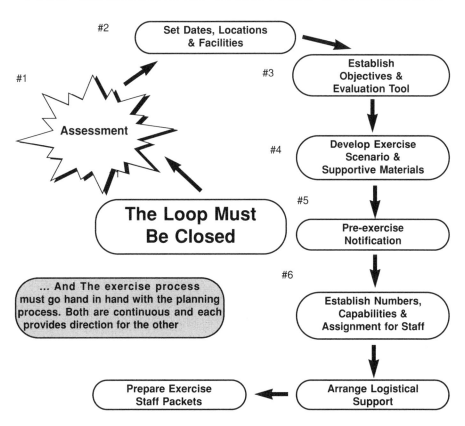

Task 1: Assessment

Long before you seek the support of the jurisdiction's and industry's chief executive, you should assess the need for and capability to conduct an exercise. Doing this assessment will keep you from taking on more than you can handle and will help you select an exercise and objectives that will contribute most to the improvement of the emergency management program. There are five different types of exercises. Each of them is progressively more difficult to conduct and will require your jurisdiction to have a greater exercise capability. You may already have that capability or you may have to develop it.

- Task 1a: Assess the Needs and Capabilities of Your Jurisdiction
- Task 1b: Selection of Exercise Type
- Task 1c: Establish Exercise Design Team

Task 2: Exercise Date, Location, and Facility

One exercise does not dramatically increase the readiness of the jurisdiction to handle emergencies. A planned program consisting of a series of exercises of increasing complexity is necessary to really improve the emergency management system.

- Task 2a: Exercise Development Checklist
- Task 2b: Exercise Development Timetable

Task 3: Exercise Objectives and Evaluation

An objective clearly and briefly states what you plan to accomplish by conducting the exercise. Developing objectives, therefore, is an extremely important task that influences the entire exercise. There are two types of objectives. General objectives express the collective actions that will be evaluated from the overall scope of the exercise. Refined objectives specify what is expected from the exercise participants. Refined objectives suggest an action taken or decision made (or should be taken or made) by exercise players.

- Task 3a: Determine Purpose or Goal
- Task 3b: Establish General Objectives
- Task 3c: Establish Refined Objectives
- Task 3d: Develop Evaluation Tool

Task 4: Exercise Scenario and Materials

The scenario must be based upon a realistic situation and circumstances. It determines sequence of events (major events) and must be developed from the community hazard analysis.

- Task 4a: Scenario Narrative
- Task 4b: Master Sequence of Events
- Task 4c: Detailed Sequence of Events
- Task 4d: Messages, Problems
- Task 4e: Exercise Agenda

Task 5: Pre-Exercise Notification

A set of basic rules pertaining to safety of all exercise participants, roles (player, controller, evaluator, etc.), actual emergencies, agreed upon levels of performance, out-of-sequence events, and time shifts is determined for the exercise. Levels of demonstration (full and partial participation) versus simulation of exercise objectives are determined.

- Task 5a: Ground Rules for Exercise Participants

Task 6: Numbers, Capabilities, and Assignments of Exercise Staff

On the basis of the scenario, objectives and jurisdictional plans, the host jurisdiction determines the number, capabilities, and assignments of exercise staff.

- Task 6a: Controllers and Simulators
- Task 6b: Evaluators

Task 7: Logistics

Logistics include both physical facilities, including communication linkages, and displays and/or materials.

- Task 7a: Arrange Logistics

Task 8: Exercise Staff Packets

The host jurisdiction prepares a packet for each staff member with information pertaining to his or her assignment, as well as information about the exercise, schedule, logistics, etc.

- Task 8a: Prepare Controllers and Simulators Assignment Packets

- Task 8b: Prepare Evaluators Assignment Packets
- Task 8c: Establish Rules for Exercise Players

Task 9: Training

Pre-exercise training for evaluators acquaints them with special or unique characteristics of the site, the off-site jurisdictions, the assignment and the exercise.

- Task 9a: Train Controllers and Simulators

- Task 9b: Train Evaluators

Task 10: Pre-Exercise Drills and Rehearsals

Once the exercise date is established, participating agencies / departments may schedule a series of drills or tabletops, as well as full-participation rehearsals prior to the exercise. These activities serve largely as training functions and help to identify potential pre-paredness problems before the exercise.

- Task 10a: Conduct Training for Players

Task 11: Pre-Exercise Briefing

A meeting is scheduled prior to the exercise so that the exercise staff can become acquainted with one another, their assignments, logistics, and to resolve any problems. In some cases, representatives of the jurisdiction present briefings on the scenario or expected exercise activities.

- Task 11a: Conduct Briefing for Exercise Staff

Task 12: Exercise Activity

The day of the exercise is the culmination of all your planning.

- Task 12a: Conduct Exercise

Task 13: Post-Exercise Debriefing

The debriefing should be very short and to the point (brief as possible); contain a positive initial evaluation of the exercise; identify where and when for the official critique; include what to expect from results; and, a thank-you to all participants.

- Task 13a: Conduct Post-Exercise Debriefing

Task 14: Final Exercise Report

The report should serve as a critique which provides very simple but important answers to the questions: "What happened and what kind of a report card did we get?" Without some kind of evaluation, an exercise would be of little value.

- Task 14a: Prepare Exercise Report

Task 15: Exercise Deficiencies

Monitor "lessons learned" on each exercise for the purpose of incorporating improvements in the emergency management system into each succeeding exercise.

- Task 15a: Track Exercise Deficiencies

Task 16: Remedial Drills / Exercises

Based upon your "report card", some type of remedial activity should occur within a period of time.

- Task 16a: Conduct Remedial Drills/Exercises

GETTING STARTED

An emergency management exercise is not a trivial task. You need time to work on it. You need the support of many other people, including the chief executive of the jurisdiction and the chief executive officer of the facility to be exercised. Therefore, before you make a commitment to conduct an exercise, either to yourself or to others, we suggest you take time to lay the ground work for a successful exercise.

The following flow chart illustrates the sequence of exercise tasks:

¹ This chapter has been adapted from the publication Exercise Planning and Evaluation, Copyright © 1990, Emergency Response Institute, Inc. Used with permission.

THE EXERCISE DESIGN PROCESS

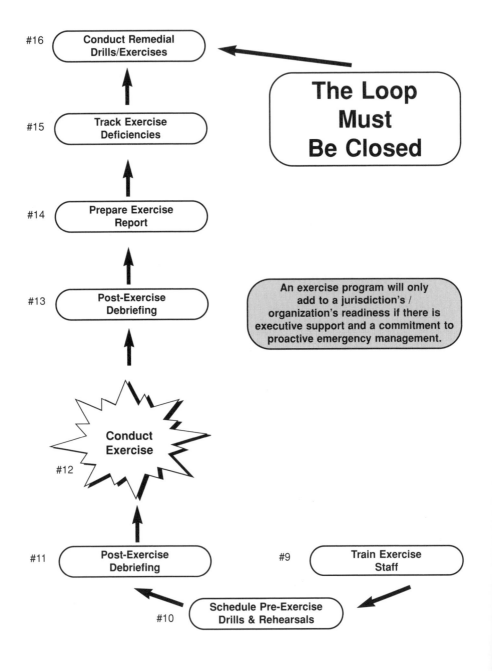

#16 Conduct Remedial Drills/Exercises

The Loop Must Be Closed

#15 Track Exercise Deficiencies

#14 Prepare Exercise Report

#13 Post-Exercise Debriefing

An exercise program will only add to a jurisdiction's / organization's readiness if there is executive support and a commitment to proactive emergency management.

#12 Conduct Exercise

#11 Post-Exercise Debriefing

#9 Train Exercise Staff

#10 Schedule Pre-Exercise Drills & Rehearsals

32

DISASTER PLAN SIMULATES PLANE CRASH INTO HIGH-RISE BUILDING[1]

by William H. Johnson and Warren R. Matthews

The thought of an airplane crashing into an occupied high-rise office building boggles the mind with the complexity of its aftermath. But when such a scenario is deliberately conceived as an emergency preparedness exercise and involves eleven months of planning, meetings and preparation, reality takes over.

This chapter chronicles just such an exercise conducted at the 62-story John Hancock Tower in Boston, Massachusetts, in the fall of 1991. It describes the preparations and planning involved, the scenario for the disaster exercise and the lessons learned.

THE BUILDING

The tallest building in New England, the slim John Hancock Tower is a megastructure that rises 802 feet above Boston's Back Bay, with floor space that can be measured in acres. The home office of the John Hancock Mutual Life Insurance Company, it houses not only a major portion of the company's corporate offices, but many tenant firms as well. On a typical workday, it contains more than 5,000 people. An observatory on the 60th floor with a panoramic view of Boston's skyline is a popular tourist attraction.

Constructed in the early 1970s, the building has five banks of six passenger elevators, plus freight / service elevators, near its central core; they are flanked by two stairways. Some of the passenger elevators are programmed as express cars that go directly to the upper floors.

Smoke detectors located throughout the building are connected to the security center and water-flow alarms go directly to the Boston Fire Department. There are fire extinguishers throughout the structure and standpipes in the stairways at each floor. The building is fully sprinklered.

Fire drills are held regularly. Occupants of the building are instructed in emergency procedures and receive emergency information from the building's public address system.

John Hancock has worked for several years to bring its in-house emergency preparedness organization (EPO) to a high level of competency. Its security department has trained its members in evacuation procedures, incipient-stage firefighting, emergency medical skills and in managing hazardous materials incidents. The EPO also includes damage-control teams of craft groups such as electricians, plumbers, elevator specialists, and heating, ventilation and air-conditioning (HVAC) engineers.

The company's strong motivation for preparedness was reinforced by recent, major high-rise fires at the First Interstate Bank in Los Angeles and at One Meridian Plaza in Philadelphia.[2]

PLANNING AND TRAINING

John Hancock's overall objectives for this drill were to exercise and evaluate its communications and incident command systems and to observe how its unified command interfaced with that of outside emergency forces.

The scenario for the disaster preparedness exercise assumed that a small airplane flying near the John Hancock Tower had developed a serious mechanical malfunction, lost control and crashed into the east (Clarendon Street) side of the building at the 54th floor. The point of impact was near the high-rise passenger elevator lobby at the north end of the building's core.

It was assumed that many people were in the building at the time of impact, working or visiting the 60th-floor observatory. It was estimated that many or most of the occupants on the floor of impact and the floors above it were killed, and that at least 50 were injured. The victims were scattered throughout the upper floors and in the stairwells.

When developing its preparedness plan, the company brought together all the agencies that would play a role in mitigating such an incident in a well-planned test of their emergency response effectiveness. In addition to John Hancock's emergency preparedness organization, the participants included the Boston Fire Department, Boston Emergency Medical Services, the Boston Police Department, and the American Red Cross, which were pre-staged. Area hospitals also participated to test their own disaster plans.

It is important to point out that the exercise was to be a tool for learning and there were to be no surprises. The scenario was fully disclosed at the planning meetings and each participating agency was encouraged to develop its own response to the simulated emergency.

Although the disaster was simulated, the participants postulated the many ways in which this type of aircraft accident would affect the tower and its building systems.

First, the building and building systems would be structurally damaged by the velocity of the impact. This would result in the loss of at least one of the two stairwells and an interconnected standpipe riser, which essentially would eliminate any water flow and effective sprinkler operation until the damage-control teams could make repairs. Fire from ignited aircraft fuel would overwhelm the sprinkler system until the fuel supply had burned off completely. The HVAC and smoke control systems would be affected and pre-fire smoke control plans would be ineffective.

A normal, orderly evacuation of the occupants would be difficult because of the loss of at least one of the two stairwells. Rescue and firefighting efforts would be routed to the only remaining means of access to the impact zone, further impeding the egress of occupants from floors above the point of impact.

It was estimated that the number of casualties (fatalities and injured) would approach 100 percent on the floor or floors of impact and 75 percent on the floors above.

Obviously, incident command would be transferred to the Boston Fire Department upon its arrival. Unless there were extenuating circumstances, such as a coinciding major incident, the Boston Fire

Department would be at the scene before the in-house emergency preparedness organization could equip its members and reach a designated staging area below the floor of impact.

The need for in-house assistance was obvious. Elevator management, plumbers, electricians, HVAC engineers and John Hancock's emergency preparedness commander would play an active role in the unified command and control of the incident.

The disaster exercise was limited to about 2½ hours to minimize disruption to area businesses and out-of-service time for the outside emergency forces. This is a fraction of the time that actual high-rise incidents have taken to resolve. In real-time, it is estimated that this incident would require from 16 to 24 hours of demanding action.

In planning the exercise, members of John Hancock's emergency preparedness organization held many meetings with key company executives. These included the director of security, the corporate safety manager, the emergency preparedness commander (who was the manager of security), the director of building operations, the general director of employee relations and the medical director. The emergency preparedness commander also met with representatives of the Boston Fire Department, Boston Emergency Medical Services and the Boston Police Department.

After these preliminary meetings, the emergency preparedness organization held a series of joint planning meetings with members of the outside emergency forces so they could work out many details and issues. These joint meetings played a major role in the overall success of the exercise. The topics discussed included safety, communications, elevator use, site security, property preservation during the drill, public relations, observers of the exercise and, most important, the roles and responsibilities of the participating organizations.

At the meetings, the participating organizations had the opportunity to bring up concerns that might otherwise have been left to chance and could have adversely affected the outcome of the exercise. Safety was a primary issue. Because this was a practice exercise, every effort was made to minimize the potential for injury to all the participants in the drill.

INSTRUCTIONS FOR DRILL OBSERVERS

John Hancock hired a consultant who specializes in emergency preparedness and response training and development to help them plan the drill.

The consultant selected seven critical areas that company observers were to watch during the exercise:

- the emergency operations center

- the tower command center

- the emergency preparedness organization's dress-out room

- the staging / command area on the 52nd floor

- incident floors 53, 54 and 55

- the EMS triage area / receiving area

- the operations of the damage-control teams.

The consultant prepared evaluation checklists and a rating scale that categorized the degree of concern for specific errors and omissions that the observers noted. He also developed general and specific performance objectives for each observed area to guide the evaluators during the exercise.

The observers were given a briefing packet containing their assignments and instructions for making and recording their observations. The instructions and the system for categorizing inadequacies were explained at a meeting held the day before the exercise took place.

Essentially, the observation team was instructed to focus on the actions of John Hancock staff members participating in the exercise and on the interaction between John Hancock's EPO and the outside forces. Evaluating the tactical actions of the outside forces was not part of John Hancock's mission. If the observers noted an unsafe act, however, they were to intervene in any way possible to prevent an injury or an accident.

Checklists prepared for each observed area included two sets of objectives: objectives dealing with general performance, such as communications, reactions and safety; and specific objectives for each area. The observers were told to evaluate all the objectives and to rate them as adequate or inadequate. Objectives that they rated as inadequate required written comments and were to be assigned to one of three categories of concern. The three categories, which were defined and discussed at the meeting held with the observation team, ranged from Category I, the least critical, to Category III, the most critical.

Category I Inadequacy designated an area of possible concern that required further investigation to determine whether corrective action had to be taken. Items in this category could be either dropped or upgraded to a higher level of concern.

Category II Inadequacy designated an area that required corrective action. It indicated a moderate-level concern that had to be resolved or corrected as soon as practicable.

Category III Inadequacy indicated the highest degree of concern. Items in this category required timely corrective action to prevent an adverse impact on safe and effective operations at the incident.

The observers were encouraged to become familiar with their specific objectives, to focus only on their area of responsibility and to note both good and bad performances. They were instructed not to distract the drill participants and to be as inconspicuous as possible.

Finally, the observers were required to present all their written remarks and category judgements at a meeting to be held immediately after the exercise.

SEQUENCE OF SCHEDULED EVENTS

At 3:00 p.m., a detailed briefing for team leaders and key security department personnel and a general meeting of all the in-house participants were held to disclose the entire drill scenario.

An hour later, building operations personnel prepared the 52nd-floor staging area by removing decorative art works, posting signs denying access to vital areas, placing floor coverings to indicate where the staging area was located and taking other actions.

At 5:30 p.m., the "victims," volunteers who were mostly John Hancock employees, arrived at the 52nd-floor staging area for moulaging – the application of cosmetic materials to simulate injuries. The moulage was applied by Boston Emergency Medical Services personnel.

An hour later, the victims were placed in various locations on the 53rd and 55th floors and in the stairwells between the 52nd and 55th floors. The locations of the victims were carefully mapped so that observers could assess the thoroughness of the rescue personnel.

At 6:50 p.m., three videotaping crews were in place to record the events. One crew was initially assigned to the emergency operations center, the second to the emergency response team's (ERT's) dress-out area, and the third to the staging area. In addition, a corporate communications department videotaping crew was stationed on an elevated platform in the lobby to record events when the outside forces arrived.

INITIATION OF THE EXERCISE

A 10-minute buffer was built into the exercise scenario to give John Hancock's emergency response team (ERT) time to dress out and reach the staging area on the 52nd floor before the Boston Fire Department was notified.

At 7:00 p.m., the simulation of the aircraft's impact on the 54th floor took place. The lead observer telephoned the emergency operations center (EOC) and instructed it to begin the exercise. The EOC started the ERT's response and activated the incident command system. The security manager assumed the role of incident commander (IC), went to the tower command center and established the tower command.

From this point on, the exercise was conducted in real time; that is, no events or variables were scheduled at specific time intervals.

Security members serving on the ERT reported to the ERT equipment room and dressed. All the team members carried an extra self-contained breathing apparatus (SCBA) air bottle with them to the staging area.

Three five-member teams of the ERT responded to the staging area two floors below the reported point of impact and designated it T-52 Command. Signs indicating severe fire and smoke conditions in Stairwell 2 prevented them from using this access to the floor of impact. Team members were forced to use Stairwell 1, where they discovered victims and immediately began evacuation operations.

When ERT 3 reached the 52nd-floor staging area, the team leader assumed the role of operations sector commander and delegated the responsibility for team leadership to a senior team member.

At this point, a telephone call was made to the Boston Fire Department (BFD), which dispatched a high-rise response to the building.

Although the BFD's plan, developed from the scenario, called for nine alarms if this were a real incident, the actual BFD apparatus responding to the drill consisted of three engine companies, two ladder companies, one rescue company, one tower company, a special unit to supply air, a district fire chief for safety, a deputy fire chief and approximately 45 firefighters.

The Boston Emergency Medical Services (EMS) and the Boston Police Department also were notified of the aircraft accident. EMS responded with 26 units and 104 EMS personnel. The Boston Police Department dispatched five units, manned by approximately ten officers, plus their command post and special services units.

John Hancock's operations sector commander waited at the service elevator lobby for the arrival of the outside emergency forces. When the BFD district fire chief arrived at the 52nd-floor staging area, incident command was formally transferred to the BFD by radio so that all emergency preparedness operations members would be aware of the transfer of command to the fire department.

The BFD then established the main command post at the corner of Clarendon Street and St. James Avenue, using their special command unit.

John Hancock's emergency preparedness commander joined the ranking BFD officer at the main command post, thus forming a unified command. This allowed John Hancock's emergency-response and damage-control teams to continue supporting fire department's activities.

After John Hancock's emergency response team had established the staging area and the tower command center on the 52nd floor, they searched for and evacuated victims to the staging area until EMS personnel arrived and established a triage and treatment area on that floor.

FIRE DEPARTMENT OPERATIONS

Fire department personnel arrived and entered the building through the main lobby. Firefighters went downstairs one floor to the concourse and freight elevator lobby and used the high-rise freight elevators to take personnel and equipment to the 52nd-floor command staging area. Their primary role was to reach the fire floor (floor 54) and to remove victims still in the stairwells.

When firefighters reached the 53rd floor, they connected 2½-inch hoselines to the standpipe riser and entered the fire floor with dry hoselines. The area of aircraft impact and the main body of fire were displayed by projected simulation. Firefighters stretched dry hoselines simulating charged lines to the impact area, which was illuminated by the simulation.

For the Boston Fire Department, the command function was a critical component of the exercise. A major objective of the drill was to observe the command relationship between John Hancock's EPO incident command system and that of the fire department, particularly the transfer of command and the interaction of the two incident commanders.

EMERGENCY SERVICES AND POLICE OPERATIONS

Like the fire department, EMS personnel entered the building through the main lobby and went downstairs to the concourse and freight elevator lobby. The EMS command established a triage and treatment sector on the 52nd floor and a treatment and loading sector at the ground-floor loading dock, from which ambulances were dispatched. The sector officers were identified by fluorescent traffic vests that designated their command.

Firefighters used the high-rise freight elevator to bring victims from the 52nd-floor triage area to the tower basement, where they were transferred to another freight elevator that went to the loading dock. From there, the victims, were taken by ambulance to several Boston hospitals.

As the planning phase of the exercise grew to include more participating agencies, area hospitals thought the exercise would be a good opportunity to test their own disaster preparedness. Many hospitals even staged additional victims nearby and timed their arrival at the hospital to coincide with that of the drill victims to evaluate the performance of their emergency staff under stress.

The Boston Police Department controlled access to the area of operations surrounding the building and rerouted traffic coming into the area. The American Red Cross was involved in keeping track of victims who were transported to hospitals.

COMMAND POST OPERATIONS

The Boston Fire Department established the main command post for the exercise, as it would if this type of incident actually occurred. Boston Emergency Medical Services and the Boston Police Department established separate command posts to carry out their own command systems.

John Hancock believes it is essential that all the emergency forces be represented in the main command post, forming a unified command, with the ranking fire department officer assuming the role of incident commander.

EVALUATION MEETING

John Hancock held an evaluation meeting for the observers and key in-house participants the day after the exercise. Each observer's checklist was reviewed and a summary sheet was completed that noted each inadequate performance that had been observed and the category of concern the observer had assigned to it.

The purpose of the meeting was to examine the performance of John Hancock's emergency preparedness organization and to prepare a corporate response for a joint post-exercise evaluation meeting to be held later that day. That meeting was attended by John Hancock's EPO leaders, participating members of the company's corporate departments and representatives of all the outside agencies.

The emergency preparedness training and development specialist acted as moderator at the joint evaluation meeting. Each participating agency was asked to comment on its actions during the exercise; John Hancock's safety manager recorded their remarks.

LESSONS LEARNED

The disaster exercise and the evaluation meeting yielded many important lessons and reinforced proper emergency actions. When this article was written, some corrective actions for the company's emergency response procedures had already been completed and others were in the planning stages.

A number of the actions taken were very successful. For example, all John Hancock participants donned full structural firefighting personal protective equipment and received clear, concise instructions from team leaders.

When the aircraft accident was reported, the security supervisor activated the incident command system and assumed the duties of incident commander. As the incident escalated, command of the incident was formally transferred at each level of supervision.

A unified command was established when John Hancock's emergency preparedness commander arrived at the fire department's main command post and reported to the incident commander.

Subdividing command before the arrival of the fire department worked well in maintaining effective incident control.

When one of the service elevators malfunctioned, the unified command made a joint decision to leave it out of service and not make repairs because the elevator machine room was located above the fire floor and would have compromised the safety of the repair team.

The exercise also uncovered a number of items to be corrected or improved. For instance, the security shift manager failed to brief his assistant and to provide clear instructions before he left the control center to take over the tower command.

In the future, all the participating agencies should be represented at the main command post established by the fire department.

Key leaders of John Hancock's emergency response team were not easily identified and should wear colored vests that identify them and their assigned activity, and they should identify themselves to arriving members of the fire department. Key ERT people include the emergency preparedness commander, the building operations manager, the safety officer, the director of security and the medical officer.

The head count of victims made by rescue and treatment teams was inaccurate. However, all the victims who were taken to area hospitals were accurately accounted for. Personnel from John Hancock's human resources department should work with the American Red Cross to keep track of victims transported from the emergency scene.

Duties assigned to ERT members should not exceed their physical abilities and stamina. Even though safety was emphasized throughout the exercise, all the areas were lighted and the victims were walked to the triage area, two ERT members required treatment for exhaustion. One of them was transported to a hospital as a precautionary measure.

The leader of each agency should use cellular phones, which provide a secure path for transmitting sensitive information and urgent messages. Numbers for these phones should be classified and given out only on a need-to-know basis to ensure that they are used primarily for outgoing communications.

Members of John Hancock's emergency response team should receive training in the proper handling and lifting of victims because the EMS would need their help in a real emergency.

The exercise also revealed the need for several additional actions. A critical-incident stress management program should be added to

John Hancock's emergency action plans. John Hancock's business resumption / disaster recovery plan should be implemented early in an incident. Lost assets should be identified, alternate business operations plans should be put into effect, appropriate notifications should be made, and resource needs should be met. These items have been incorporated into the emergency preparedness plan.

SUMMARY

If the simulated aircraft crash at the 62-story John Hancock Tower had actually occurred, it would have crippled the structure and stretched the capabilities of both the in-house emergency preparedness organization and the outside forces to their limits.

For the most part, John Hancock found its employees ready in terms of task level training, communications and incident command. The emergency preparedness organization learned from this exercise how well agencies can work together in a major emergency. Several actions that were identified as inadequate during the review and evaluation of the exercise can be improved. Cooperation among all the participating agencies was excellent and we feel that, as a result, each participant feels more confident.

An effective emergency preparedness organization responsible for a structure like the John Hancock Tower must include teams with craft skills, such as the damage-control teams, in addition to the emergency leaders and responders.

The incident command system for a megastructure should include as members of the command staff essential building personnel such as the emergency preparedness commander, the facilities manager, the security director and the safety manager. This type of staff can advise and support the incident commander of the outside forces.

ORGANIZING YOUR COMPANY'S EMERGENCY RESPONSE

If you are responsible for organizing and controlling emergency response in your workplace, visualize a major fire or some other life-threatening event taking place there and list the aspects of the situation that worry you most. You have just assessed your building's greatest needs and have identified the starting point for an emergency preparedness plan.

Each organization should develop an emergency plan that meets its own specific needs. These may range from an evacuation team to a full-scope emergency organization trained and equipped to handle fires, hazardous materials, medical problems and other emergencies.

An emergency preparedness plan requires several components:

- identification of potential man-made or natural emergencies
- development of standard operating procedures for handling emergencies
- development of an incident command system and training in its use
- training for team leaders
- training in skills at all task levels
- integration of the emergency preparedness organization with the outside forces responding to an emergency.

EPILOGUE

On August 11, 1992, an emergency occurred at the John Hancock Tower when a fire in an electrical transformer on the seventh floor sent smoke up through portions of the 62-story building.

When Boston Fire Department officers arrived, they took command, evaluated the situation and ordered evacuation of the entire structure. More than three thousand employees and tenants were evacuated by stairway. During the operation, 72 people were injured but only two required hospitalization overnight.

John Hancock's emergency preparedness organization feels that its training, and particularly the level of preparedness that it developed during the disaster exercise, prevented the actual emergency from becoming more serious.

WORLD WAR II BOMBER STRIKES EMPIRE STATE BUILDING
by Casey Cavanaugh Grant, P.E.

If you think the aircraft crash scenario used in the emergency preparedness exercise at the John Hancock Tower was a bit farfetched, you might want to consider the case of the bomber that flew into the side of the Empire State Building in 1945.

Early on the morning of Saturday, July 28, 1945, the three-man crew of a U.S. Army Air Corps B-25 bomber headed its two-engine aircraft south from the Army Air Corps base in Bedford, Massachusetts.

During its approach into New York City, the aircraft encountered considerable fog. The crew established radio contact with LaGuardia Field, but the pilot disregarded advice to land there and started for nearby Newark Airport. He also disregarded a Civil Aeronautics Administration regulation that required aircraft over Manhattan to maintain a minimum altitude of two thousand feet.

Visibility throughout the area was estimated at 2½ miles, which allowed less than a minute of apprehension time if the plane were at a cruising speed of 250 miles per hour. At 9:52 a.m., the aircraft flew out of a patch of fog and the horrified crew saw a tall structure looming directly in their path. Despite a final, desperate attempt to climb, the bomber crashed into the north wall of the 102-story Empire State Building.

The impact ripped a hole approximately eighteen feet by twenty feet in the building's exterior wall at the 78th and 79th floors. Part of the landing gear, a portion of one of the wings and a radiator from the building traveled across the 78th floor and went through the south wall, where they plummeted to the roof of an adjacent twelve-story building, starting a fire in a penthouse apartment. An engine and other parts of the landing gear crashed into an elevator shaft and fell to the subbasement.

	B-25 Mitchell Bomber	Boeing 727	Boeing 747
Wing Span:	67.6 ft.	108.0 ft.	195.7 ft.
Weight, Maximum:	36,047 lbs.	209,500 lbs.	800,000 lbs.
Fuel Load, Maximum:	1,400 gals.	9,730 gals.	570,285 gals.
Cruising Speed:	230 mph	599 mph	608 mph

Flaming gasoline from the aircraft's 1,400-gallon fuel tanks splashed throughout the 78th and 79th floors and onto the exterior of the building at least five floors above and below the point of impact. Flames shot as high as the 86th-floor observatory, lighting up the tower with frightening brilliance.

Fortunately, it was a Saturday morning and only a skeleton workforce was in the building. Furthermore, the 78th floor was not occupied by a tenant; it was temporarily being used to store various building supplies.

This was not the case on the 79th floor, however, where seventeen employees of the National Catholic Welfare Conference War Relief Services had reported to work. Ten of them, who were at their desks at the north end of the floor, were fatally burned by the spray of flaming gasoline. The fire flashed rapidly toward the south end of the floor, where the other seven employees were seriously burned, one fatally. These deaths and those of the three-man crew of the plane brought the final toll of victims to fourteen. Twenty five other occupants of the building were injured.

A bank of ten express elevators and one freight elevator extended up through the building. Parts of the aircraft and debris from the building cascaded down several of the elevator shafts, starting fires near the ground floor. Four of the passenger elevators became inoperative. One elevator plum-

meted from about the 75th floor to the subbasement when all of its cables were severed. The elevator operator survived the terrifying drop but was seriously injured.

One of the aircraft's engines penetrated one of the two stairwells and broke an eight-inch-diameter standpipe in the stairwell. The stairwell remained tenable, however, and occupants of the upper floors were able to use it to escape. Firefighting operations were not seriously affected by the loss of the standpipe because another eight-inch standpipe in the second stairwell remained functional.

The New York City Fire Department received numerous calls reporting the crash and sounded four alarms in eight minutes, which brought approximately twenty five fire companies and forty apparatus to the scene.

Arriving fire officials faced three separate fires. The primary fire involved the 78th and 79th floors of the Empire State Building. The second fire was in the lower portions of the elevator shafts. And the third, a serious fire, was atop the adjacent twelve-story building at Ten West 33rd Street. On each of the four alarms for the major fire in the Empire State Building, one or more companies was detached to fight the blaze in the adjacent building.

The fire on the 78th and 79th floors was reportedly under control in about nineteen minutes and was completely extinguished forty minutes after impact. Twelve hoselines from the Empire State Building's standpipes were used to control the fire: one line at the 65th floor, which was directed into the elevator shafts; three lines directed onto the 78th floor; six lines directed onto the 79th floor, where the fire was most intense; and two lines used at the 80th floor. In addition, one outside line was brought in to control the fire on the first floor.

The fire in the penthouse of the adjacent building was controlled by three hoselines connected to the standpipes of the twelve-story building, in addition to the building's automatic sprinkler system, which was damaged by falling debris.

Built in 1931, the Empire State Building was the world's highest structure when the accident occurred. The crash, along with the ensuing fire that ignited substantial quanti-

ties of flammable liquids, occurred 913 feet above street level. Yet when the situation was under control, the building's 56,000-ton structural frame had withstood the impact of the bomber with relatively little damage. the damage to the building was eventually estimated at more than $500,000 (in 1945 dollars), of which only about twenty percent was caused by fire damage.

In this situation of "World War I bomber versus high-rise building," the building survived the fury of the impact relatively intact. If this situation occurred today, however, the result would probably be different.

This particular incident involved an aircraft that, by today's standards, would be considered comparatively small. If you compare the aircraft size, crash momentum and flammable liquid fuel load of the B-25 Mitchell Bomber that crashed into the Empire State Building with those of two larger, conventional aircraft (see table) – while ignoring other factors such as different building construction techniques and different aviation regulations – it becomes evident that the John Hancock Tower might not be as lucky as the Empire State Building.

[1]   Reprinted with permission from *N.F.P.A. Journal®* (*Vol. 87*, #6), Copyright ©1993, National Fire Protection Association, Quincy, MA   02269. *N.F.P.A. Journal®* is a registered trademark of the National Fire Protection Association, Inc., Quincy, MA 02269.

[2]   See "Los Angeles High-Rise Bank Fire," *Fire Journal*, Vol. 83, No. 3, (May / June 1989), p. 72, and "High-Rise Fire Claims Three Philadelphia Fire Fighters," *N.F.P.A. Journal®*, Vol. 85, No. 5 (September / October 1991), p. 64

33
REHEARSING YOUR CRISIS MANAGEMENT PLAN[1]
by Alvin Arnell

PROLOGUE

Webster defines a crisis as a "turning point for better or worse;" as a "decisive moment" or "crucial time." It is also defined as "a situation (incident, occurrence) that has reached a critical phase."

Consider testing of a crisis management (control) plan as analogous to rehearsing a play, or making a movie: scene-by-scene; act-by-act. The plan is the script and the identified vulnerability scenarios are the scenes and acts. Therefore, this chapter will relate to testing in theatrical terms rather than testing terms that might be confused with those tests applicable to a data center or information processing organization's disaster recovery plan. The setting is first to define a crisis and its effects and implications on the credentials of the organization.

Many disaster recovery administrators and coordinators will read this document, and perhaps consider testing their disaster recovery plans using the methodology described here. Effectively, a test is nothing more than a scene (small component test), an act (a more comprehensive performance test) and a play (a rehearsal of reality, mirroring a probable disaster). A crisis management plan is a series of "scripts" preparatory to staging a "show" for the media, customers, community and perhaps governmental regulatory agencies.

Expectation . . . is the objective for the development of a crisis management plan or disaster recovery - business continuity plan. The commonality between the two results in:

- the *expectation* that the organization can maintain its operating performance in a "business as usual" manner

- the *expectation* that any crisis or disaster will be completely transparent to anyone dependent on the normal performance of the organization or on the ability to provide critical information processing capability, network and functional department operation, with little or no interruption or interference

- the *expectation* that with the systematic adherence to the plan's criteria and action plans that the organization will be capable of surviving any level of crisis or disaster impact

- the *expectation* that the plan will provide the structured activities and strategies: the script, that will assure complete recovery without any stigma (chronic crisis)

- the *expectation* that the plan will provide the guidance and that personnel will perform in the same manner as they did during testing / rehearsal.

Crisis Management is the managing of crisis within the organization, and more important the effect of any form of adverse incident / disaster that gains a high profile, either negative or positive, with personnel, the community, customers, government agencies; and, which has a direct, unfavorable, antagonistic impact on the credentials and credibility of the organization.

There is often a missing link in the contingency planning process. While this chapter is specifically directed towards the rehearsal (testing) of a crisis management plan, the incongruity is that few companies have taken an initiative in developing any plan of this nature. Crisis management is likely to be far more critical to ensuring the ongoing, stable performance of an organization at the time of any catastrophe than a disaster recovery plan.

The crisis management plan will have little or nothing to do with any adverse incident relating to information processing, information flow or information dissemination. This may exclude such areas as life-threatening situations (hospitals, EMS, police emergency) or financial services (banks, stock exchanges, etc.). Contrary to the disaster recovery plan for information processing, the crisis management plan is dedicated to preventing the loss of credentials, credibility and stature of an organization at the time of an undesirable or unexpected event (a pervasive, emotional and psychological process).

UNDERSTANDING THE CRISIS MANAGEMENT REQUIREMENT

Another paradox: management and present day planners commonly have little or no knowledge of crisis management. If you don't have a plan; if you don't understand the necessity of such planning; and, if you don't know how such a plan applies to your organization's ability to maintaining your operational performance, corporate stature, credentials, credibility and personnel morale —- how can you design a plan — how can you test a non-entity?

In order to better understand the nature and rationale of a Crisis Management Plan, it is important to compare this planning process with those most of the readers of this book encounter:

- *Prevention / Security Plans:* plans designed and developed from a business impact analysis which determined the potential and probable disaster sources. These plans cover all aspects of protection and preservation of existing operations, and guide management in the "hardening" of operational sites to avoid interruption.

- *Emergency Response Plans:* actions taken immediately upon the recognition of an emergency. The primary objective of these plans is to protect the safety, health and welfare of personnel.

- *Data Center Disaster Recovery Plans:* the plans designed to guide disaster recovery action teams to recovery any central computing operation that has experienced a disaster. These plans are usually designed to transfer information processing resources and capability to a secondary, backup facility.

- *Business Unit Disaster Recovery Plans:* business unit plans are used by each of the functional business operations of the organization to recover critical business activities. These may be standalone plans which may or may not have little or no dependency on central computing operation.

- *Network Disaster / Recovery Plans*: Specific plans designed to re-establish the organizational network in order to maintain the flow of information. These plans cover all of the areas of activity and are totally integrated with all of the previous plans described. The network plan may cover the minimum of recovery of a small group of workstations performing interrelated functions; a local area (LAN) network interfacing a larger more complex group of interdependent departments or divisions; or, a wide-area network (WAN), serving an entire organization.

- *The Crisis Management Plan*: this plan is designed to provide management with a working tool to protect the credentials, credibility and business stature at the time of any unexpected, undesirable catastrophic event that will create an unplanned visibility.

The primary objectives of a Crisis Management Plan are:

- to manage unexpected, undesirable, adverse visibility caused by one or more catastrophic events during the first minutes, hours and perhaps days of the incident

- to provide accurate information in order to avoid escalating the situation into an uncontrollable, acute crisis.

The significance of this planning is demonstrated early in the crisis situation where misperceptions, errors and mistakes are eliminated and avoided. Planned, panic-free responses have a unique capability of ensuring the dissemination of accurate, untainted misconceptions and erroneous assumptions.

CRITICAL SITUATION SCENARIO DEVELOPMENT & CONSEQUENCE

The critical situation scenario is used for three aspects of the crisis management plan:

1. to understand unexpected or undesirable situations, conditions, events that could cause a significant internal or external crisis;

2. for preparation of communications at the time of an incident and the script to be used at the time of a rehearsal of the crisis management plan; and,

3. for preplanning of disclosures and intelligence to be disseminated at the time of an adverse incident, and selection of individuals to represent the company in the event of a crisis.

When rehearsing the critical situation scenario, various scenarios with the accompanying material should be selected. Do not limit rehearsals to a single obvious scenario. Do select some scenarios that are improbable. This will tend to draw in more participants and specific technical or legal specialists.

CRISIS MANAGEMENT REHEARSAL PLANNING

The success or failure of any plan is its ability to perform as designed, to mitigate the implications of the crisis and to reduce the potential crisis from escalating to the acute / chronic phase. Plans will not perform properly if they are used only when needed. Updating changes in organizational operations based on rehearsal results is vital to making a plan viable and effective.

Plan expectations direct the plan components. Rehearsals make them work and add significant benefits to other plans. It is management's responsibility to determine what is to be expected from the plan. But there are limitations to how much any one or two "rehearsals" can achieve in determining whether a crisis management / containment plan will work. Each test should be designed to achieve one (but certainly no more than two) objectives, recognizing that each of the plan tests will have different objectives and expectations. By splitting rehearsals into small controllable components, many of the plan elements can be demonstrated without going to a major test procedure at the outset.

One scenario can be run with only a few of the active participants to perform their tasks, while another scenario may engage the entire organization from corporate headquarters to branch offices, divisions, and international operations. The rehearsals will assuredly bring out information that was overlooked, or new situations that were not apparent at the time of the plan development.

Testing will divulge significant insight to other areas of the organization. In addition, the completion of rehearsals provides management with concrete results that the planning process they have supported has the ability meet their expectations.

ESTABLISHING THE PLAN SCOPE AND CORRESPONDENT REHEARSAL LEVELS

Some aspects of an organization's business, products or services are more prone to crisis than others. For example, in the chemical industry over-the-counter products are usually under a higher level of scrutiny than those sold in commercial quantities. A one-quart can of a product improperly used by the purchaser can cause more unwanted visibility than an error in a commercial quantity.

While we recognize that any impropriety in either situation will be widely scrutinized in the event of a failure, the likelihood of class action lawsuits would probably be more devastating to a company than the recall of a product from industry. Consumer advocate and protection organizations, local, state and federal watchdogs are active in greater numbers now than ever before.

Other aspects of consumer and industrial protection can be found in corporate use of consumer call-in and complaint departments. These departments are used to head off major crises by dealing with the consumer (private or industrial) on a one-on-one basis. Therefore, an outstanding intelligence source about potential crises can be the information gleaned from these activities. The scope of crisis management plan rehearsals can often be based on these consumer / industrial complaints.

Planners designing and implementing tests have to recognize that preparation and anticipated results vary from department to department, product to product, and so forth. Test programs very from simple "table-topping" to full-blown rehearsals of a specific department, division or business activity. Component testing usually can highlight areas for reconsideration.

REHEARSING INCIDENTS CAUSED BY "ACTS OF GOD" VS. "ACTS OF MAN"

The key to successful testing is the ability to "crystal-ball" outcomes. Attempting to test acts of God may be virtually impossible. No one can foretell the overall effects of an earthquake, flood, or other significant causes for interruptions — unless the organization is directly related to the outcome. For example, an architectural / engineering firm designing an earthquake-resilient building will have a great deal to answer for if what they have produced is proven incapable of withstanding an earthquake. Yet, many crises caused by earthquakes are common to all organizations.

BASIC REHEARSAL CRITERIA

Establishing the proper levels of protection, preservation, security and risk reduction avoids the probability of short-changing your organization in crisis management planning. The script outline for rehearsal of the crisis management plan should include at least the following:

- management
- department involvement
- critical impact assessment
- board members
- division, branch management
- legal department
- participant personnel
- critical incident scenario development
- government agencies
- applicable regulatory agencies
- customers / clients
- community leaders
- shareholders
- financial resource (external, banks, etc.)
- industry associations
- vendors
- union officials
- sales / marketing personnel
- corporate and consulting public relations

PLAN TEST CRITERIA

The crisis management (control) plan should be rehearsed against the following criteria:

- identify the person or persons that will be the spokesperson for the company (at divisions; at branch offices; at international facilities). Is the spokesperson a public figure respected by the media?

- identify the risks and vulnerabilities in terms of their effects on the organization, individuals within the organization, shareholders, customers, the community, government regulators, the environment, the health, welfare and safety of anyone who is involved with the product manufacturing, product use, services, etc.

- identify alternates in the event the primary spokesperson is not available

- identify the key critical scenarios, based on the highest risk vulnerabilities. There should typically be about six to twelve key critical vulnerabilities

- identify whether these key critical risks / vulnerabilities are likely to change within the next six months to one year

- identify and prepare the counteractions for each — thus ensuring that at the time of the event the company can go from the crisis phase to the crisis resolution phase with few complications

- identify all of the possible remedies or solutions from the simplest risk to worst-case scenarios

- identify any crisis potential that may create an environmental problem, such as contamination of the building, the area, air or ground water

- identify all external support resources that will be involved in the event of an environmental or other emergency

- identify any policy, condition or potential emergency that will lead to organized opposition

- identify all of the corporate regulatory requirements, permits or licenses that may be affected by an environmental or similar emergency (local, state and Federal Environmental Protection Administration)

- define all of the primary releases that will be required for the media, personnel, customers, clients, community, government agencies based on the critical assessment and scenarios

- do a factual, in-depth study of all of the potential vulnerabilities and crises. Such a study has to be performed from the top down

- senior management has to be involved and support the entire program from concept to final initiation

- identify all of the "opportunities" that will be available if the organization performs in a factual and open manner at the time of an emergency. This should be part of each of the scenarios

- management should appoint the prime qualified person within the organization to manage the emergency, as well as one or more qualified alternates

- poll all of the companies within your industry to determine the support you can obtain at the time of an emergency

- identify your base audiences (within the scenario) and encourage them to participate at the time of an emergency. This would normally include personnel, customers, clients, emergency services, community organizations, national and international organizations where applicable

- select and prepare those persons who will be the first on the scene at the time of an emergency. This might not be those who have been specifically involved in the overall planning or implementation of the plan. This could include but is not limited to senior management, engineering, operations managers, divisional managers, etc.

- establish a schedule for testing various components of the plan, updating schedules, plan revision meetings, etc.

- financial management should be involved in the development of the plan to determine the costs involved in all of the public relations and savior actions to retain the reputation, credentials and market recognition and share at the time of an emergency. Cost can play an important factor in the extent of actions taken to preserve the corporate entity

Your procedure may include all of the factors to accomplish the tasks necessary to make the plan work, but there are other considerations which should be rehearsed:

- the first person on the scene or available to speak on behalf of the company may not be a spokesperson who has been trained to represent the organization

- the media and other outsiders will probably arrive on the scene of the emergency much ahead of proper spokespersons from the company, particularly in any incident involving an aircraft, a major fire, a terrorist attack, etc.

- the lack of availability of a qualified spokesperson will direct the media to the most accessible people on the scene.

THE ACTUAL REHEARSAL PROCEDURE

Develop a test plan. The expense of performing a full dress rehearsal of the crisis management plan, especially when there are a number of departments, divisions or subsidiaries involved, could be quite costly in time and critical manpower use. Therefore it is generally most appropriate to rehearse modular components or a specific scenario. Successful rehearsals break down into small scenes, so many of the elements of one scenario will accentuate the deficiencies and benefits of another approach.

The preparation and expected results are usually different with each of the scenarios (or adverse incidents). In scene rehearsal, rather than the entire play rehearsal, consideration is given to:

- identifying the organization and its operation before the rehearsal (or, before the potential incident occurs)

- restoring the status of the company to the level before the rehearsal (or, how the company operated and performed prior to the incident).

Another consideration when conducting a dress-rehearsal of the crisis management plan is that you can expect considerable disruptions throughout the organization if personnel are not forewarned about the rehearsal. A full dress rehearsal is usually not required if sufficient component rehearsals are performed, limiting the operational interruption to a minimum.

THE REHEARSALS AND PERSONNEL TRAINING

Rehearsals ensure that all personnel of the organization directly related to plan implementation receive complete training. The most important functions to emphasize are:

- emergency response: what to do and whom to call

- limitation on divulgence of information to non-company personnel

- all of the components of the crisis management plan

- all of the action plans and recovery activities

- each individual's responsibilities and contribution to the plan performance

- identification of sub-crises and proper reporting procedures

- identification and communication with peers, subordinates and others within the scope of each individual's activities

- emphasis on the security of information: non-divulgence of information by personnel not trained in responding to the media, governmental agencies, community representatives, etc.

- distribution of letters from management (and posting throughout all facilities, departments) to all personnel on the performance expected of them under duress / crisis

- the entire organization should be aware of all of the ramifications and implications of misrepresentation and misconstruing of information erroneously presented by non-authorized personnel to the media or other requesters of information

- distribution of a short overview of the plan limited to specific branches, departments, etc. of the company.

TECHNICAL TRAINING FOR REHEARSALS

Selected personnel should be trained to act in various assignments as participants in the actual plan implementation. Others should be assigned responsibilities to perform containment and control tasks to limit (mitigate) the damages, impact, effect on employee morale and loyalty, etc. in the event of a crisis emergency.

It is difficult in this short article to describe all of the training components. But if crisis management planners would take a page from the notebook of those involved in disaster recovery planning, they will find how comprehensive a plan of this nature has to be.

The crisis management plan generally assumes the most offensive, destructive, widespread crises imaginable. The first dozen of the crisis vulnerabilities are to be taken, and the results measured against the material and validation covered above, as the criteria for establishing a rehearsal.

THE ACTUAL SEQUENCE OF CRISIS PLAN REHEARSAL

The crisis management plan is designed to perform under the "worst case" crisis. In previous sections of this document we discussed the "rehearsal" of component sections before any full-blown test is performed. If planners have performed their crisis vulnerability analysis properly, everything from the most minor crisis to a major catastrophe has already been identified. The plan should be able to utilize subsets of the master plan for less-than-catastrophic events. Clearly, the normal culture and operating performance of the company will be completely different once a plan is in place.

Autonomous groups, previously reporting back to management after the fact, will now have to simulate initiation of plans or subsets of plans at the time of a simulated catastrophe. The responsibility for their actions will be with those directly accountable for the plan implementation. By invoking subsets of the plan at the time of a minor incident — that will go public — people within different functions of the corporation will call and rely upon plan management.

SCENE AND ACT CRISIS PREPAREDNESS REHEARSAL

Preliminary to a Full Dress Rehearsal

Following the concept of preparing for a stage play or movie, the first thing the planners and participants are required to do as part of the preparation for larger, more extensive rehearsal is to read through the "script". This form of "static" logical rehearsal assures a reasonable level of the script's (plan's) completeness and correctness. This provides the opportunity to do the "first-cut" of the content and procedures.

A script analyst (perhaps an individual from upper management) should act as a "devils advocate" in determining that all of the content meets the policy and standards of the company. Another person should take the role of an "auditor" and prepare a checklist / questionnaire that the entire plan (script) can be continually measured, certified and validated against in the future when changes are required.

The "script" reading / static "table-topping" rehearsal is one of the most effective methods of culling out all of the superfluous material, correcting errors and completing the plan factually.

Scenes - Acts - and Full Dress Rehearsal

Scene Rehearsal: the next step in rehearsing a crisis management plan is to verify if all of the scenes (scenarios) cover all of the probable key critical crisis conditions which have been identified. Each scenario is rehearsed (statically) to verify its completeness as well as the potential effects on the financial, productive and moral aspects of the incident.

Act Rehearsal: the "act" covers all of the scenarios identified as critical crisis vulnerabilities and the "staging" (actions) to be taken should any one of the scenarios come to pass.

Dress Rehearsal (the dynamic test): once all of the scenes and acts have been carefully rehearsed, a complete dress rehearsal involves all of the participants of one or more scenarios, one unit at a time. The exception may be if the specific rehearsals and scenarios are interactive, interdependent or interrelated, or a result of one scenario creating issues in other areas. The dress rehearsal includes but is not limited to the action plan, the distribution of resources (personnel and financial), the use of arms-length critics to act as representatives from the media, community, governmental agencies, and so forth.

Testing / Rehearsing the crisis management plan: This program can be viewed in terms of a theatrical performance:

- *script reading* — table topping: total review of the entire crisis management script scene rehearsal - reviewing one scene (scenario) at a time

- *act rehearsal* — reviewing those scenes (scenarios) that have a causal effect on other scenes (scenarios)

- *dress rehearsal* — performing a full test taking one scenario at a time, including all participants (internal and external, domestic or international operations).

- *script improvement and modifications* — few crisis management plans operate without flaws. Updates and modifications are continually required as a result of rehearsals as well as from organization changes, responsibility changes or new products / services.

CONCLUSION

Creating a crisis management plan that is capable of being properly rehearsed is in itself a major test of an organization's desire to maintain its reputation, credentials, credibility and stature within a community and with its customers / clients. Sun Tzu (The Art Of War, 500 B.C.) understood the importance of preparation: "... those who face the unprepared with preparation shall be victorious."

Time, effort, management support, personnel and financial resources have to be allocated to develop plans and rehearse them to the degree that the company will not falter at the time of an unexpected or undesirable incident. Corporations fighting to maintain a solid profit bottom-line are less prone to throw resources into areas that do not produce profits. Yet, planning and rehearsals need not necessarily require extensive resources. Prudent and cohesive plan development and rehearsals can produce effective and productive plans and significant success in their testing and rehearsal. Rather than throwing "bucks" into a problem, it makes more sense to make the available resources more productive.

34
TESTING EMERGENCY PLANS AND CAPABILITIES: TWO CASE STUDIES
by Roger W. Mickelson

INTRODUCTION

Testing the emergency response capabilities of any organization requires a continuing commitment by senior management, definition of objectives, careful construction of a scenario focused on achieving those objectives, observation of actions, and analysis of the results to derive those important lessons learned and allow the organization to develop corrective actions to improve capabilities. It is a closed loop system – what capabilities we want to examine (setting objectives), how we assess achieving objectives, what was not done well, how do we fix the problems?

This process, in much more detail and disciplined rigor, and the steps used in designing exercises to test capabilities can be applied to a wide variety of crisis management simulations – they work as well for earthquakes, radiological accidents, hazardous materials spills, technological breakdowns, terrorist actions, and military conflicts – and they have been used in such cases. Two major exercises sponsored by national companies are summarized in the case studies below. The names of the companies are omitted; their commitment and dedication to improving response capabilities reflect a foresighted, proactive desire to learn to deal with crises prior to a real emergency.

INFORMATION WARFARE

"What do you mean, the phones don't work?
The phones always work! Get somebody up here
who can tell me what the hell is going on! I'm the Governor,
and I want some answers — RIGHT NOW!"

Corporate Commitment; Setting Objectives

Key major telephone corporation executives recognized the need to examine local and corporate capabilities to react to a crisis that could create a breakdown in standard telephone service. After preliminary discussions, their managers chose a few key and specific objectives to examine capabilities (policies, plans, procedures, and supporting systems) designed to respond to a major service interruption in a state capital. This site was chosen because of economic, technical, distance, and, more importantly, political implications of widespread outages.

Scenario

The scenario wove demands for ransom for employees, explosions in the central switching equipment area, ensuing fire, injuries among the gathered and confused employees coming on shift, and general chaos as local and long distance services are totally disrupted.

6:24 a.m.	"This is Diego Sanchez. I got two of your guys here in the telephone office and want $300 million and safe passage for my team out of the U.S. — or your people die! Get me your boss's phone number and get the money now!"
6:27 a.m.	Local telephone company management begins series of calls to police, local officials, emergency managers, and corporate headquarters.
6:30 a.m.	The arriving shift supervisor notices a truck leaving garage. Security services guard confirms the sighting and notes the absence of his guard on shift.

6:34 a.m.	First police cruiser arrives; the crowd at the entrance is confused and milling around – unwilling to enter to begin the daytime shift.
6:40 a.m.	As police investigate, two major explosions in the main central office inflict several minor injuries and the telephone system – 911, direct dial, long distance, and operator services – ceases to function.
6:50 a.m.	Radio and television crews begin to arrive as police establish safe stand-off distances to allow fire and rescue teams to enter the smoldering entrances.
7:00 a.m.	Additional explosions result in toppling antenna tower across the main street; additional injuries occur. Police lines and SWAT teams deploy to seal the site.
7:08 a.m.	The disaster makes the early morning national news – stay tuned for details.

The response continues, with police, FBI, company employees, and firemen responding to an uncertain, but dangerous situation. The local phone company response team initiates technical, media affairs, and resource actions to alleviate the situation and restore normalcy. Corporate officers, including the Chairman and President of both the telephone and the umbrella corporation were notified immediately and directed that emergency plans be activated and teams assembled to respond.

The disaster was the most newsworthy event on that quiet Friday morning; media, union, family, public, stockholder, and government queries and demands build to a crescendo – the technical restoration appears to be straightforward, although neither quick nor simple. However, the external implications of political, legal liability, economic, and social threats to the solidarity of the corporation require immediate, strong, and continuing attention at the highest corporate levels. The long term direct financial implications – interruption of electronic bank transactions affecting social security recipients, major bank-to-bank fund transfers, investments, payments, credits, and government welfare transfers for state and regional recipients are estimated to be in the tens of millions of dollars and could create a flood of lawsuits and potential liabilities.

Lessons Learned — Return on Investment

The intense pace of exercise events, diverse nature of problems presented, and mountain of associated issues with what had been initially perceived as purely a technical telecommunications engineering problem revealed significant gaps in approved emergency response plans and procedures. At the same time, the incredible aplomb and innovation displayed by managers at local, regional, and corporate levels showed an incisive grasp of dealing with the host of external issues confronting the corporation.

The 45-minute verbal discussion of results immediately after the exercise and the subsequent written report identified many corrective actions to improve corporate policies, plans, and procedures. They also sensitized all participants to the importance of proactively dealing with the public, stockholders, media, and government calls – how to deal with stress induced external to the immediate catastrophe.

The corporate foresight of the potential value of the exercise, setting of key objectives, and full commitment and participation created a payoff in the identification of needed improvements. With the improvements made as a result of this exercise, any future telecommunications catastrophe could be dealt with more efficiently and with greater confidence in the company's crisis management capabilities, both locally and at the corporate level.

MEETING ECOLOGICAL THREATS – OIL SPILL RESPONSE

"This is Captain Morgan, Master of the tug Bullet, calling Coast Guard Marine Safety Office (MSO), San Francisco. An inbound freighter that had a steering casualty hit us at 1:25 p.m. It hit the number 5 port tank of a barge under tow, releasing at least 1000 barrels of fuel oil number 6. We have 109,000 barrels total at risk. Position is 1/8 mile east of buoy number 12 in San Pablo Bay near the Carquinez Strait. Maintaining steerage; moving South out of the channel."

Corporate Commitment

A national Oil Spill Recovery Organization (OSRO) is in its third year of developing a comprehensive exercise and evaluation program to meet Federal and State guidelines. They have completed over 30 major exercises and more than 15 table-top drills. Their President cites exercises and drills as, 'the crucible in which oil spill response capabilities are forged." Continued top-level dedication and participation, refinement of objectives to reveal areas requiring polish (having steadfastly improved plans, procedures, and systems since 1990), and increasingly complex involvement of government and industry organizations involved in oil spill response are their focus.

The OSRO is subject to federal, state, and client scrutiny to validate capabilities required by the Oil Pollution Act of 1990 (OPA 90) and similar state and territorial directives. This particular exercise, conducted and evaluated in 1993, involved all parties: the Captain of the Port, San Francisco; California's Office of Oil Spill Prevention and Response (OSPR); and a petroleum transporting company.

Scenario

The initial situation, reflected in Captain Morgan's call to the Coast Guard, was a simulated oil spill in San Pablo Bay resulting from a collision between an inbound freighter and the tug / barge transporting fuel oil number 6 (Bunker C), a heavy petroleum product. Outside the dredged channel, the bottom shoals very gradually, with shallow water complicating recovery operations and prediction of the trajectory of the spilled oil.

Management of the response is complicated by time and distance – the shipper and the OSRO offices are located a few hundred miles away, although an OSRO oil spill response vessel (OSRV) and other equipment is based in the Bay area. MSO San Francisco is relatively close to the site of the oil spill; and OSPR is headquartered in Sacramento, expediting government presence and control. A local cleanup co-operative, the primary responder for the client, is first on the scene and initially represents the client company.

1:30 p.m.	Captain Morgan initiates a series of calls to the MSO, client, and Co-op.
1:40 p.m.	The client calls the OSRO to activate a comprehensive oil spill response package; the client is patched through to the OSRO manager's phone

and details of the spill and initial response request are discussed.

2:00 p.m.   Initial media calls begin to flood the OSRO home office and the Co-op at their headquarters in the Bay area. Government, environmental, and public queries follow, as concerns for environmental and economic damage rise.

2:15 p.m.   The Co-op dispatches all available recovery vessels, skimmers, boom, and support boats to the scene; the first vessel on the scene initiates a site safety characterization and assessment.

2:30 p.m.   Six Co-op skimmer vessels and OSRVs commence skimming operations.

2:45 p.m.   First State officials arrive and assume initial overall control of the response; U.S. Coast Guard MSO representatives arrive shortly thereafter. Both build their staffs and provide a Federal On Scene Coordinator and State On Scene Coordinator to coordinate management of the spill response.

3:00 p.m.   OSRO skimmers are staged and deployed to be mounted on quickly contracted vessels of opportunity; the OSRO response vessel arrives and begins skimming the thickest, heaviest oil. Shoreline protection planning is initiated.

3:30 p.m.   First surveillance overflight reports slow spread of oil toward Carquinez Strait due to ebbing tide offset by fresh water flow. Tug, leaking barge, and freighter have moved south of traffic channel; tug and barge at anchor and initiating source control (stopping the leak).

4:25 p.m.   The OSRO manager and spill management team arrive and integrate with the client, Coast Guard COTP, and OSPR to track and recover the oil, plan for next day's operations, protect key environmental areas on the shoreline, manage the response, and collect recovered oil / water emulsion.

The field exercise continues for approximately 24 hours, with shifting tides, currents, and winds spreading the oil, threatening and oiling additional coastal areas, including environmentally sensitive areas and U.S. Navy facilities at Mare Island. Issues of recovery, pleasure boat cleanup, closure of the Carquinez Strait (with significant commercial implications), and handling of media and public queries are dealt with cooperatively by the Unified Command and the integrated Incident Command System. The plan for Thursday's operations is developed late Wednesday and the operational plan for Friday and the longer term General Plan are completed on Thursday. Estimated costs are provided to the client, operations are supported and sustained, and the Unified Command approves the draft plans for complete operations for the next several weeks, subject to daily review and control.

Lessons Learned – Improved Capabilities and Compliance with Federal Law

This drill marked a watershed in the ongoing series of increasingly complex and complete exercises. As announced by the Director of the Office of Oil Spill Prevention and Response, "this is the first industry-sponsored area exercise meeting the Federal and State requirements, including achievement of the National Preparedness for Response Exercise Program guidelines," thus complying with the directives implementing the Oil Pollution Act of 1990. Although successfully meeting all stated exercise objectives, the exercise revealed needs for more complete and timely documentation, education of government and industry organizations concerning OSRO plans and management processes and review of the Area Contingency Plan. Additional findings noted refinements and improvements that can be made to internal communications and procedures to increase the timeliness of comprehensive spill management and recovery operations.

35

VITAL RECORDS TESTING[1]

Federal Emergency Management Agency

The company security officer, records manager and internal auditor should test / evaluate the vital records program at least once a year and note any program defects or problems in a joint test results report to be sent to the proper company officer for information and remedial action.

DETERMINING TEST OBJECTIVES

The test determines if the currently operated program will provide needed information under circumstances simulating disaster or emergency conditions. Every effort should be made to make test conditions as realistic as feasible.

Broadly, the tests should verify that vital records needed after a disaster are:

- current
- protected sufficiently against natural disasters, nuclear detonation and other possible perils
- retrievable as needed in usable form.

More specifically, the tests should determine that the company's various vital information needs can be satisfied in a typical emergency situation. As examples:

- employees can be paid and proper deductions made for taxes, the retirement fund and other payroll accounts

- the company's cash position and the location of its banked funds can be determined

- the company's assets, accounts receivable and payable ledgers are all current

- the order entry, engineering, production and customer account information needed to resume production and sales activities are available and current.

PREPARING AND CONDUCTING THE TEST

After scheduling the test, determine where it will be held, who will participate, and how long it will last. Restrict advance knowledge of the test date to as few people as possible. Keep the test period as short as possible. The amount of time required for the test will vary. A large company may need several days to complete it. A small company may need no more than an afternoon. Reduce to a minimum participants' absence from their regular duties. The test should be located off company premises, if possible, to eliminate intrusion of normal day-to-day business matters. It may be held at a motel, an executive conference center, the company alternate headquarters site, or in a conference room made available by the local emergency management agency.

Well in advance of the scheduled test date, arrange for necessary test participant team support, working space, couriers, microfilm, copying equipment and access to data processing equipment. Also, arrange for several company executives not scheduled to participate in the test to act as judges. They should be familiar with the records used in the test. They must be able to determine if the problems posed by the test have been answered successfully.

After the participants arrive at the test site, explain the test conditions. Emphasize that the problems posed must be answered by records currently included in the Vital Records Protection Program. Give the questions to the test team.

TYPICAL VITAL RECORDS TEST PROBLEMS

Assume that the facility has been completely destroyed during the night, with nothing salvageable. Demonstrate the company's ability to perform tasks such as the following:

notify all managers to report to an emergency center for reorganization planning

notify all other employees not to report to work until further notice

continue paying company personnel on time

send alternate shipping instructions to vendors with whom orders have been placed

prepare a list of sources of supply for a specified product

produce engineering drawings and the bill of materials for a small number of specific products

prepare an insurance claim statement covering the complete destruction of the manufacturing building

prepare a list of vendors in order to replenish operating departments

produce a current statement of assets and liabilities and a statement of income and expense

produce a list of commission balances for each manager and sales representative by employee number

Allow time for test team members to determine what records will be needed to answer these questions.

As the requested records arrive by courier from their various locations, they must be reproduced or reconstructed in useful form. If the records are on microfilm, prints must be made of the first ten images on each reel. These prints must be inspected by the test judges to determine that they are sufficiently legible for use in performing the specified test task. If the records are on computer magnetic tape, the test must print out successfully the first one hundred records on each reel. The judges must determine that the printout adequately reproduces these records.

TESTING VITAL COMPUTER RECORDS AND OPERATIONS

Vital computer records will be used to satisfy many of the basic test problems. But a comprehensive evaluation of the Vital Records Protection Program requires supplemental testing of vital records computer processing. Devise tests that will:

- compare a clear copy of the tapes for selected vital records processing programs against a copy of the programs currently in use to determine that protected computer program documentation is current

- demonstrate that computer audit trails are being maintained in vital records computer programs

- determine that the alternate computer and its associated supervisory programs still are compatible with the company computer facility

Additional aspects of computer facility operations should be tested. These will be determined by company data processing management policies.

Adapted from Disaster Planning Guide for Business and Industry, Federal Emergency Management Agency Publication 141.

36
THE BOTTOM LINE

Most professional contingency planners would assert that recovery plans are of little value without testing. Some, more progressive professionals would further argue that testing is the very heart and soul of contingency planning – that an untested plan is at least as dangerous as a loaded weapon in untrained hands.

The consensus of the experts who contributed their knowledge and experience to this book is crystal clear: testing is vital to successful recovery from disruption. Further, no amount of plan development or refinement can ever displace testing. Always remember that the principal goal of recovery testing, consistent with the goal of continuity planning, should be the successful management (or ideally, avoidance) of the significant impact of any disruption, whether anticipated or not.

Philip Jan Rothstein

V.

CONTRIBUTORS' BIOGRAPHIES

ALVIN ARNELL

Alvin Arnell is President of DIA*log(R) Management, Inc., devoted to assisting corporations throughout the world in developing and implementing programs for business restoration, crisis management, disaster prevention, security and emergency response.

Mr. Arnell is the creator and author of the RES'Q^{sm} Disaster Recovery / Business Restoration Modular Component Planning Methodology. He has presented this methodology at seminars and workshops for over fourteen years. He is author of The Handbook of Effective Disaster / Recovery Planning (McGraw-Hill), which has been adopted by over ten universities. He is also the author of Standard Graphical Symbols for Science and Engineering (McGraw-Hill).

Mr. Arnell has devoted a significant amount of research and development in the area of crisis management planning. His forthcoming book, Crisis Management Planning - Preparing the Unprepared Before It Hits The Fan follows the same modular / component approach.

His experience in corporate planning and O.S.H.A. Administration safety planning led him to develop emergency response training programs and to installing disaster prevention and security measures for the paper converting and other specialized industries.

ROBBIE ATABAIGI

Robbie Atabaigi is a Disaster Recovery Coordinator with The Home Depot in Atlanta, Georgia. Previously, Robbie held the position of Contingency Planning Specialist with Equitable Real Estate Investment Management, Inc. She has travelled throughout the United States to conduct in-house training and has conducted presentations for various disaster recovery user groups.

Robbie is the 1994 President of the Atlanta Chapter of The Association of Contingency Planners, and serves as a member of the South East Business Recovery Exchange (SEBRE) Administration Committee.

Robbie has over seven years of experience in disaster recovery and over eighteen years in the data processing field.

KENNETH J. BAUMAN

Kenneth J. Bauman has 18 years of technical and marketing experience in the computer software industry. He has held management positions with software vendor firms offering products that support a wide variety of computer platforms.

Mr. Bauman is currently Director of Sales at Computer Security Consultants, Inc. (CSCI), an international firm specializing in business recovery planning and risk assessment. CSCI offers consulting services for these areas and is the developer and direct supplier of RecoveryPAC and RecoveryPAC II, personal computer software products that automate business recovery plan development and maintenance. CSCI also develops and markets RiskPAC, a personal computer-based software product that automates and manages the process of risk assessments.

JOAN A. BLUM

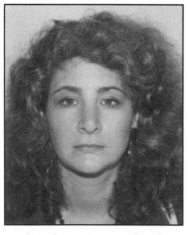

Joan Blum is currently in the Client Servicing Group of the Private Advisory Services at Bankers Trust Company, where she serves as a Technology Consultant. Previous roles at Bankers Trust included Disaster Recovery Manager for the Technology Strategic Planning Group, where her responsibilities included establishing the strategic direction for contingency planning for all technology areas worldwide.

Ms. Blum has served on the Business Advisory Board of the Contingency Planning Exchange. Articles by Ms. Blum addressing business continuity have appeared in periodicals including Disaster Recovery Journal.

Ms. Blum holds a B.S. degree in Mathematics and Computer Science from Brooklyn College and an M.B.A. with a concentration in Operations Research.

JAMES CERTOMA

James Certoma is a Vice President at United States Trust Company, a commercial bank and trust company in New York City. He is responsible for corporate contingency planning. His duties include development, maintenance and testing of the corporate contingency plan and support of the business units and data center in the formation of their specific plans.

Mr. Certoma is the 1994 Chairperson of the Executive Committee of the Contingency Planning Exchange, a group of contingency planners in New York City with a membership in excess of 1000 professionals. The Contingency Planning Exchange conducts quarterly meetings which address current contingency issues. He has spoken on the subject of contingency planning to various trade organizations and has written and contributed articles for professional journals. He is the former chairperson of the Business Continuity Committee of the New York Clearing House Association. This committee is composed of senior managers from major N.Y. banks who discuss common business continuity and contingency planning issues with particular emphasis on the New York City infrastructure.

Mr. Certoma earned a Bachelors Degree in Industrial Engineering from Columbia University and a Masters in Business Administration from the State University of New York at Buffalo.

RONALD N. CHAMBERLAIN

Ronald Chamberlain has spent the last twenty two years specializing in the air handling industry with American Air Filter Company, Cummins Engine Company and, for the past eight years, with Munters Moisture Control Services. He helped develop and build Munters MCS from its inception in North America. He has served as the Northeast Regional Manager and is presently the National Training Manager for Water Damage Recovery.

Mr. Chamberlain holds a B.S. in Business Administration from Bryant College. He has been the spokesperson for MCS on many occasions including the M.I.T. Museum-sponsored program on Disaster Prevention, Response and Recovery.

MICHAEL G. COURTON

Michael Gardner Courton is president of The Courton Group, a firm that specializes in disaster recovery and business continuity planning.

Mr. Courton has over ten years in the data processing field with seven of those years as a disaster recovery specialist. His experience includes developing plans for major data centers as well as integration of departmental computing, operational areas, telecommunications, and business units.

Mr. Courton has served on the Executive Committee of the Contingency Planning Exchange since 1988 and was the Chairman of that organization from 1991 to 1993. He also serves as Vice President on the Board of Directors for Trail Blazers Camps Inc., where he oversees the programming and planning function.

He earned a B.S. in Computer Science from Lock Haven University with major work in Management Science.

DAVID G. DOEPEL

David Doepel is a mental health professional who has specialized in the
human response to traumatic
events. He has both practiced and
researched in the area of crisis management since 1985 in Australia and
the United States.

He has published and lectured extensively on this topic,
addressing both academic and corporate audiences. He is a
founding director of NEDRIX, a New England disaster recovery
professional organization, and an affiliate of the Center for
Corporate Response-Ability, Washington, D.C.

Mr. Doepel is also the president of EchoBridge Productions,
a Massachusetts-based communications company and is the pro-
ducer of the award-winning educational documentary series,
"Understanding Psychological Trauma."

CHARLES ERWIN

From 1979-1983, Mr. Erwin served as Area Coordinator for the Tennessee Emergency Management Agency, field office in Johnson City, Tennessee. Mr. Erwin was the Administrator of Training and Education for the Tennessee Emergency Management Agency, Nashville, Tennessee, 1984-1989.

Mr. Erwin has been serving as a contract planner for the Yakima Valley Office of Emergency Management, Yakima, Washington, June 1990 to present. He has assisted E.R.I. in the development of numerous "local government based" emergency planning programs to include: exercise design; emergency operations center management; damage assessment; disaster planning.

ALAN FREEDMAN

Alan Freedman is Vice President, Technology Strategic Planning for Bankers Trust Company, one of the world's largest money center banks. In that role, he is accountable for Global Disaster Recovery and Business Contingency. Since joining Bankers Trust in 1976, he has managed development of the Bank's International Funds Transfer systems; managed the Bank's New York and New Jersey data centers; and, designed and implemented the infrastructure support systems critical to the Banks' computer technology.

Mr. Freedman serves as Chairman of the Board of The Uninterruptible Uptime Users Group, a national, educational forum with a mandate to promote a better understanding of the design, implementation, operation and management issues involved in achieving high levels of uninterrupted computer uptime.

He has been quoted in *The New York Times; Japan Economic Journal; InformationWeek; Datamation; Computerworld; Wall Street Technology; American Banker; Bank Systems & Technology; Global Investment Technology; InfoWorld; Power Quality*; and, many other publications. He has been a featured speaker at the Department of Energy / E.P.A. National Workshop on Energy-Efficient Office Technology; Dun & Bradstreet Recovery Planning Seminar; Treasury Management Association; The Nippon Club; International Power Quality Conference; and, numerous other symposia.

Mr. Freedman holds a B.A. degree from Marietta College, with post-graduate study in law, data processing and business management.

CASEY CAVANAUGH GRANT, P.E.

Casey Cavanaugh Grant, P.E., is the National Fire Protection Association's Chief Systems and Applications Engineer.

JUDITH A. HINDS

Judith Hinds is a Contingency Planner at The Depository Trust Company in New York. Since 1985, she has been involved in data center recovery planning and testing, operations area business resumption, and other information technology projects.

Ms. Hinds is a founding member and former chairperson of the New York-based Contingency Planning Exchange. She currently serves on the C.P.E. Executive Board as membership chairperson. She is also active in the Association of Records Managers and Administrators (A.R.M.A.). She has published articles in disaster recovery publications and spoken at several industry events.

Prior to joining The Depository, she held administrative positions with organizations in the fields of community service, education and international health care. Ms. Hinds holds a B.A. from Oberlin College, a M.A. from Radcliffe College, and a PhD from Harvard University.

WILLIAM H. JOHNSON

William H. Johnson is the corporate safety and loss prevention manager for the John Hancock Mutual Life Insurance Company in Boston, Massachusetts.

PAUL F. KIRVAN

Paul F. Kirvan is Vice President of The Kingswell Partnership, Inc., a telecommunications consultancy with offices in the U.S. and U.K. that focuses on disaster avoidance, disaster recovery and business continuity planning. Mr. Kirvan has been in telecommunications for over 27 years, with experience in telecom management, technical planning, training, and publishing.

Mr. Kirvan has published over 200 technical articles and several technical manuals on telecommunications management and disaster recovery planning. He developed the TC/DRP software which is used to design voice recovery plans. Mr. Kirvan also teaches seminars on telecommunications and local area network contingency planning; he has taught over 1,000 delegates in the U.S. and U.K. He is a columnist with *Communications News* (U.S.) and *Communications Networks* (U.K.) magazines, and recently was appointed U.S. Editor to the SURVIVE! U.K. quarterly journal.

Mr. Kirvan holds a B.S. degree from The Pennsylvania State University, and is a member of SURVIVE! Inc.

WILLIAM J. KROUSLIS

William J. Krouslis is an Assistant Vice President of Chubb Services Corporation, a management consulting firm and developer of the first state-of-the-art contingency trading facility, ChubbCTF. He has over 20 years experience in a variety of business, management and safety disciplines and has applied this expertise to a wide range of industries and projects in the disaster recovery field.

Mr. Krouslis has spoken in a multitude of forums around the country on a variety of Disaster Recovery issues. Such forums include the International Disaster Recovery Symposium & Exhibition, the Uninterruptible Uptime Users Group, the New York Mail Order Merchandise Show, the New York State Society of CPA's, and the Downsizing Exposition.

Mr. Krouslis holds a B.S. in Fire Science from the City University of New York. He is a Certified Disaster Recovery Planner, Certified Safety Professional, Certified Fire Protection Specialist and is a Principal Member of the National Fire Protection Association's Technical Committee on Disaster Management.

PATRICK LAVALLA

Patrick "Rick" LaValla was employed by Washington State Department of Emergency Management from 1972 through 1984 as: Director, Puget Sound Earthquake Preparedness / Planning Project, 1982-1984; Director of Washington State's response to the Mt. St. Helens Disaster, 1980; Operations Manager, Department of Emergency Services, 1979-1982; Search and Rescue Coordinator, Department of Emergency Services, 1972-1979; Chairman, Search and Rescue Council, 1974-1981.

During the past nine years, Mr. LaValla (and E.R.I.) has worked for state agencies, federal agencies, local governments, emergency response organizations, foreign countries and corporations assisting and directing the development of: disaster plans; training and education programs; and, related emergency management services.

As a principal in and co-founder of ERI, Mr. LaValla (along with Messrs. Stoffel and Erwin) has written, co-authored and edited over 30 training manuals and books covering the full spectrum of emergency management, disaster planning and emergency response.

JAMES N. LOIZIDES

James N. Loizides is Vice President and Division Manager for Chubb Contingency Trading Facility, a Division of Chubb Services Corporation located in New York City.

ChubbCTF provides a full trading room hot site service for their customers. Their digital trading environment provides trader turrets, market data and support services.

Mr. Loizides was the key consultant hired by the Wall Street Telecommunications Association's Hot-Site Consortium to formulate the traders' requirements for disaster recovery.

He has been in the data processing and financial services industries for over 25 years and has worked for banks, brokerage and services companies in support of trading operations.

JAMES E. LUKASZEWSKI

James E. Lukaszewski, A.P.R., P.R.S.A., is co-founder and chairman of The Lukaszewski Group Inc., a New York-based consulting firm specializing in management communications. As an expert in crisis and high-profile corporate communications management, he personally advises top corporate executives.

Mr. Lukaszewski is frequently retained by senior management to direct on-location efforts and manage high profile problems in the communities across the United States and Canada in which his client companies have operations. He helps prepare spokespersons for editorial board meetings, local and network news interviews including *20-20*, *Sixty Minutes* and *Nightline*, financial analyst meetings, legislative and Congressional testimony.

He is an Assistant Adjunct Professor of Communications at New York University's Management Institute and a civilian advisor to the International Disaster Advisory Committee, U.S. Department of State, and to the United States Marine Corps. He is a nationally recognized speaker on crisis management, ethics, media relations and public affairs topics. He is an accredited member (APR) of the Public Relations Society of America and a member of its College of Fellows.

Mr. Lukaszewski is the author of several books and more than 130 articles.

WARREN R. MATTHEWS

Warren R. Matthews is an emergency preparedness and response training and development consultant. He is an associate of Professional Loss Control, Inc. of Kingston, Tennessee.

ROGER W. MICKELSON

Mr. Mickelson is a Principal Member of the Professional Staff of Systems Research and Applications Corporation (SRA) and serves as the Director, Operations, Training, and Exercise Division. He is directly and substantively involved in developing and supervising commercial, national, state, local, and regional policies, plans, and procedures related to natural disasters and technological accidents; emergency preparedness, mitigation, and response; crisis management; and, logistics operations and sustainment. His principal efforts have been in testing those capabilities through structured exercise and evaluation programs, identifying systemic deficiencies and lessons learned to provide corrective action programs in order to improve emergency proficiency and capabilities prior to an actual crisis.

Mr. Mickelson has prepared key portions of operational, procedural, exercise, training, and evaluation plans for commercial clients, Federal Emergency Management Agency, White House offices, Department of Defense, and other government organizations. He has planned, conducted, and evaluated over forty table top, command post, and field training exercises related to chemical, nuclear, oil spill, terrorist, and national security response. He is the author of numerous emergency preparedness and disaster response exercise policies, plans and procedures for commercial and government clients. He has served as the Assistant Emergency Coordinator, Department of Defense; Nuclear Accident and Incident Control Officer (various locations); and as a Senior Fellow, Naval War College Center for Advanced Research.

DAN W. MUECKE

Dan W. Muecke is Vice President, Technology for Advanta Corporation. Previously, he was Vice President, Technology Strategic Planning at Bankers Trust Company where he had responsibility for information technology strategic planning, disaster recovery, and security. He has over 25 years experience in network design and operations supporting the delivery of highly reliable information services. He has spoken at International Communications Association, Communications Managers Association and COMnet Conferences on disaster recovery of network resources. He has been quoted in *Information Week*, *Communications News*, and *Computerworld*.

Mr. Muecke is a past director and member of the International Communications Association as well as past president and board member of several specialized telecommunications equipment user groups. He is a member of the I.E.E.E. Communications Society.

Mr. Muecke holds a B.S. and M.E.E. degree from Rensselaer Polytechnic Institute and an M.B.A. from Monmouth College.

MELVYN MUSSON

Melvyn Musson is a business continuation planning and crisis management specialist with over thirty years experience in insurance, loss control and risk management consulting areas.

He is presently Vice President of Business Continuation Planning Consulting Services with American Risk Protection Consultants. He has held similar positions previously with two major worldwide insurance brokerage companies.

Mr. Musson has extensive experience in the development of emergency response, business continuation and crisis management plans for various industries, including manufacturing and distribution (nationally and globally), financial institutions, telecommunications, retail and health care.

Mr. Musson is a member of the National Fire Protection Association's Technical Committees on Disaster Management, Protection of Computer Operations and Records Protection. He is also a member of the National Coordinating Council for Emergency Management, The American Society for Industrial Security, The Information Systems Security Association and is an Associate Member of the Society of Fire Protection Engineers.

Mr. Musson is a Certified Disaster Recovery Planner (C.D.R.P.) and a Certified Information Systems Security Professional (C.I.S.S.P.).

JOHN E. NEVOLA

Mr. Nevola is the Business Recovery Services Center Site Manager of one of the IBM large systems business recovery centers in support of the Integrated Systems Solutions Corporation, Business Recovery Services offering. I.S.S.C. is a wholly owned subsidiary of the IBM Corporation.

He started his data processing career in 1965 as a network systems programmer with Bell Labs in Holmdel, New Jersey. After two years in the U. S. Army, John spent two years as a programming consultant before joining IBM in 1970. He held a variety of middle management positions in Information Systems before being named site manager of the Systems Support and Operations function in Franklin Lakes in 1982. He retained that position until April 1989, when he was reassigned to the business recovery services center position he currently holds. The Franklin Lakes data center was moved to Sterling Forest, NY in September 1993.

A frequent speaker at various disaster recovery user groups and at SHARE, he has been widely quoted as a recognized expert in the disaster recovery field. Since the Wall Street fire in August 1990, he has appeared in the *Wall Street Journal*, *The New York Times*, *Computerworld*, *Networking Magazine* and on the BBC. His articles have been published in *Disaster Recovery Journal* and *Crisis* Magazine.

JOHN SENSENICH

John Sensenich is Director, Product Development for Sungard® Recovery Services Inc. He is responsible for developing, packaging, and marketing the company's mainframe hot site recovery services. His duties also encompass sales support, sales training, market research, and subscriber communications.

Prior to becoming director, product development, Mr. Sensenich held various positions within the company, including Director of the Philadelphia MegaCenter and Manager of Customer Support. He has more than 20 years of experience in the data processing industry.

He earned an associate's degree in business administration from the University of Pennsylvania's Wharton School of Business and a bachelor's degree in business administration from Southern Methodist University.

Mr. Sensenich is a frequent guest speaker for various disaster recovery industry and business groups, delivering presentations on topics such as "Contingency Plan Testing," "The Evolution and Future of Commercial Disaster Recovery Services," and "Exploding the Myths About Business Recovery."

ROBERT F. SHRIVER

Robert Shriver (C.I.S.A., C.S.P., C.D.P., C.M.C.) is the National Co-Director of Information Technology Consulting Services at McGladrey & Pullen, a national C.P.A. and consulting firm. He performs and directs projects related to disaster recovery planning, computer security and information technology planning. He has over fifteen years of disaster recovery related experience. He has published four books on disaster recovery topics.

Mr. Shriver specializes in the technology considerations relating to disaster recovery planning such as evaluating hot sites and data communications strategies. He has been involved with the design of over twenty PC-based disaster recovery planning software systems.

Mr. Shriver holds a B.A. in Physics and Mathematics and an M.A. in Operations Research. He has participated in developing standards for the A.I.C.P.A.

DAVID A. SOBOLOW

David A. Sobolow is a Senior Consultant based in Bethpage, New York. He has more than twenty years of experience in data processing and has focused on Information Security and Contingency Planning for the past twelve years.

Mr. Sobolow was Manager of Data Security for American Express and FIserv. He is the editor of Recovering Your Business (© 1993 TAMP Computer Systems, Inc.). His clients include Chase Manhattan Bank, Morgan Stanley, Bristol-Myers Squibb, Diversified Technology and Multiple Technologies.

Mr. Sobolow is a member of the Contingency Planning Exchange and served as a member of the Board of Directors for the Long Island Chapter of the Data Processing Management Association (D.P.M.A.). He has been a frequent participant at seminars conducted by the Computer Security Institute (C.S.I.), the Information Systems Security Association (I.S.S.A.) and the International Information Integrity Institute (I4).

Mr. Sobolow holds a Bachelor of Science Degree in Computer Science from New York Institute of Technology. He has attended additional courses provided by St. Johns University.

ROBERT STOFFEL

Robert "Skip" Stoffel has over 25 years of practical, hands on experience in all aspects of emergency management and response at local, state, and federal levels. Mr. Stoffel worked at the Washington State Department of Emergency Management from 1972-1977 as project director and training officer for the state's emergency preparedness education program. From 1977-1981, Mr. Stoffel served as the Director of Emergency Management for both Chelan and Douglas counties in Washington state. Mr. Stoffel is a principal in and co-founder of ERI.

MARVIN S. WAINSCHEL

 With more than 25 years of experience in business and data processing, Mr. Wainschel's ideas have had a significant impact on the way the Disaster Recovery industry views corporate crisis management. His advice on matters of business continuity is sought by experts in this field, and he sits on the business advisory board of the Contingency Planning Exchange.

Many of the visionary concepts in the Disaster Recovery industry originated at McWains Chelsea, a planning and research company founded by Mr. Wainschel over 10 years ago. His recently published book, <u>Knowledge at Risk</u>, is a comprehensive treatment of business continuity.

Mr. Wainschel is a frequent speaker at contingency planning associations. His articles have been published in *AQP Journal, Contingency Journal, Disaster Recovery Journal* and *Quality Times.* He has been quoted in *Computerworld, Information-Week, Service News, Computer in Banking* and *Bank Systems and Equipment.* He is a Certified Disaster Recovery Planner.

GEOFFREY H. WOLD

Geoffrey H. Wold (C.P.A., C.M.A., C.M.C., C.D.P., C.I.S.P., C.I.S.A.) is the National Co-Director of Information Technology Consulting Services at McGladrey & Pullen, a national C.P.A. and consulting firm. He specializes in disaster recovery planning, computer security and information technology planning. He has nearly twenty years of disaster recovery related experience. He has been a featured speaker at several disaster recovery conferences and has published several books and articles related to these areas including four books on disaster recovery topics.

Mr. Wold directs all aspects of organization-wide disaster recovery planning projects. He has worked with over one thousand clients in developing organization-wide business resumption and continuity plans. He has designed several PC-based disaster recovery planning software systems.

Mr. Wold holds a B.A. in Mathematics and an M.B.A. in Accounting. He has participated in developing standards for the A.I.C.P.A. and is involved in a number of other industry committees and task forces.

BUSINESS CONTINUITY BOOKS AND RESOURCES FROM ROTHSTEIN ASSOCIATES INC. — www.rothstein.com

PRINCIPLES AND PRACTICE OF BUSINESS CONTINUITY: TOOLS AND TECHNIQUES,
by Jim Burtles

From basic principles to advanced best practices, the reader will engage in all of the activities associated with the development, delivery, exercise and maintenance of an effective business continuity program. The included CD provides extensive tools, templates and other valuable resources.

www.rothstein.com/new/nr800.htm

A RISK MANAGEMENT APPROACH TO BUSINESS CONTINUITY: ALIGNING BUSINESS CONTINUITY WITH CORPORATE GOVERNANCE, by David Kaye and Julia Graham

"Business continuity is a vital area of modern risk and resilience management for any organisation. This book provides an ideal introduction to the subject for both the practitioner and for leaders and managers in general. It is also the core text for the Institute of Risk Management's (IRM) own business continuity qualification." - Steve Fowler, CEO, Institute of Risk Management.   www.rothstein.com/data/dr778.htm

BUSINESS CONTINUITY: BEST PRACTICES - WORLD-CLASS BUSINESS CONTINUITY MANAGEMENT by Andrew Hiles

Endorsed by the Business Continuity Institute International (BCI) and Disaster Recovery Institute International (DRII), This book is a guide to implementation of World-Class Business Continuity Management within an enterprise. It may be used as a step-by-step guide by those new to Business Continuity Management or dipped into by the more seasoned professional for ideas and updates on specific topics.   www.rothstein.com/data/dr770.htm

ENTERPRISE RISK ASSESSMENT AND BUSINESS IMPACT ANALYSIS: BEST PRACTICES, by Andrew Hiles

This book demystifies risk assessment. In a practical and pragmatic way, covering techniques and methods of risk and impact assessment with detailed, practical examples and checklists. It explains, in plain language, risk assessment methodologies used by a wide variety of industries and provides a comprehensive toolkit for risk assessment/business impact analysis.   www.rothstein.com/data/dr600.htm

AUDITING BUSINESS CONTINUITY: GLOBAL BEST PRACTICES, by Rolf von Roessing

"Not only provides a general outline of how to conduct different types of audits but also reinforces their application by providing practical examples and advice to illustrate the step-by-step methodology, including contracts, reports and techniques. The practical application of the methodology enables professional auditors and BCM practitioners to identify and illustrate use of good BCM practice whilst demonstrating added value and business resilience." – Dr. David J. Smith, MBA LL.B(Hons), Business Continuity Institute.

www.rothstein.com/data/dr601.htm

COMPREHENSIVE BUSINESS CONTINUITY MANAGEMENT PROGRAM: BUSINESS IMPACT ANALYSIS, BUSINESS CONTINUITY PLAN AND CRISIS/RISK MANAGEMENT PLAN DEVELOPMENT TEMPLATES ON CD-ROM, by Douglas M. Henderson

Includes advice for all development steps from Information Collection, through the Business Analysis, to the actual Business Continuity and Crisis Response documentation and finally the ongoing exercising and maintenance processes.   www.rothstein.com/data/dr789.htm

BUSINESS CONTINUITY MANAGEMENT FRAMEWORK™ CD, by Andrew Hiles

Extensive, easily-tailored modules reflecting a combined total of over 100 years of consultancy experience - modules that are most relevant to any situation, culture, organization and infrastructure. Contains documents, examples, checklists and templates covering each of the DRII/BCI's core disciplines, model project plans, questionnaires, business recovery action plans, organization schematics and role descriptions.   www.rothstein.com/data/dr476.htm